# HEROES AND LEGENDS
# OF WORLD WAR I

*Books by Arch Whitehouse*

Wings of Adventure
Hell in the Heavens
Hell in Helmets
Crime on a Convoy Carrier
The Real Book of Airplanes
Fighters in the Sky
The Years of the Sky Kings
Tank
The Years of the War Birds
Bombers in the Sky
Combat in the Sky
Subs and Submariners
Adventure in the Sky
Squadrons of the Sea
Billy Mitchell
Action in the Sky
Legion of the Lafayette
Amphibious Operations
Decisive Air Battles of World War I
John J. Pershing
Heroes and Legends of World War I

# HEROES AND LEGENDS OF WORLD WAR I

## by Arch Whitehouse

*Illustrated with 32 photographs and 4 maps*

*Doubleday & Company, Inc.*
*Garden City, New York, 1964*

Library of Congress Catalog Card Number 64–11399
Copyright © 1964 by Arch Whitehouse
All Rights Reserved
Printed in the United States of America
First Edition

*To*
*Ruth Terhune Whitehouse*

# CONTENTS

## Chapter XII                                                    292

## Chapter XIII                                                   319

# INTRODUCTION

This is not a strictly chronological history of the Great War, but a presentation of its highlights and legends.

In these pages I plan to present fairly remembered battles, national crises, bloody campaigns, many heroes—and a few heroines—all brought up to date in the hope the reader will gain a clearer view of World War I. This conflict was, after all, the first modern war, one in which modern weapons were conceived and first employed. None who took part had ever engaged in such an experience before. It was largely fought by civilian armies since the professional soldiers were either wiped out during the first few weeks, or were withdrawn from the carnage to train others for the ordeal.

The platoons, battalions, squadrons, batteries, and flotillas were built up from all levels of society. Every trade and profession was represented.

These volunteers and conscripts set a new pattern, and some wrote new pages of history. Because they were unfamiliar with military dogma or protocol, many of them wrote a straight story, ignoring the restrictions and traditions of the Colonel Blimps. Thus, even skilled historians have difficulty deciding which is wheat and which is chaff.

Generals who had gained world-wide renown, later were shown to stand on feet of clay. The true stories of many heroes have been forgotten, and new variations of their histories substituted in the rush to put out revised accounts for popular consumption. Many headlined airmen with lengthy victory scores are now being debunked and deflated, and newcomers have taken their places. Hundreds of combatants who were modest and inarticulate after the Armistice have during the past few years become verbose and professionally expert in their late middle age. As a result, we have a world conflict that is made up of varying portions of truth and legend.

World War II with its fleet of Superforts, its blockbusters, its rocket fighters, and atomic bombs may have been a global fracas that made the 1914–18 campaign look like a preliminary bout, but it was not in the same league when it came to the production of word-of-mouth legends. It never produced an Angel of Mons, a Phantom Piper of Polygon Wood, or a touching story such as that of the Virgin of Albert Cathedral. World War II gave us Buzz Beurling, Pappy Boyington, Kobber Kain, and the Abbeville Kids, but it never had a girl who flew a red-nosed S.E.5 scout, a Gurkha with a silver knife, or a spectral soccer player.

All legends, cheerfully admitted. Not one word of truth to any of these stories, one may argue. Perhaps, but not always. Who can determine how much imagination has been worked into the *accepted* stories of any war? How reliable was the account of Sergeant Alvin C. York's heroic assault on the enemy during the Battle of the Argonne? What the citation officials wrote was considerably elaborated from the simple statement made by this conscientious objector after he had returned to his little church in the Tennessee hills.

Consider the case of Major Charles W. Whittlesey who skillfully brought his 308th Infantry Regiment out of the Argonne trap to complete the story of the Lost Battalion. Today, we know the battalion was never lost. It was only thought to be. Major Whittlesey was awarded the Congressional Medal of Honor, but shortly after the Armistice, this hero disappeared from a transatlantic liner. The historians have presented many explanations for this act—presuming it was suicide—and here again, it is difficult to separate fact from fancy.

What about the case of Nurse Edith Cavell? Was she given a fair trial and rightfully executed? Did Douglas Haig actually admit that the British Army had its back to the wall?

What about the German atrocities in Belgium during the early days of the war? Was that Allied propaganda or were the Kaiser's troops as ruthless as those of Hitler? Who actually won the Battle of Jutland? Were British and French airmen Fokker fodder all through 1915–16? Should the Battle of the Argonne have been fought?

Myth and mystery. Truth and legend.

It is openly acknowledged that histories written at the time were hurriedly produced for an immediate market; details and accuracy were not important, and there was little time to check the facts. The public wanted to read of victories, defeats, strategy, and, more important, the deeds of the individuals concerned. National pride colored many of these records: defeats were usually gallant stands, and victories hard fought and attained against tremendous odds.

Truth may be stranger than fiction: a point the reader must decide for himself, for most of the legends included here are the sort grownups delight in passing on.

There must be further justification for a book of this kind. Military historians have always been accused of rattling the rifle bolt, but as long as military conflict produced such history in its effort to maintain the structure of nations there will always be a natural appetite for tales of heroism. How well military historians discharge their duties may pose a question. Most of us have seen more than our share of war and few of us relish the prospect of another, but what is more important is that no matter how much we hate war, the more likely we are of being involved in the next campaign. Once we are committed, that war has to be won, for in defeat there are many things worse than war.

*Arch Whitehouse,*
*Montvale, New Jersey,*
*May 11, 1963*

# HEROES AND LEGENDS
## OF WORLD WAR I

# ON THE LAND

# CHAPTER I

## A Side Street in Sarajevo

The assassination of a second-rate Austrian Crown Prince has long been regarded as the international incident that triggered World War I. Whether Francis Ferdinand, Archduke of Austria-Este, was that important politically is highly debatable, for until his sudden demise he was a comparative unknown. History discloses that he was a strong, hard, uninspired man who was in constant disfavor at the Hapsburg Court, and had defied monarchical tradition by marrying beneath his station. His "morganatic" wife, who died in trying to save his life, possibly was the only person in the world who had any affection for this caricature of a ruler.

Sophie, Duchess of Hohenberg, a title grudgingly bestowed on her, was an attractive woman but a member of the despised Slavic people. Emperor Franz Josef of Austria, the Archduke's uncle, made certain she never received recognition in the Royal Court and she was reminded continually that she had married the man, not the prince, and that her children could never succeed their father on the Hapsburg throne. Because of these family rebuffs, Francis Ferdinand spent most of his time at his country home in Konopischt with his wife and children. It must have been a frustrating existence, that of a large frog in a small puddle, but early in 1914 the drab routine was enlivened by a visit of the German Kaiser, Wilhelm, and a small entourage.

According to legend, it was this visit that resulted in an alliance between Wilhelm and Francis Ferdinand, and later rumors indicated that other Hapsburgs were determined to have the Crown Prince disposed of quietly before he could succeed his eighty-four-year-old uncle, the Emperor Franz Josef, and drive all of them from their small chancelleries of power.

The overture of this operatic intrigue makes interesting reading. During the first six months of 1914 a series of conferences were held at which European rulers and high ranking statesmen considered the simmering political situation. Many members of the Triple Alliance—France, Great Britain, and Russia—had been discussing the aggressive programs openly arranged between the Central Powers—Germany and Austria-Hungary. The Balkan situation was very touchy and the Albanian regime under Prince William of Wied had shown evidence of complete failure. Turkey, already in secret collaboration with Germany, was aiming to regain control of the Aegean Islands that had been awarded to Greece. Turkey also had outraged Athens with her atrocities against the Hellenes in Asia Minor.

Germany openly sought conflict with France, and only by plain speaking and severe warnings that she would stand by France was Great Britain able to avert war earlier. Adjustment of the Moroccan question was made by treaty, and Germany was forced to accept compensation elsewhere in return for recognition of a French protectorate over Morocco.

Prussian pride had suffered many reverses and the history of the Central Powers is besmirched with defeats, errors, and unfortunate guesses. In the first of the Balkan wars, Germany was firmly behind Turkey, but she went down to defeat. In the second Balkan upheaval the Central Powers again were on the losing side when they supported Bulgaria. These setbacks reduced German and Austrian influence and placed new obstacles along the strip of control the Central Powers had hoped to establish between Berlin and Baghdad. With all this, a new assertion of power against Russia and Serbia became necessary if the military party in Germany was to save face.

A bewildered chauffeur gave the Central Powers a dramatic and timely opportunity.

On the morning of Sunday, June 28, 1914, the Austrian heir-apparent was to make a ceremonial appearance in the town of Sarajevo, Bosnia, the discontented province that was then part of Austria. Francis Ferdinand had been advised not to go into this area, and one variation of the story is that the Crown Prince declined to take the risk, but certain members of the Hapsburg family taunted him with charges of cowardice and goaded him into final acceptance. The truth of the matter is that in a country where elaborate and stringent police control was the custom, the Austrian heir and his wife were sent into an openly rebellious district with inadequate protection.

The Bosnian plot had been concocted for several months. In April, Gavrilo Princip became acquainted with Nedjelko Cabrinovic, Trifko Grabez, Vaso Cubrilovic, and Cestes Popovic, students in Belgrade, Serbia, where the assassination plan was conceived.

Princip and Cabrinovic were assigned to collect bombs and other weapons. Then followed a program of amateur cloak-and-dagger activity that lasted for more than a month. During this time Cabrinovic made a contact with Major Voja Tankosic, a member of the Narodna Obdrana (a Serbian anarchist society), who supplied six bombs, four Browning pistols, a quantity of ammunition, and, to complete the deal, a vial of cyanide of potassium with which to kill themselves *after* the assassination in order to keep the secret of their organization. At that time, however, anarchist tradition went out the window, for five of the chief conspirators were captured and brought to trial.

Another ingredient of the plot was the fact that the bombs—actually grenades—used in the assassination came from the stores of the Serbian Army depot at Kragujevac, sixty miles southeast of Belgrade. Throughout his subsequent court testimony Trifko Grabez referred to them as "Kragujevac bombs."

Early on that fateful day as the Crown Prince's entourage moved slowly in procession through the town, Nedjelko Cabrinovic hurled one of the grenades, but it missed the Crown Prince's vehicle and exploded and injured the occupants of the following carriage.

The wounded were patched up, and the parade continued on to the Town Hall where the Mayor of Sarajevo had arranged a formal reception. On one page legend has it that Francis Ferdinand, in a haughty speech, dressed down his hosts for the lack of sufficient protection, but refused their entreaties not to ride back to his hotel in an open vehicle. Another version is that he was unable to touch his lunch and cringed in a shadowy corner, stating that he would under no circumstances make another trip in an open carriage. However, officials satisfied him that his safety would be assured for the rest of the day.

It was agreed finally that the Archduke and his wife should be driven to the railroad station at good speed over a circuitous route, but somewhere along the way the chauffeur became lost, and as he crept slowly through back streets, ran into a surprised Gavrilo Princip who, after Cabrinovic's failure, was skulking for cover.

As the royal chauffeur sought a familiar route, Princip stepped up to the car, drew his pistol, and started shooting. The Duchess threw herself in front of her husband and died from the first bullet. The second bullet hit the Archduke, who, before he died, is said to have gasped, "Vienna will give that young man a decoration for this."

Princip, who was consumptive, died in prison, but what happened to Cabrinovic is not clear; he was later reported to be an Austrian, not a Serb, and supposedly a spy in the police service.

The burial of the royal pair was lacking in the usual pomp and few dignitaries of any importance turned up for the funeral. But the assassination was enough for the Court of Franz Josef to forge a chain of argument against the Serbian government. Francis Ferdinand, who had dreamed of a powerful Austria, may not have conspired with Kaiser Wilhelm, but he was such a disreputable man it was easy to accuse him of plotting against European peace.

The Balkans breathed again, and Austria was satisfied that the Archduke Francis Ferdinand would conspire no more, and most people believed that true peace was at hand. Instead, Europe was to be drenched in blood for more than four years in payment for the death of this petty tyrant.

## Assault on Liége

The opening battle of World War I was the German assault on Liége during which the Belgians made one of the most heroic stands of that conflict. Historians do not agree as to the actual military value of this defense and resistance from the forts surrounding the gallant city. Many state that but for this long forgotten stand, the German armies would have swept on down and overwhelmed France before any effective opposition could be established; that she would have been beaten without having an opportunity to fight.

Of military importance or not, Liége's resistance was an event of rare moral and spiritual value. Belgium's brave stand was proclaimed throughout the world, and the depravity of Germany's aggression was highlighted in a manner no publicist could have matched. The great heart of the Belgian people equaled the honor which the German government had declared to be an empty word. The stand at Liége gave birth to the phrase "Brave Little Belgium."

The city of Liége, at the time a wealthy metropolis of eastern Belgium, stands on a broad river valley, the most obvious road from northern Germany into France. German plans had long included this pathway of invasion, and as early as August 3, 1914, her troops were crossing the Belgian border, seizing small frontier towns, such as Visé, and overcoming little Belgian outposts. By the morning of August 4 they were in front of Liége and demanding its surrender.

General Otto von Emmich, commander of the German VII Army Corps, concentrated on the plains before Herve from where he planned his attack on Forts Barchon, Evegnée, and Fléron. These strongholds were three of the twelve surrounding the city that formed a circle of concrete and steel thirty-three miles in circumference. Six of these redoubts were large forts, the remainder somewhat smaller. Built on the heights surrounding the city, about six miles from its center, they commanded the River Meuse, all the railroads, and highway approaches.

Each fort was armed with eight heavy guns or mortars, and four lighter caliber quick-firing guns. The chief weapons were shielded in steel cupolas designed by the Belgian military engineer and general, Henri Alexis Brialmont. Each stronghold had accommodations for 169 to 200 men. The steel and concrete redoubts were connected by an intricate trench system, practically a chain of lighter fortifications. In 1914 these forts were considered impregnable against all known artillery, and it was agreed generally that they could hold out for weeks against heavy siege guns. Each fort was a triangular mass equipped with revolving turrets that could "disappear," that is to say, be retracted for loading between rounds.

It was this formidable complex of defenses that the Germans had to capture or destroy before they could expect to take a permanent hold on Belgium.

At the time of the invasion the Liége fort system was held by approximately 22,000 Belgian troops, under the command of one of the war's most gallant soldiers, General Gérard Mathieu Leman. Actually, 50,000 men were needed for an adequate defense, but there was no time to assemble such a force. Aware of this, the Germans anticipated little difficulty in taking the three most easterly redoubts, Barchon, Evegnée, and Fléron. Furthermore, believing that little or no resistance would be met, the enemy prepared a timetable that presumed that Brussels would be taken by August 3, and Lille by August 5. But these calculations were rudely upset since Brussels had not fallen by the time of their opening attack on Liége.

On the night of August 4, the German VII Army Corps, then composed of 40,000 men, massed opposite the open country areas between the three forts. German artillery had shelled these structures a short time before, but the heavy concrete and steel took this hail with little effect. Some of the ammunition was poorly aimed, other shells were fitted with the wrong nose caps and exploded on impact instead of after penetration. There was no aviation capable of furnishing close reconnaissance, and the German infantry was ordered to advance with the understanding that the way had been opened by the artillery.

These peacetime professional soldiers advanced in close formation, shoulder to shoulder, like troops in a ceremonial marchpast. The Belgians made the most of the parade and with their rifle fire mowed down the oncoming troops like scythes reaping grain. One battalion formed up too close to the Belgian trenches and was wiped out before the order to advance could be given. When the spaces between the three forts were filled with marching Germans, the Belgians, from their trench fortifications, cut them down row by row. Men of the rear ranks had to struggle over mounds of dead and dying in their vain efforts to charge the defenders' positions.

Powerful searchlights illuminated the advancing columns and Belgian machine guns and light artillery swept wicked fire into the masses of struggling men. Not one German got to within fifty yards of the emplacements, and when it was seen that they had been halted and were being ordered to withdraw, the enthusiastic Belgians charged with the bayonet, drove their enemies into the dark, and then captured hundreds of prisoners.

So terrible was this first German defeat, General von Emmich was compelled to plead for an armistice to bury his dead. No longer trusting the Germans, the Belgians refused, knowing that General von Emmich would make other uses of any temporary cessation of hostilities.

The following morning, August 5, the invaders attempted another artillery attack, but the forts returned the fire and, since their garrison artillery outranged the German fieldpieces, the enemy suffered another setback. Several German big guns were totally destroyed and many others damaged. The German

General Staff then decided to send for heavier siege guns, and until these arrived attempted to gain possession of Belgian forts on the eastern bank of the river or even penetrate into the city itself. To carry out this plan General von Emmich called on the IX and X Army Corps which enabled him to extend his attack southward between Forts Flémalle, Boncelles, and Embourg.

With this extension of the German effort, General Leman sensed that he could not hold three German Army corps with the small force at his disposal; his problem was an efficient deployment of what forces he had available.

On August 5, General von Emmich made his first demand for the surrender of the city after he had laid down a preliminary bombardment, but General Leman refused to throw down his arms, and again flung back his adversaries as fast as they came marching through the spaces between the redoubts.

By early morning of August 6 the German big guns had been brought up and placed in position. They fired not only on the forts but poured hundreds of shells on the city itself, and panic broke out among the civilian population as the heavy barrage continued for seven hours. The roof of the cathedral was destroyed, many people were killed and hundreds injured. This cruel attack and its effect were so terrible, it was evident that to resist was folly, and the city surrendered although the forts were still intact.

Before the enemy marched into Liége, General Leman had withdrawn the bulk of his troops beyond the banks of the Meuse, but had left his forts well garrisoned and able to protect themselves. Thus the civilian city of Liége was in the hands of the Germans, but in the military sense its forts were intact and showered terrible execution on the enemy whenever he came within range of the guns and rifles of the Belgian troops sheltered there.

The entry into the city was carried out with due ceremony. The German troops goose-stepped in parade order and kept cadence to patriotic songs. Had it not been so tragic, the scene would have been ludicrous to the sidewalk watchers.

Stringent orders were issued and pasted on billboards and walls, and it was announced that if one shot was fired for any reason, the whole city would be devastated. Of course these orders could not be applied to the forts that still held out with guns that could shell the roads along which the enemy must advance. Beyond the circle of forts, the main Belgian force was advancing from Louvain to defend the right bank of the Meuse which, up to then, the Germans had failed to reach. The enemy had captured Liége using 120,000 men, but this army was in a difficult position since it was impossible for them to march out of the city in any sizable force, except at night. North and south of the city the Belgians had destroyed all the bridges over the Meuse, and as fast as the invaders erected pontoon bridges, artillery fire from the forts broke them up.

It was evident that the forts would have to be taken or destroyed before any planned advance could be started. A number of siege howitzers were brought up and the circle of redoubts blasted until they were piles of rubble. This was carried out in a grim systematic manner; each fort was bombarded as German infantry crept up gradually, isolated one from the other, and eventually became masters of the ground that separated the targets. At night more powerful batteries were brought in until the German infantry could strike from the forts' rear sides which had not been built to resist heavy attacks. While the main forts were cut off from the rest of the defense system, the troops inside courageously went about their routine business. Although shells could not penetrate the deeper galleries, they did destroy the electric generators, and all work and defense had to be carried out in total darkness. The ventilating systems were also damaged and the air was foul with the stench of acrid powder.

This attack and defense continued until August 14 when many new 21-cm siege guns opened up and continued a bombardment for twenty-four hours. The Belgians had no idea where the guns were emplaced, so had no targets to shoot at. Great shells bounced off the concrete and steel cupolas, splintered sheets of flame, and billowing smoke probed through every crack in the walls, and the garrisons had to concentrate in the large central gallery where they were comparatively safe.

Some time later, when General Leman was a prisoner at Magdeburg, he said that on the morning of August 15 bombardment by the 21-cm guns was started and one shell wrecked an arcade under which his general staff was sheltering. Horrible gases were discharged by this particular shell, and many of the officers appeared to be asphyxiated by the fumes.

(The next year when the Germans used poison gas at Ypres someone recalled the shells that had been fired into the forts at Liége, and debate arose as to whether such lethal fumes had been used at that time.)

After General Leman had ordered his inspection in the late afternoon of August 15, a new bombardment started in which siege mortars were used—weapons that hurled missiles that weighed almost a ton and exploded with a force never encountered before. As Leman moved back into the deeper shelter area, fighting smoke and fumes, a terrific explosion went up, and he stated afterward that he tried to get back to the bulk of his troops. En route he came upon some soldiers whom he mistook for Belgians, and as he called to them he fell unconscious from the fumes and gases.

A combination of enemy shellfire and embers from the internal fires had exploded a powder magazine in the large Loncin fort, the center of which collapsed in a cloud of flame and dust. Indescribable devastation resulted. A wild torrent of concrete, twisted steel, and burning walls crushed everyone beneath it. This was followed by an eerie silence, and then those who still lived saw German infantrymen streaming up and threading their way through the ruins.

General Leman was found unconscious but still breathing, and the Germans carried him out on a stretcher. Another enemy force was stopped by the sound of shots, and when a number of

portable electric lights were turned on, it found itself faced by
a handful of survivors who had massed at one end of the cor-
ridor. It must have been a fantastic sight for these valiant defenders were black with burned powder, their faces streaked
with blood, their uniforms in tatters. Twenty-five of these heroic figures, still clutching their arms, stood to resist the enemy.
Touched by this tableau of courage, the Germans made no attempt to mow them down, but hesitated, piled their own arms,
and rushed forward to aid the gallant defenders who were half-
asphyxiated by smoke and gases. In Fort Loncin alone, 350
men were dead and more than a hundred were seriously
wounded.

In commemoration of the gallant defense of Liége, the French
nation subsequently conferred the Legion of Honor on the city.
Independence was shown to be still treasured, an ideal worth
dying for. Honor was proven to be more than an empty word
for Belgium's little army had resisted "to the uttermost."

## Belgian Atrocities

Legend is intertwined with fact in the defense of Liége.
Whether poison gas was actually used may never be known,
but German prisoners taken some time before the first gas attack at Ypres on April 22, 1915, intimated that canisters of poison gas had been unloaded behind the German lines many
weeks before. And to top this, the Germans had long claimed
that the British were either planning or were ready to open
a poison-gas campaign, which in itself should have been sufficient warning that the Germans were only awaiting a suitable
situation in which they themselves could employ this new type
of warfare.

Whether a magazine explosion brought about General Leman's capture and put an end to the defenses is questioned in
German accounts that report that General Leman had disabled
his last three guns and exploded the supply of shells kept by
the guns in readiness, that he had burned all plans, maps, and
papers relating to the defenses, had destroyed food supplies,

and then had attempted to retire with one hundred men to another fort, but was cut off.

Believed to be dead when first found, General Leman was carried out, but, on recovering and looking around, is reported to have said, "It is as it is. The men fought valiantly, but please put in your dispatch that I was unconscious," to which General von Emmich replied, "You have fought gallantly, and nobly held your forts." General Leman then said, "War is not like maneuvers," a reference to the time the two generals had been together during previous Belgian war games. When General Leman attempted to unbuckle his sword, General von Emmich said, "No, keep it. To have crossed swords with you has been an honor."

Crocodile tears were shed by German Chancellor Theobald von Bethmann-Hollweg during an official address to the Belgian government in which he said, "The fortress of Liége has been taken by assault after a gallant defense. My Government deeply regrets that the attitude of the Belgian Government toward Germany has led to sanguinary encounters. Germany does not come to Belgium as an enemy. It was only when it had been forced by circumstances and in presence of military dispositions made by France that the German Government was obliged to take the grave step of penetrating into Belgium and of occupying Liége as a *point d'appui* (point of support, or basis) for further military operations.

"The Belgian Army having preserved in the most brilliant fashion the honor of its armies by its heroic resistance against a greatly superior force, the German Government now asks H.M. the King and the Belgian Government to spare Belgium the continuation of the horrors of war. The German Government is ready to enter into any kind of convention with Belgium which can in any way be made compatible with the difference between itself and France. Germany reaffirms in the most solemn manner that she has not been actuated by any intention to appropriate Belgian territory; such an intention was foreign to her. Germany is still always ready immediately to evacuate

the kingdom of Belgium as soon as the situation in the theatre
of war permits her to do so."

That month of months closed in gloom with the fall of Liége,
Namur, and Brussels, the sack of Louvain, and the repulse of
the Russian raid into East Prussia at Tannenberg, following in
rapid succession.

But the Belgian government rejected Germany's offer to spare
its country from the horrors of war, and continued to raise an
army for opposition against the passage of troops "necessitated
by the enemies of Germany."

Germany then began her world-wide proclamations of Belgian treachery. The people whose land they invaded, were said
to have fired on German troops, taken part in combat while wearing civilian dress, killed the wounded, and shot doctors who
were attending the injured. The lamb refused to be slaughtered
by the wolf or to lie still while being devoured by the wolf.
The population of Antwerp was said to have destroyed German
property in a "barbarous manner," some civilians had even cut
the telegraph and telephone wires, while wearing everyday
clothing.

The Germans were unable to understand these Belgian actions, and countered with new "atrocities." Wounded soldiers
were found outside villages, hands bound and their eyes put
out. No one ever learned the names of these victims, near what
villages these incidents took place, or who discovered the un-
happy situations. A young woman stepped up to the German
chauffeur of a military automobile and when his back was
turned, shot him dead. Her name was not revealed, where it
happened, or the name of the German chauffeur.

The German newspapers conducted a definite campaign and
because the neutral world could read it in print, a percentage of the incidents was believed.

The American Minister to Belgium at the time, Brand
Whitlock, sent a full and revealing account to the United
States Secretary of State of the German troops' behavior during

those early weeks. He wrote: "During the whole of that terrible month of August and during part of September eastern Belgium was the scene of such happenings, from the deliberate and systematic organized massacres of civil populations, with isolated murders and outrages, violations of women, and those nameless deeds one cannot bring one's self to mention and yet somehow hears, down to the sack of wine cellars by drunken soldiers."

Once a Belgian town was subjected to fire and the sword, it was easy for a drunken soldier to bellow, "Someone fired a shot at us!"

But Brand Whitlock's report was not made public until September 12, 1917, five months after America entered the conflict, and as was to be expected, German apologists denounced the paper as just another contrived justification for our declaration of war.

A German, Major General Disfurth, settled the whole matter of Belgian atrocities with: "No object whatever is served in taking any notice of the accusations of barbarity leveled against Germany by our foreign critics. Frankly, we are and must be barbarians, if by this we understand those who wage war relentlessly and to the uttermost degree. There is nothing for us to justify and nothing to explain away. Every act of whatever nature committed by our troops for the purpose of discouraging, defeating and destroying our enemies is a brave act and a good deed and is fully justified . . . Germany stands as the supreme arbiter. The commonest, ugliest stone placed to mark the burial place of a German grenadier is a more glorious and venerable monument than all the cathedrals of Europe put together."

## The Angel of Mons

In Great Britain Lord Horatio H. Kitchener asked for 500,000 men—and got them. In fact, the recruiting stations were overwhelmed with volunteers, and many who had left their jobs had to be sent home again to await openings and the manufacture of uniforms, a situation that made popular the music-hall ditty "Sister Susie's Sewing Shirts for Soldiers." Recruits were seen drilling with wooden guns while wearing bowler hats, Newmarket leggings and out-at-the-elbows Norfolk jackets. These amateurs developed a spirit worthy of the Regulars, and as one wag wrote, "Feed them like princes, pamper them like babies, and they'll complain all the time, but stand them up to be shot at and they'll take it as a joke, and a rather good joke, too!"

The Russians, who had joined the carnage, were supposed to have won a great victory in southeast Poland at Przemyśl, but because no Englishman could pronounce that name, the success was more often transferred to another area that was less of a tongue-twister. The Russians also provided the first absurd legend of this war.

Since no one knew exactly how many men Russia could put into the field, it was easy and reassuring to believe that the Czar would send a few thousand soldiers to Belgium or France to help out there. Why not? Censorship was clamped down tight everywhere and it was reasonable to assume that something important would have to happen if all those German atrocities were to be dealt with.

And so began the tall tale of a quarter of a million Russian soldiers passing through Great Britain on their way to France. Everyone seemed to know about this massive migration. Whispers were heard on street corners, small groups in pubs discussed it, everyone knew someone who had actually seen these strapping Cossacks, and the matter was settled to the satisfaction of all concerned when a railroad porter solemnly declared, "How do I know these Rooshuns really came through? I was on the platform when the train went through, and then when it came back all the floors and seat cushions were still covered with snow. Snow, off their boots. If that ain't proof, what is?"

Unfortunately, by August 31, the Russian army of invasion that had marched into East Prussia was soundly defeated by General Paul von Hindenburg at Tannenberg, and all hope of succor from the North melted with the mythical snow from the Russian boots.

British troops had their first real test of battle at Mons, the
capital of Hainaut Province in Belgium. This famous engagement began on August 23, 1914, and by the next day the greatly
outnumbered "Contemptibles" began their historic retreat,
marked by the Battle of Le Cateau, that ended on the Marne
where a Franco-British offensive turned the tide.

It was here that the Coldstream Guards encountered the
Angel of Mons. The Coldstreamers—never refer to them as the
Coldstreams—were first organized by Oliver Cromwell in 1650,
and from the point of age are the senior Guards regiment of the
British Army. These men were first-class Regulars, highly trained,
but, more important, inspired by great regimental tradition.

Moving in their long-planned "around the right end" thrust,
the Germans were fighting with rare caution but determination.
The French were hampered by a lack of reliable information,
and although a General Sordêt's cavalry corps had moved
ahead, it was blocked off by better armed German cavalry and
cyclist corps, and when French divisions tried to move forward
they were cut to ribbons by unexpected enemy forces.

In the ensuing mixup, infantrymen fought with revolvers or
the bayonet. At Ethe, light artillery was used point-blank in the
streets. One hundred Frenchmen, spaced at ten-yard intervals
on a one-thousand-yard front, halted five German battalions at
Neufchâteau for almost an hour, but finally had to retire with
the satisfaction that they had at least held up the enemy wheel-
ing action at a critical period.

The next French army that moved up faced an unpleasant
predicament, for on its left wing there was only a handful of
troops to hold important ground to the west and north. General
Charles Louis Marie Lanrezac had no choice but to appeal to
the British, who had only just landed and were grouping at
Tournai. The German General Alexander von Kluck believed he
had an excellent opportunity to outflank General Lanrezac, but
his information was scanty, and he was astonished to find four
British divisions blocking him.

The BEF had crossed the Channel and landed at Le Havre

under the protection of the Royal Navy. The Imperial German Navy had made no attempt to interfere, since General Helmuth von Moltke had insisted that he wished to deal with this puny force straight away and put it in the same bag as the French in the great victory that was sure to come.

The British enjoyed some protection behind the Mons-Condé Canal, but could not prevent the enemy from crossing east of Mons since there was no true joint of the French and British armies. This forced a withdrawal of the British right flank, and the move was made so hastily soldiers of infantry, cavalry, and artillery fought in a complex of black slag heaps, pithead buildings, and the engine houses of a large coal field. Cavalry was hampered under these crowded conditions, and artillery batteries had no field of fire. In fact, one British battery was hauled to the top of a slag heap to find a target.

On Sunday, August 23, 1914, the town of Mons responded to the church bells, and ignorant of what was about to happen, went hopefully to the services.

General von Kluck had an excellent opportunity to outflank the Old Contemptibles, but he was under the command of General Karl von Bülow, an elderly, cautious man who was trying to prove he was a born fire-eater, although adverse to taking risks. He forbade General von Kluck from swinging wide, and this timorous decision compelled Kluck to send his First Army head-on against the British. This proved to be unfortunate for the Tommies put on one of their amazing fifteen-rounds-rapid-fire displays that mowed down their enemies like chaff. The defense was so devastating, the Germans were convinced they had walked into a "machine-gun army," although at this time the British had but two machine guns to a battalion. It was superb musketry that stopped the enemy at Mons—for a short time.

"Our rushes became shorter," a German corporal admitted, "and finally the whole advance came to a stop. We suffered bloody losses and the attack gradually came to a close."

But sheer weight prevailed finally, particularly in the salient

formed by a loop in the canal north of Mons. And so it was
decided to withdraw by night to a position two and one half
miles south of the town. By midnight British General Sir John
French learned from General Lanrezac that he had been ordered by superiors of his Fifth Army to retreat—a withdrawal
that was to begin in the early morning of August 24. The French
had been heavily engaged all day long and had had to face
possible attacks from the east and north simultaneously. General
Lanrezac also explained that the French withdrawal from the
Ardennes by the armies on his right made his position doubly
dangerous.

The British leader had no choice. He had to issue parallel
orders, for there was no possibility of making a stand south of
Mons: he would have to go along and accept the hazards of
a long retreat. The BEF withdrew skillfully without the loss of
one gun, but the troops were puzzled and worried by a retirement that made little sense to them, for they thought they were
victorious. The French also withdrew well, but the German
First and Second Armies pressed closely on their heels. When
the British reached the Mormal Forest in northern France they
split into two corps and passed on either side of it, not knowing
there was a sheltered road through it that would have afforded
cover to at least one corps. It was during this part of the movement that the Coldstreamers experienced their astonishing encounter with the Angel of Mons.

When the retreat started the Coldstream Guards were the
last to be withdrawn, and in the half-light of a false dawn they
became lost and wandered about trying to make contact with
their main body. When it was obvious that they were completely
out of touch, they dug in, determined to make another stand
with the daylight.

"Wot the 'ell are we retreatin' for?" one Guardsman is said to
have demanded.

"How should I know? We're probably going to attack 'em
in the rear."

"I was having a glorious time," another grumbled. "Just like knocking down a set of skittles."

"Well, it looks like we're in a fine mess 'ere. Nobody seems to know where we are."

At that moment when one of the Guardsmen looked up to make certain his digging lined up with that of the next man, he noticed a warm glow just ahead. For a second he thought someone was moving about with a farm lantern.

"Who's that messin' about out there, carrying a light, the damn fool?"

"Some bloody-fool French farmer."

"We ain't in France. This is Belgium, so they tell me."

"Who knows? . . . Coo! Look at that!"

The glowing nimbus moved in closer and the Coldstreamers perceived the dim outline of a female figure. As it became more distinct, they decided that they were looking at an angel. It looked exactly like any angel they had ever seen in a regimental chapel: tall, slim, and wearing a white flowing gown. She had a gold band around her hair and Eastern sandals on her feet, a pair of white wings were folded against her slim back.

"Crikey!" one of the Guardsmen gasped. "What sort of game is this?"

"She's beckoning to us," another muttered slowly.

"What's she want?" the first Guardsman inquired tonelessly.

No question about it, the angel was inviting them to follow her. She moved closer to the digging and her signal was more insistent.

No one remembers who first crawled out of the shallow slots, but one by one the Coldstreamers lined up, after hauling out their rifles and entrenching tools, and followed the glowing figure across an open field.

"Did you ever read about anything like this in your Sunday-school papers?" a puzzled Tommy asked over his shoulder.

"Keep moving, and ask no questions."

The angel moved on, her right hand still making that inviting gesture until she came to a halt on the upper rim of a sunken road.

The Guardsmen looked down in surprise. "How did she know this road was here? It wasn't here when we tried to get out of this mess," one of them said. "Bloody funny to me."

"You're right, chum. I was leading the patrol that went out this way. We was lookin' for a pathway like this, but it wasn't 'ere then," a young corporal insisted.

"Well, 'ere it is now. Come on."

The vision led the way until all the Coldstreamers reached the end of the sunken road, then she floated up the bank and pointed toward a covering copse a few dozen yards away. She smiled—and vanished.

Not questioning this strange visitation, the Guardsmen were gratified to escape and join the other British forces. Their defense and eventual stand enabled Generals Joffre and French to re-form and dig in around Le Cateau.

Within a few days the story had trickled all along the front and for a time the Angel of Mons was accepted as a friendly token of the Almighty. What made the story more puzzling was that no one ever found that sunken road again. The Coldstreamers pored over every available map but could not find one on which it was traced.

Today, no one can explain how the Coldstream Guards escaped at Mons, but they did. Members of the present-day regiment no doubt scoff at the legend and argue that those were weary, battle-tortured men whose minds were fertile soil for any kind of hallucination, but those same Coldstream Guards went from Mons to a very exposed position outside Ypres (now Ieper) and held it, unrelieved, for three weeks!

## Miracle of the Marne

To neutral observers, glancing over newspaper war maps, it looked as though the Germans were winning hands down, but the position of the Allies was not so perilous as it appeared. British musketry had inflicted severe losses on the invaders, and in all the areas of retreat the enemy had captured but thirty-eight guns and only a few prisoners. General von Moltke was disturbed by this and demanded to know why no great victories had been scored. "You have advanced, yes," he bellowed at his field commanders, "but where are the spoils? Where are the prisoners? Where are the big guns?"

The First Battle of the Marne unquestionably saved France and civilization. Autocracy and Prussianism were for the time destroyed. This campaign was chiefly a French operation, and although the British were close at hand, they had no great share in the victory. It was Sir John French's task to halt the British withdrawal and make some sort of stand against General von Kluck's two-corps army.

Simultaneously with this British stand, French General Michel Joseph Maunoury's new Sixth Army was to assault the flank and rearguard of General von Kluck along the Ourcq River. General Joseph J. C. Joffre, as commander in chief, had planned this for September 5, but General French, after inspecting his weary troops—his cavalrymen were falling out of their saddles fast asleep—requested forty-eight hours in which his heroes of Mons could gain some rest. But such a delay was out of the question since there was some chance that General von Kluck's army might join up with those under the German Crown Prince. Thus, the French went ahead on their own with only a few British regiments available to fight in the area left of Château-Thierry.

It should be understood that this war had already presented mass-and-movement problems that no commanding general had encountered before. The German Schlieffen Plan that included the invasion of Belgium, was already far too involved to be executed with the available communications. Wireless was comparatively new, and what portable sets were at hand were ill-fitted for field operations. Military telephony was also in its infancy and most unreliable. French cavalry had already been cut to ribbons, and only a few cyclists or motorcyclists provided any trustworthy picture. The modern soldier will ponder on the use of the airplane—it was here that the Royal Flying Corps gained

its first laurel. The reconnaissance, carried out by their old unarmed biplanes, was the one factor that brought on the enemy
downfall. General Joffre knew almost to the minute what move
General von Moltke would make next, or where his real strength
lay.

Joffre first fixed a limit for the movement of the retreat, a line
through Bray-Nogent-Vitry and the region north of Bar-le-Duc.
His forces were to withdraw no farther, but would attack as soon
as there was a possibility of bringing about an offensive disposition, permitting the co-operation of all French forces. Such a
situation had arisen by September 5.

"The hour has come," General Joffre told his troops. "You will
advance at all costs, and die where you stand rather than give
way."

Basil H. Liddell Hart, noted British historian, has stated that
no battle has caused more controversy, produced so wide a shelf
of literature in so short a time, or given rise to more popular interest and legend than that of the Marne.

There is the assertion that "Papa" Joffre conceived the idea of
his counteroffensive *after* General Joseph Simon Gallieni's initiative had set up the opportunity. And still another group insists
that after Joffre's first attempt to stage a counteroffensive had
failed, he had given up all hope of victory, and that but for
Gallieni's determination and personal persuasion, the French retreat would have continued.

It is fairly obvious that the German redistribution of troops
would have been carried out, leaving no open flank to break
through, had it not been for Gallieni's assault from the outskirts
of Paris.

A similiar controversy ensued on the German side for years.
Much of this was based on the lack of reconnaissance and information available to General von Moltke, and his decisions
made under stress of his unenviable position. Knowing that the
French would have to make a stand somewhere, he worried
himself frantic trying to learn exactly what General Joffre was
doing. Hesitating, he acted overly cautious and finally came to

the conclusion that the main strength of his enemy lay in the region of Paris; first to protect the capital, and second to threaten the right flank of the German Army. He, therefore, commanded his First and Second Armies on the right wing to wheel right, move on the eastern side of Paris and then halt, an action designed to cover the rest of the armies against French attacks from that quarter. The other armies were to continue their progress, but the Third was to halt when it reached the Seine.

As so often happens, these orders were not delivered in time to be wholly effective by September 5. But time waits on no man, and during that afternoon General Maunoury's new Sixth Army came upon General von Kluck's corps that had been disposed as a right-flank guard. Outnumbered, the Germans retired for a distance of six miles. This was the first engagement of the Battle of the Marne, a conflict that was to detonate or fizz up and down the front for nearly a week from Verdun to Compiègne, a distance of more than one hundred miles.

To simplify the general engagement, it might be explained that Maunoury's persistent stripping of Kluck's First Army, one corps after another, must have saved Paris. The German Third Army had to be withdrawn from its original front, leaving a gaping hole on the right of Bülow's Second Army, a space lightly held by some cavalry, one infantry brigade, and a few Jaeger battalions.

It was into this gap that the British Expeditionary Force, now six divisions strong, marched to what might have been one of the most rewarding assaults of British arms. Unfortunately, the Royal Flying Corps was operating for General Joffre farther south and Sir John French had no idea how weak the opposition was ahead of him.

Had they known the true situation they might have gone to glory. Instead, the BEF advance moved at the rate of eight miles a day, when twelve would have been enough to sever General von Kluck's three corps from the rest of the German Army and permit General French to make a timely attack from the rear while General Maunoury was hammering at their front.

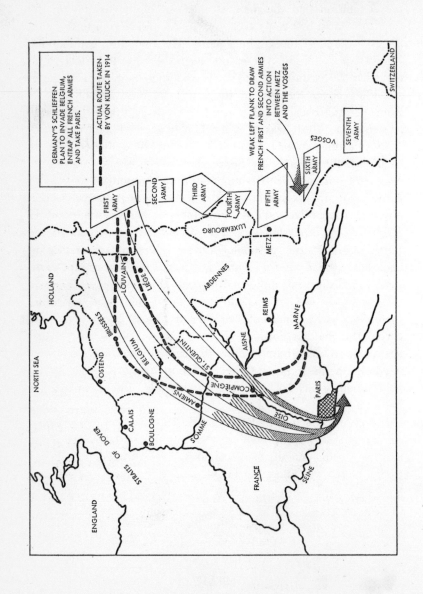

GERMANY'S SCHLIEFFEN
PLAN TO INVADE BELGIUM,
ENTRAP ALL FRENCH ARMIES
AND TAKE PARIS.

ACTUAL ROUTE TAKEN
BY VON KLUCK IN 1914

WEAK LEFT FLANK TO DRAW
FRENCH FIRST AND SECOND ARMIES
INTO ACTION
BETWEEN METZ
AND THE VOSGES

FIRST ARMY

SECOND ARMY

THIRD ARMY

FOURTH ARMY

FIFTH ARMY

SIXTH ARMY

SEVENTH ARMY

VOSGES

LUXEMBOURG

METZ

ARDENNES

REIMS

AISNE

MARNE

ST. QUENTIN

COMPIEGNE

OISE

PARIS

SEINE

FRANCE

AMIENS

SOMME

BELGIUM

BRUSSELS

LOUVAIN

LIÉGE

OSTEND

HOLLAND

NORTH SEA

CALAIS

BOULOGNE

STRAITS OF DOVER

ENGLAND

SWITZERLAND

Prior to all this, a new French Ninth Army was fighting the Germans along Petit-Morin where the enemy had the best of the exchange. No matter what the French generals did in this area, they had little success. How much this contributed to the situation farther north is an interesting point.

General von Moltke was suffering a variety of tortures. For one thing he was under the impression that several more British divisions had been transported across the Channel "along with thousands of Russian troops" who were believed to be disembarking at several Belgian ports. His meager wireless communications were being jammed by French antennas erected on the Eiffel Tower, and the German leader began to lose his nerve.

Distraught, bewildered, and incapable of commanding on such a wide front, he made a decision that has been discussed by military experts ever since. He sent one of his staff officers, Colonel Hentsch, the Chief of Intelligence, on a four-hundred-mile round trip from Luxembourg, new base of the German Western Army headquarters, to analyze the general situation at the front. Obviously, Moltke was in a panic, for he sent Hentsch on this trip with written instructions and full authority to order, in case of necessity, a withdrawal to positions behind the Vesle River.

Colonel Hentsch left about noon of September 8 to visit in turn the five German armies west of Verdun. With full powers to co-ordinate the retreat "should rearward movements have been initiated," he called at the headquarters of the Fifth, Fourth, and Third armies that afternoon and learned that those commanders were satisfied with their positions. Continuing on, he spent the night with General von Bülow, the Second Army commander, where he found a dreary atmosphere of gloom, and when he left the next morning, September 9, it was apparent that orders for a retreat would be given soon. One air reconnaissance had shown that six enemy columns, one French and five British cavalry units, were approaching the Marne. This worried General von Bülow who realized that this mobile force actually was entering the critical gap in the German line. According to general reports, he issued an order to retreat by 11 A.M. and had sent General von Kluck a report of his decision.

Meanwhile Colonel Hentsch was driving north over a road cluttered with transports of all kinds, and it required almost five hours to cover thirty-seven miles. In fact, he was held up at one point by a British air attack, indicating that some lone flight of the Royal Flying Corps of that early date was carrying out more than a routine reconnaissance. In all probability the airmen dropped a primitive form of road grenade.

With all this delay Hentsch never saw General von Kluck, but the general's chief of staff advised him that orders for a retirement had already gone out and General von Moltke's emissary simply added the direction of the retreat—to the northeast.

Later on General von Kluck's chief of staff argued that these retirement orders were the mistake of a subordinate and that he had ordered only a swing back to the left in view of the fact that the British were almost behind him. He stated, too, that Colonel Hentsch, knowing General von Bülow's situation, gave the orders to retreat. These charges and countercharges were made after the Armistice when Hentsch, who died before the war ended, was not available for comment. A court of inquiry, held shortly after the retreat, agreed that the emissary had carried out his mission according to the instructions issued by General Moltke.

Actually, the German withdrawal began at two o'clock that afternoon. The roads had been cleared completely, and neither General von Kluck nor General Kuhl, Prince Rupprecht of Bavaria's chief of staff, troubled to request a written order so eager were they to get away. General Kuhl admitted later that the imminent breakthrough of the British and French made the retreat inevitable. British penetration had indeed forced General von Kluck's army to retreat north, widening the gap still more.

The Battle of the Marne, therefore, was a strategic, not a tactical victory. Few German prisoners were taken, and most of these were inebriated soldiers trapped in wine cellars. Yet the Marne proved to be one of the vital battles of history. The Germans had come within an ace of successfully employing their Schlieffen Plan, and ending it with the complete defeat of the French. They had lost the opportunities awarded by striking the first blow—and the violation of Belgium's neutrality. Their defeat was largely moral, for in the higher leadership of Moltke, Bülow, and Kluck, they were never able to produce leaders with the skill, courage, and drive of Joffre, Foch, and Franchet d'Esperey.

Had other French commanders of lesser rank not been content to enjoy this return of fortune and shown more decision and skill in swelling the results of this victory, there is no telling what the over-all result might have been. Instead the Goddess of Victory suddenly smiled in the other direction. A German corps that had been marching over a zigzag course from Alsace, and another that had been engaged in the siege of Maubeuge where the French garrison surrendered on September 7, suddenly appeared and filled the gap between the German First and Second Armies. Some hot fighting resulted, but by now the Allies had decided to slow down, and their advance was brought to a halt. They could not know that the Germans had been ready to move back all the way to the Oise, an area of more than twenty miles between Soissons and La Fère, if they could not form a new front on the Aisne.

An interesting study might be made of the part played by Verdun during this Battle of the Marne. Verdun's garrison intervened actively on General Maurice P. M. Sarrail's right, and the 72nd Division under a General Heymann harassed and held back the German columns while a General de Morlaincourt, supporting a General Coutanceau, attacked in the direction of Dombasle. During the bombardment of Fort Troyon, General Coutanceau sustained the defenders' courage with pressing messages and ordered General Noël de Castelnau, Commander of the Second Army, to the rescue.

Speaking of legends, we have one in our family, a typical epic of a hero who almost reached the pinnacle of glory, but war is a lottery, and the winners are usually the luckier ones rather than the most worthy. Their time brackets are propitious, and what they do is noted by those responsible for the wording of the citation; the measure of their gallantry depends on who witnesses the incident.

During the First Battle of the Marne, my uncle, Sergeant Arthur Whitehouse, who was manning one of the few machine guns allotted to his regiment, gallantly hung on to his post until he was the only man of his gun team left alive. Unquestionably, he fought well with outstanding valor and maintained the traditions of the Lancasters (The King's Own). One of his superior officers recommended him for the Victoria Cross, but another commissioned gentleman, who valued field tactics above the courage of one heroic soul, charged the sergeant with disclosing his company's position and demanded that he be court-martialed. Somewhere between these divergent viewpoints a happy medium was reached; my uncle was deprived of his sergeant's stripes, but given the Distinguished Conduct Medal—an award that could be bestowed on any regimental baker who had turned out his quota of loaves of bread during his particular period of wartime servitude.

This is the epic of the Whitehouse family, and whether it be truth or legend, none of us could vouch today, for Sergeant Whitehouse was killed in World War II while serving as a motorcycle despatch rider, but we would not swap the tale for half a dozen Victoria Crosses.

### Bloody Wipers

With the German Army in retreat, or at best making desperate stands, or holding rearguard positions, the Allies failed to realize their great opportunity. They settled down in billets, instead, and figured how soon they might cross the German frontier. Sir John French lost a sterling chance when he failed to advise his troop commanders of their favorable advantage or the necessity for speed. General Joffre performed no better, but what was to be expected of a man who refused to talk on a telephone?

Owing to the hole in the German front, British cavalry moved up with no trouble, but instead of crossing the Aisne River, General Haig's cavalry corps unsaddled and settled in billets. The French cavalry actually reached the river where there was an opening forty miles deep that exposed critical German communications to their assault. But believing they were riding into possible danger, the French horsemen under a General Conneau, actually retired.

Failure of the higher command to appreciate the situation was given as the explanation of these desultory movements, and by the time the troops were ready and anxious to move on, German reserves had filled in the gap. No organized attack was prepared, no plan was available, no objective seen, and no arrangements for further co-operation were completed. The available divisions simply blundered into their next battles.

This allowed the Germans to rebuild their front. The deep trench systems were being dug, and the machine gun chattered its first full chorus of martial discord. The enemy line was strung with barbed wire and gradually built into an impregnable barrier. When General Joffre had completed his formal message of success to his government, an epistle that was to haunt him for the rest of his career, there was no enemy gap to march through. His so-called race-to-the-sea was a pathetic series of sidesteps, each so uninspired and obvious, the enemy had no trouble in brushing them aside.

While the Belgian Army still hung on to Antwerp and maintained a continued menace to German communications, it seemingly never occurred to Joffre that this situation might be developed, or to send French forces to reinforce the Belgians.

The British saw the opportunity, but Lord Kitchener refused to send any of his eleven Territorial divisions, saying they were not ready for front-line action. When the Germans began bombarding the Antwerp forts, the First Lord of the Admiralty, Winston Churchill, took matters into his own hands, after pleading with the C-in-C, and sent over a handful of Royal Marines and Naval volunteers. These men made a gallant effort, but

could not save Antwerp—most of them were killed or captured—
but they did help the Belgian Army to slip away and evade annihilation. The time gained was also the salvation of the Channel
ports.

The German general, Erich von Falkenhayn, who had replaced General von Moltke, was aiming to sweep down the Belgian coast, while General Joffre was timidly using his narrow
outflanking movements, and take the ports so vital to Britain's
communication with France. Surprisingly, these cities had been
left untouched during the weeks that Germany could have
seized them without much opposition. Antwerp did not fall until October 10, 1914, and nearly a week more passed before enemy forces, reinforced by four newly raised Army corps, started
their drive for the coast.

General Joffre urged King Albert of Belgium to withdraw his
forces from the coast and join some fictitious wing in Flanders.
King Albert refused the appeal and persisted in holding a line
that would protect the Channel ports. The Belgian Army had to
hold the enemy for ten days when the Germans swept down from
Antwerp and struck at the Yser line, and only by opening the
locks and allowing water from the sea to flow in was it able to
stem the German attack.

This forced the enemy to turn inland toward the Ypres sector
where, fortunately, the main British Army had been transferred
from the Aisne to serve with a French army as the left tip of
Joffre's latest ouflanking maneuver. On reaching Ypres, Sir
Douglas Haig's cavalry corps attempted to advance but met a
new German offensive made by comparatively raw troops while
General von Falkenhayn's war-experienced armies were practically idle between the Aisne and the Vosges. Colonel Wilhelm
Gröner, Chief of the Field Railways, advised General von Falkenhayn that he could move six army corps to the German right
wing, but the general turned down the offer. These troops might
have broken through the thin British line and brought the war
to a speedy close, but once more the German High Command

saved the Allies. And to add to this military tangle, General Erich Ludendorff was asking for reinforcements to start his wedge blow at the Russian flank near Lodz. Again General von Falkenhayn vacillated and missed this chance by delaying until his troops had bumbled their way into defeat at Ypres.

This First Battle of Ypres has to be read several times to be believed. While a puny British force moved toward Ypres with small idea of what enemy power lay before it, Generals Foch and French were comfortable in their château headquarters sublimely issuing orders to "continue the advance," ignoring the fact that their troops were clinging frantically to any fold of ground or natural cover to keep from being overrun.

By the time reality had set in and it was explained that the Allies were *under* attack, not making one, a lull in the enemy assault was awaited, upon which General French sent Lord Kitchener the word, "The enemy are vigorously playing their last card." By October 24, General French ordered his own offensive to be resumed and reported that the battle was practically won, and that the Germans were incapable of making any strong and sustained attack.

But in response the Germans staged a series of heavy blows against the British line. After two days of this a breach was forced at the southern flank, but this hole was filled by a few scratch troops who held on until Haig's center was pierced and broken. General French appealed to General Foch for help, but the Frenchman replied, "General French, your lines are pierced. You have no troops available. You have no alternative but to advance," and with that General Foch gave a half promise that his troops would try to counterattack to relieve the pressure.

Luckily for General Haig, the Germans reacted the same as had the British when they faced a wide gap; they did not know how to exploit their success and while they halted, the British counterattacked, as did the French, and the situation was saved. The French effort was not truly a victory for they lost Messines Ridge on their southern flank, and the German offensive in this area reached its climax on November 11.

As winter came on, the action subsided. The miracle of the
Marne had been followed by the miracle of Ypres. Outgunned
and outnumbered, the British had stemmed the German rush to
the sea, the road to Calais had been blocked, as had that to
Paris. Japan had scored a telling victory at Tsingtao in China,
and with it went Germany's scheme for an Oriental empire. Turkey had joined the Central Powers, and the war was already cost-
ing Great Britain one million pounds a day.

But it is interesting to note that at this time a proposal to
change the name of Berlin Road in the Lewisham district of
London was rejected by the residents.

### That Phony Christmas

The first war Christmas seemed to apply a warm embrocation
to the wounds and sorrows. It was decided that "for the sake of
the children" the holidays should be celebrated as usual, a theme
quickly adopted by all the shopkeepers in Britain who responded with alacrity. Early in December colorful signs reading:

BUSINESS AS USUAL<br>
DURING ALTERATIONS<br>
TO THE MAP OF EUROPE

were seen in all the busy towns, and barrel organs ground out
chromatic variations of "Tipperary," "Meet Me in the Shadows,"
and a particularly discordant atrocity, presumed to be "La Mar-
seillaise."

London was especially gay that Christmas. Everyone already
in khaki was hoping for the best, and making the most of this
opportunity to go on the "razzle" before being selected for the
next overseas draft. The shops and stores were well stocked, and
there was no suggestion of rationing. The theatres were packed,
and Christmas trees were on sale at every corner. *Peter Pan* was
at the Duke of York's Theatre with Madge Titheradge playing
the title role, *Hullo Tango!* was packing them in at the London
Hippodrome, and Sir Gerald du Maurier (the distinguished ac-

tor-father of novelist Daphne du Maurier) was starring in a re-
vival of *Raffles* at Wyndham's Theatre.

The shock of Mons and the Aisne left an ache in the hearts of
the middle-aged, but the young people were still exhilarated by
the progress of events—*and* the standings of the football leagues.
By now, no one believed that it would all be over by Christmas,
but everyone was putting on a good face, trusting that the New
Year of 1915 would bring brighter prospects. Only one undis-
tinguished penny-a-liner, scribbling for *Punch,* had the temerity
to predict that the war would go on until Christmas 1918. His
name has never appeared in any military anthology.

That Christmas brought a swath of dreadful weather and for
days southern England was lost in a pea-soup fog. A number of
gales and blizzards swept away the murk, and with it went
church steeples, billboards, house roofs, and hundreds of age-old
trees. Many small fishing smacks, nosing out from the East Coast,
were sent to the bottom. All this disturbance was charged to "all
them big guns going off all over France." Today, meteorological
phenomenon is blamed on atomic tests, or jet planes shattering
the sound barrier.

Those who were already in military service and undergoing
training in England were fortunate if they could get home for
forty-eight hours during Christmas week. Actually, there were
very few men in khaki to be seen on the streets, although recruiting had more than satisfied Lord Kitchener. But there were not
enough uniforms to supply the long lines of volunteers, and hundreds had to be sent home to await supplies, or they reported
willingly to military depots and drilled in whatever they wore.
Still, the Yuletide was enlivened by the military, and the odor of
stiff leather, dubbined boots, polished bandoliers, and Brassoed
buttons wafted through the shops and restaurants.

"Are we downhearted?" soldiers on one side of any street
would bellow.

"Nao!" those on the other side would respond.

By December 1914 there was a great deal of talk of capturing

Germany's world trade, and a scheme to manufacture aniline dyes was considered by the government. Wide studies of German industrial products were undertaken, and everyone was certain that British skills would soon reproduce enemy goods that would compete in quality and price. Christmas also suggested an attack on the Nuremberg toy market, and one ambitious manufacturer of Stoke-on-Trent began to turn out dolls' heads, but when it was suggested that Sheffield attempt to produce cheap "German-type" cutlery for the foreign market, all interest in this questionable venture dissipated.

With all the talk of war in the air, England was not raided until that Christmas Eve. A small patrol of German aircraft did approach Britain on December 21, but the pilots thought better of the venture and dropped their bombs into the sea before they reached the coast. Then, in the early morning of December 24, a small German biplane sneaked through the Channel mists, and made a wide turn over Dover. A very primitive bomb was dropped. It fell in the garden of a Mr. T. A. Terson, who lived near the St. James's Rectory, and exploded, doing little damage. This was the first time in history that Albion was raided from the air.

The raiders came again on Christmas Day. A monoplane, probably a Taube, was seen flying high over Eastchurch and approaching Sheerness. The antiaircraft guns went into action and three British airplanes went up to intercept, but with what is not known; the aircraft of that day had not progressed to the armed-fighter stage. No bombs were dropped but the raid did create new interest in a proposed Anti-Zeppelin and Air-War Insurance policy to be offered as a circulation builder by the London *Daily News*.

The Air Arm of the British Navy retaliated with a raid on the German Zeppelin sheds at the seaport of Cuxhaven, 315 miles from the coast of England. After being transported across the North Sea aboard several naval vessels and lowered into the water, a flight of seven seaplanes roared off and attacked the

German naval installations and shipping lying in the Schillig Roads. The naval flotilla was composed of light cruisers, destroyers, and submarines.

The Germans tried everything in the way of counterdefense. Garrison batteries and guns aboard their warships greeted the British fliers. Two Zeppelins hove into view during the furor, and escorted by four German seaplanes, evaded the British planes and set course for the British Navy flotilla well offshore.

The raiding British seaplanes scored remarkably well, considering the equipment they carried. The bombs weighed twenty pounds apiece and did little damage, but the observers gathered much important information concerning the disposition of German Navy vessels. The British naval force cruised about just outside the enemy's main naval base for eight hours, but other than a halfhearted attempt by the Zeppelins, and a more resolute effort by a number of German seaplanes, no attempt was made to drive them off.

Three of the British seaplanes were picked up safely by their mother ships, and the crews of three more were rescued by British submarines. The fourth crew was saved by a Dutch trawler. Flight Commander C. F. Kilner and his observer, Lieutenant Robert Erskine Childers—author of *The Riddle of the Sands*, an early imaginary account of a German raid on England—made a valuable reconnaissance, reporting the presence of seven battleships, three battle cruisers, and a large number of other warships at Wilhelmshaven. One of the pilots, interned temporarily in Holland, was Flight Commander Francis Hewlett, son of the novelist Maurice Henry Hewlett. He had been taught to fly by his mother, who in 1909 was a member of the group that organized an aviation school at Brooklands outside of London.

This aviation action is presented to illustrate how far war-in-the-air had progressed in the campaign that had been under way for less than six months. (More detailed features will be given in the Air section of this book.)

That Christmas of 1914 will always be remembered for the preposterous tale of German-British fraternization between the lines, a story that writers have revived in one form or another over the years. It is interesting to note that few actual facts are ever offered, and that the incident is usually credited to some fictitious organization such as the Wessex Regiment. There is no such regiment in the British Army.

For months, after 1914, I tried to track down this fable, but I never met a British soldier who would admit that he had taken part, nor have I found an account of this Christmas Eve adventure in any regimental history. Likewise, the legend never has been written into any German war history, and it is never stated where the Christmas gathering took place, but it is always on the Wessex Regiment's front. However, should some reader have access to more reliable information, this version is offered, compounded of the many heard or read over the years.

According to the hoary fable, that Christmas Eve lowered with all routine measures being observed. Sentries were on the firesteps. A few soldiers huddled down for an hour's sleep before their guard-duty time came up.

As the story goes, the men of one British regiment first noticed a number of small lights set up along the German front lines, and these were added to as the evening wore on. As night fell voices were heard and then music—accordions or concertinas, and harmonicas perhaps—but as the Tommies listened they realized that their opposite numbers were welcoming the Yuletide with Christmas carols. More lights were added to the long string.

As the night wore on the British noticed that the string of lights apparently was raised higher, and as their night sight improved the sentries saw that the glow came from lanterns being held up on the bayonets of rifles. The singing became more audible.

One sentry inquired cautiously over his shoulder, "What do you make of it, Sergeant?"

The three-striper climbed up on the firestep and peered through the barbed wire.

"Cool Must be bloody balmy. Keep an eye on 'em."

The sentry waited and studied the situation. "They're climbing up on top and seem to be Christmas caroling. Do you think it's a game, Sergeant?"

"Keep an eye on 'em!"

The sentry huddled behind his barrier of sandbags, and to his bewilderment sensed that the same sort of thing was going on along the British line. Soldiers in khaki were crawling out of their trenches and boldly standing up, waving their water bottles.

"Here's a fine bloody to-do, Sergeant," the sentry muttered. "Now our blokes are going out there."

The NCO leaped up on the firestep again, and to his disbelief saw British and German infantrymen threading their way through their barbed wire. The singing became louder as the old carols rang along the front. Small groups of British and German soldiers stood together for a while, beating time to the singing. Tommies poured hot tea and their Christmas ration of rum into German mess cups, and Jerries sloshed dollops of schnapps into their coffee and offered the mixture to the Britishers. The caroling continued as a few rocket and star shells lit up the scene. Angry voices from superior officers on both sides snarled through the barbed wire, demanding the miscreants to return to their posts.

But the story is too pat. It has been written and polished too many times. Admittedly, Christmas does encourage forgiveness, sentiment, and fraternity, but anyone who ever served in the trenches will question that this holiday party took place. The author was not in France at this time, but in conversations with men who were in the British lines that Christmas, not one encountered any evidence of the incident. In fact, most of them stated that they had not heard of it until some time later, after being wounded or returned to England for leave or rest. There the fable was widespread—as was the story of the Russians traveling through England with snow on their boots—especially in military hospitals and pubs.

I have always doubted this particular legend, and my disbelief is continually heightened by every magazine illustration that accompanies the story of this Christmas fraternization. In these gay and graphic pictures, the artist usually shows the Tommies wearing steel helmets, when in fact that piece of equipment was not adopted by the British Army until the spring of 1916.

But again, there may be some logical explanation for this mythical gathering. Recalling that particular Yuletide, I remember talking to Tommies home on leave, and when they were asked how things were "out at the front," one or two would always employ that form of reverse-English humor which might go: "Out at the front? Oh, we have a lovely time. Dangerous? Not a bit of it. In fact, you ought to have been out there on Christmas Night. We called everything off and had a good old get-together out there in no man's land. Made a proper night of it, we did. Share and share alike, sort of thing. Old Jerry had some booze of some sort and we let him have a snift of our rum ration—that is we did, until the officers found out about it and then we all had to duck back into the trenches before the sergeant major started taking any names."

It would go on like this with suitable winks at the more outrageous features, until it was time for someone to order another round.

But more often the Tommy just back from the front would respond with: "Garn! You know who started that one, don't you? Them pacifists would put *anything* in the papers. I carn't see myself hobnobbing about no man's land wiv a pack of 'Uns . . . Christmas, or no Christmas!"

# CHAPTER II

*Birth of the Tank . . . Carnage at Neuve-Chapelle . . . The Gurkha and His Silver Knife . . . Dry Land Drowning . . . First Amphibious Operations.*

### Birth of the Tank

The deadlock along the fighting front at the end of 1914 aroused the concern of the general staffs of all belligerent nations, since they had no tactics with which to wage this type of warfare. Barbed wire and the machine gun, plus the entrenching tool, had revolutionized their trade and cast in discard their old staff college theories of open warfare—at least for the time being. There was one large fallacy in their views; all believed that the machine gun was the greatest killer in the line, but records kept by the medical services disclosed that the artillery shell caused more than 50 per cent of all wounds. And why not? With so many men crowded into the limited spaces of the trench system, shrapnel (to use a generic term) had a very profitable target, particularly along the Western Front. The rifle, hand grenade, and the bayonet accounted for many more, but the machine gun spoke with authority, and it was difficult to displace. In all too many instances, wounded men were apt to explain that they had been hit by machine-gun fire, when in fact their injuries may have been inflicted by an individual rifleman.

The high casualty figures threatened to bankrupt all available manpower before a decision could be reached, and both sides searched for an answer to this wasteful situation.

One man, Lieutenant Colonel Ernest D. Swinton, who at the time had the task of feeding the British Press with a few daily morsels of war news, had watched the pathetic efforts on both sides as they attempted to make advances through the natural and artificial barriers of the front line. As the official correspondent, using the by-line "Eyewitness," Swinton had seen what deep trenches, barbed wire, artillery barrages, and machine-gun fire could do to a battalion of infantrymen trying to root out the enemy. He realized that something had to be done if ever the war was to be won.

Swinton was a very experienced soldier and engineer who began his career during the Boer War in South Africa. Due to his journalistic talents he was asked to edit a machine-gun handbook being written by a Captain Applin of the 14th Hussars.

During this chore Colonel Swinton learned that one of his fellow officers who had spent his leave in Germany had heard that a factory in Spandau was engaged in the manufacture of 38,000 machine guns. Swinton looked into the matter further and found that the weapons actually were Vickers-Maxim guns, an improved version of the old Maxim gun, invented by the American, Hiram Maxim, who had gone abroad to sell his weapon.

This revelation of Germany's intent aroused Swinton, but when the information was placed before the British War Office the matter was greeted with smirks of disbelief, and then ignored. The Vickers-Maxim was a lightened and speeded-up version of the original Maxim gun. The Maxim Gun Company, organized in 1884, merged with the Nordenfelt Company of Germany in 1888, and this combine was absorbed later into Vickers Sons' and Maxim in 1896. The German version of the Vickers-Maxim gun was called the Spandau, marking the city of its manufacture. Not until Mons, Ypres, the Aisne, and other charnel ventures had taken their toll, did the War Office remember the warnings from Spandau.

Since the Boer War, Swinton's orderly mind had tried to conceive a weapon that would triumph over the machine gun.

More machine guns or heavier weapons were not enough. What was needed was a mobile fort that would traverse enemy earthworks, tramp down barbed-wire entanglements, and save the lives of the attacking forces. Specifically, he aimed to lessen the waste of life that was going on all along the front. By the end of November 1914, the Allies had lost nearly a million men, a fantastic toll, never eclipsed in so short a time throughout the war. Nothing in World War II equaled it.

But what sort of war machine could put an end to this carnage?

Colonel Swinton had tried for nearly fifteen years to visualize a weapon that would save his British Army, and his efforts are a classic in human effort and official bullheadedness. The idea that Swinton's brainchild might shorten the war had no effect on the War Office. The possibility of the use of poison gas had been known months before the outbreak of the war, but when the first gas attack was launched in April 1915, not one British Tommy had anything resembling a gas mask, or even a simple impregnated pad to protect himself.

Colonel Swinton, the typical British clubman-soldier who followed all sports with restrained enthusiasm, was an inveterate letterwriter and corresponded with people all over the world. One such contact was a Mr. Marriot, a mining engineer working a farm in South Africa, who, in his efforts to simplify his transportation problems, had come across an American agricultural machine known as the Holt Caterpillar tractor.

"This machine," he wrote to Swinton, "has surprising powers of crossing rough country. It can traverse narrow trenches or holes in the ground and is so powerful it can drag a five-furrow plow set at maximum depth through marshy soil."

This suggested a picture of a land destroyer, a vehicle that could penetrate the enemy's wire, straddle his fortifications, muzzle his machine guns, and open the way for some sort of breakthrough. The picture was not yet completely in focus and the structure ill-defined, but it held the basic idea of the future war tank.

Late in October 1914, Colonel Swinton was recalled to Britain, and while driving from the war area to the port of Boulogne he pondered on his idea and was gradually creating an armored vehicle that would help to break the bloody deadlock. As he approached the outskirts of Calais he suddenly remembered Marriot's tractor and the fact that the Holt Company had an agency and assembly plant in Antwerp. It might be a good idea to pop into Antwerp and have a look around the Holt plant. Antwerp? Good heavens! The Germans had taken Antwerp only ten days before! What an opportunity for them. If they ever considered the same problem, they'd be totally blind not to see the answer in this Holt tractor mechanism. On to London! Lord Kitchener would leap at this idea.

By the time Colonel Swinton was aboard a Channel steamer to Folkestone he was positive the key to the problem was in Holt's caterpillar tractor, but the reception he got at the War Office would have driven most men to wholesale mayhem. After explaining the actual war-front conditions to Colonel Maurice Hankey, Secretary to the Committee of Imperial Defense, and adding his idea for a fighting machine that might break the deadlock, Colonel Swinton asked to see Lord Kitchener. The C-in-C was "unavailable," so Swinton wrote out a detailed explanation of his proposed weapon, and hoped that Hankey would get it to Kitchener's attention. It was then that Hankey explained that someone in the War Office had come across the Holt tractor idea as early as 1909 and had ordered several—for transport purposes.

Nothing came of his first effort, and Swinton returned to France to witness the horrors of the Second Battle Of Ypres, April 22 to May 25, 1915. He saw how German 5.9 shells, pounded over in long salvos, were turning strong men into screaming idiots.

When Swinton got to London again he learned that Lord Kitchener had scoffed at his land destroyer plan, being positive that the British Tommy eventually would crash through—as he had always done—it was just a matter of time.

But Colonel Swinton would not be rebuffed, and he next took his idea to General Sir George K. Scott-Moncrieff, Director of Fortifications and Works. This Royal Engineers expert promised to "look into the matter," but did nothing of the sort.

In June 1915 the "Eyewitness" post created for Swinton was abolished and the gathering of war news was left to more professional journalists. He was sent home once more where he continued to work on his "machine-gun destroyer," for he realized now that his tractor vehicle would have to be armored to withstand the steel-cored and armor-piercing bullets the Germans were using. More important, he recommended that these machines be built secretly in England, moved up to the railheads by train or road, and distributed at night along the action front.

Some general talk of Swinton's idea reached the front, and in time General French demanded to know how soon a number of these machines could be built and put into action, and with this inquiry some interest was stirred. The first workable models of Swinton's basic plan were designed by Lieutenant W. G. Wilson of the British Navy, and Mr. W. A. Tritton of Messrs. W. Foster & Sons, an engineering firm at Lincoln, England.

The original proposal to use a Holt tractor was tried, but it was found unsuitable for the width of the trenches to be straddled. Mr. Tritton then devised a new and much lengthened tractor system; the hulls were rhomboidal, or lozenge-shaped, and because of their length could cross trenches more than eleven feet wide. As a matter of fact, these first British models were far superior in crossing trenches than any armored vehicle since devised.

The first model was named H.M.S. *Centipede*, since, after all, this project was under way only through the good offices of Mr. Churchill who was using Admiralty money. A second version, developed to fill new requirements, produced a comic anomaly when for production identification it was called the Female. The Number 1 machine, however, had been dubbed "Mother," but at the same time had to assume the production title of Male.

All these models were wooden mockups, but Mother was eventually adopted as the first design for a war tank in which Lieutenant Wilson had devised the lozenge-shaped hull with tractor treads running around the complete body. The so-called Female was developed to protect the Male, and was armed with one Hotchkiss machine gun and four Vickers .303 weapons, mounted so as to offer a wide arc of fire.

The Male vehicle was an impressive monster weighing thirty-one tons, and since it was to lead all attacks, it was covered with 0.4-inch armorplate over its most vulnerable areas. The rest was protected by plates of 0.2-inch metal. An armored sponson, or gun turret, was bolted to each side, and British Navy six-pounder guns were mounted in these ports. This weapon fired a shell weighing six pounds and was fitted with a sensitive fuse and loaded with amatol, a most suitable explosive for this type of work. To all intents and purposes, the six-pounder was a quick-firing gun, and in trained hands could spray a target with high explosive, canister shot, or armor-piercing missiles.

One weak feature of the Mark I tank was its steering system. A pair of four-feet six-inch wheels were mounted at the rear and kept in contact with the ground by a set of depressive springs. To make a slight turn this tail was swung to one side by means of wire cables operated manually by the driver. For sharper turns the steering tail was lifted hydraulically and the machine was steered through its secondary gearbox.

These early tails were vulnerable to shellfire, and being outside the armored hull were subject to other hazards. All too often they snapped off under the punishment encountered in moving over shelled areas.

The Male, which became the Mark I of the British Army, had its faults and weaknesses, but considering the rugged path its developers had to negotiate before a prototype could be bolted together, it was a miracle of military effort. Nothing comparable to Colonel Swinton's destroyers had ever moved

across the face of the earth before. No weapon had been designed that could create so much havoc, and unquestionably
Swinton's tank was the ultimate weapon of its era, particularly
in a war that had dug in, settled down, and taken cover behind
miles of trench and dugout systems. As primitive as it may seem
today, it filled a military need greater than had been faced before. Had time permitted a full and complete period of training
and development of a proper program of tactics, World War
I might have been won before the United States decided to
cast in its lot with the Allies in April 1917.

Little did military men realize it at the time, but Colonel
Swinton's idea, so many years in reaching fruition, should have
made the bayonet charge as dead as the Grecian phalanx. But
barbed wire, deep entrenchments, and concrete pillboxes are
not as defiant as the stodgy minds of military men. Looking
back, it is incomprehensible that both sides continued to waste
men and munitions trying to break through the defensive weapons both had devised. The war tank was nothing new. Variations of the land ironclad had been drawn on paper, described
in magazine articles, and in several instances workable models
had been placed on display before military men who should
have snatched at this great opportunity.

But the history of military thinking is a shocking record of
blindness, indecision, ignorance, and the determination to
shackle any logical advance—except through the expenditure of
blood and bodies.

In a later chapter it will be shown how Colonel Swinton's
tanks performed in their first engagement.

## Carnage at Neuve-Chapelle

Through the months of January and February 1915 the British and French accepted the stalemate and used the time to
realign and build up their forces. As soon as a period of reasonable weather appeared, the French opened a fierce and bloody
campaign in the Champagne sector. Gains were negligible and
losses great; the assault cost both sides 90,000 killed, wounded,

and taken prisoner, and the attack had to be broken off by March 17.

Still Field Marshall Joffre was determined somehow to pierce the German line and began to eye the commanding heights of Vimy Ridge in the Artois area. If this could be taken, the marshal intended to push on to the center of the enemy's road and rail junctions at Douai. He requested that General French open a new attack on the Ypres front, but the British were having troubles of their own with the mess developing in the Dardanelles, the lack of artillery shells, and the general delay in equipping new troops, and Sir John felt that whatever aid he could give before Ypres would be insignificant as far as any push against Vimy Ridge was concerned.

However, once he had talked himself out of that arrangement, he suddenly decided to open a new offensive slanted toward the village of Neuve-Chapelle where the enemy was believed to be not too strong. There was no real justification for this attack, but any form of active warfare came as a relief after those winter months of 1915.

Early March brought some periods of clear weather and mellow spring breezes began to dry up the countryside, and once his artillery batteries were finally supplied with a few rounds of ammunition, General French decided to make his move. The operation was to be carried out by two army corps, the British IV and the Indian, which had been moved up secretly on a line between Rue d'Enfer and Richebourg-Saint-Vaast. About 350 French and British field guns had been made available for the attack.

The town of Neuve-Chapelle lies four miles east of La Bassée and about a mile west of a high ridge that sweeps down from the general direction of Lille. The little river Des Lays flows between Neuve-Chapelle and this high ground on which is situated the village of Aubers. Pietre nestles on the side of the Lays farthest from Neuve-Chapelle, and south of it is the Bois de Biez in which the Germans had dug strong positions that could be defended by a bridgehead over the Lays.

If Neuve-Chapelle could be won, the fateful Aubers Ridge might be taken in the next stride and put the Germans in a hazardous position and threaten their hold on Lille. But this was wishful thinking since the Germans had built Neuve-Chapelle into a village fortress with every house turned into a strong point and a number of country villas outside the village strengthened and interconnected with trench systems that linked up gardens and orchards. This complex was supported by many machine guns.

At the same time, back in England, those of us who had volunteered for machine-gun teams, were being trained on 1895 models of the old Maxim gun at ancient Kentish redoubts that had been erected to withstand an earlier threat of invasion by Napoleon. We had little live ammunition to fire, but learned the mechanism and sequence of action by manually running through a number of expended rounds fitted with wooden bullets. I clearly remember my sergeant-instructor explaining dolefully, "You men face a hopeless task. I am supposed to teach you how to become machine gunners in one month. In peacetime it took three years to learn this new science. God help you!"

Instead, our training was spread over two weeks, a course in which a lone Maxim gun was shared by each ten-man group. When this instruction was completed our photographs were taken standing around the weapon to prove that we had graduated and were presumed to be expert machine gunners. We also were awarded embroidered badges to stitch on our sleeves and were told that now we would be paid twopence extra a day for our daring. This affluence never materialized.

A short time later I was sent to France where I never saw a Maxim gun, but was given a French Hotchkiss, and later, while taking a hurried course in the recognition of poison gas, was given some rudimentary training on the Vickers and Lewis guns. Once I had digested this military lore, I developed a keen instinct for self-preservation and applied for a transfer to the Royal Flying Corps as an aerial gunner. I was fortunate in that I selected the lesser of two evils.

It can be seen that the British Tommies faced a grim task in storming Neuve-Chapelle, but since some artillery was now available their chances were considered to be better than even. The Germans had shown them how to flatten an area with shell-fire before the infantrymen went "over the top," so it should be simple to reverse the trend and straighten out that salient.

The British IV Corps was under General Sir Henry S. Rawlinson, and the Indian Corps under General Sir James Willcocks. These troops were to be supported by some cavalry, the artillery, and some infantry from the general reserve. At the same time troops of Britain's Second Army were ordered to keep the enemy occupied and try to prevent the moving of their reinforcements from their front to the main point of the attack. These diversionary moves were as rewarding as the Neuve-Chapelle thrust, for the village of L'Epinete near Armentières and a few adjacent farms were captured.

The main attack began on March 10 when four hundred field and heavy guns opened with their hellfire. The bombardment was very effective as literally thousands of shells exploded in the German area. This wall of fire and steel fell on the several lines of enemy trenches, and the defenders were driven mad with terror. The concussion was terrific and, gradually, as the range was extended, the lyddite shells poured into houses, farms, and barnyard buildings, hurling great sections into the sky. By now the trenches had disappeared, and a short halt was called to learn of the fire effect and to set up new ranges.

The Indian brigades, in particular, made a glorious charge ahead to clean up the battered opposition. Other troops did not have such an easy path, as in some sectors the shellfire had not destroyed the barbed wire, and men of the Middlesex Regiment and the Scottish Rifles were especially hard hit.

### The Gurkha and His Silver Knife

It was during this attack on Neuve-Chapelle that the famous story of the Gurkha with the silver knife was conceived. A Gurkha, one of those gallant but strange Indian fighters who carry a great curved knife at their belts, was the hero of another grim legend. The Gurkha knife is a variant of the Malay kris, and one of the unwritten rules concerning its use is that it must never be withdrawn from its scabbard without being bloodied before it is returned.

As usual, there are several variations to this story, but since it has been corroborated to some extent by German sources, the Neuve-Chapelle version may have some substance.

A Gurkha patrol was sent out early in this attack to round up a few representative troops of the enemy, put them out of action, cut the shoulder straps—epaulets—from their uniforms, and then return. This was to identify the regiments—divisions—facing them, an item of information for the Intelligence sections.

One Gurkha of this patrol was said to own a silver knife, and there had been much talk concerning this weapon, its value, and how many of the enemy it would dispose of. Since his arrival in France, however, the owner had not had an occasion to unsheath the blade. The instant he and his companions crept out of their trench, the beautiful weapon was disclosed, of course, as every member of the patrol glanced at it and was fascinated by the glints of light that flashed off its blade every time a shell exploded overhead.

But there was some concern for such a beautiful knife. Was it really as sharp as a regulation weapon? Would the owner risk its delicate tracery and design in hand-to-hand encounter? What if he were killed; who would be lucky enough to pick up this superb, delicate weapon?

Once the Indian patrol broke into the enemy slots, the owner of the silver kris went to work with a vengeance, as, with perfect artistry, he moved along each trench and with a professional swipe practically sliced off the head of every unfortunate he met. In a few minutes his sergeant had enough enemy shoulder straps to make a blanket, and blew his whistle for the recall signal.

But the Gurkha with the silver knife continued on through bay after bay, his flashing blade hissing with automatic precision. That was the last seen of the man with the silver knife, but not the last that was heard of him. The German High Command complained for weeks that a whole tribe of Indian savages was at large, hacking off the heads of unsuspecting German soldiers. A complaint was filed with the International Court at The Hague, but no one ever found the missing Gurkha or his silver blade.

This would be just another World War I legend, if Margarete Munsterberg, a woman reporter for the popular Berlin *Kriegs-Rundschau,* had not filed a story in which she stated: "At Neuve-Chapelle Indian troops rushed ahead—seemingly unarmed. In the preceding days numerous Indian troops had deserted to our lines, hence our troops believed that in this case they were dealing with deserters, so did not shoot. This sin of omission was thoroughly revenged; for close before our positions the Indians began to throw hand grenades and attacked the garrison of our trenches with knives."

I heard this story of the Gurkha with the silver knife shortly after I arrived in France, and was fascinated by it. I wearied every Indian soldier I met for further explanation, but this is all I could learn. A Gurkha, armed with a silver kris, had simply gone over and had never stopped killing until deep in enemy country when, in all probability, he was finally overcome. His silver weapon was never recovered.

Although they had been surprised and their main positions had been overrun, the Germans holding Neuve-Chapelle put on a brave stand. The spirit of the British soared for they believed that the enemy actually was on the run, but, once more, upper-staff handling was amateurish and there were too many delays in the movement of troops, and here and there unfortunate hitches in the plan added up to tragedy. The Germans were able to rush up some reinforcements, the British drive simmered down, and after three days only a mere dent had been punched in the enemy line—a bulge a mile and a quarter wide and one thousand yards deep. When the Germans attempted a counterattack, they also suffered dreadful casualties, making the losses about equal.

But with this questionable success, the British did glean some hope for the future. They sensed that if enough artillery shells could be produced, they could make any attack succeed. They realized that mistakes had been made, but despite their losses, were determined to try again and do better. They were convinced of one thing; the enemy was now assigned to the defensive and would have to accept that situation for many, many months. He was well occupied in the East, but General von Falkenhayn was to be persuaded to try a new battle experiment, a new type of warfare that relied to some extent on favorable meteorological conditions; conditions, he was told, that might be found opposite Ypres. It was here that Germany might have won the war on April 22, 1915, but once more failure to take advantage of a temporary situation forfeited this amazing opportunity.

## Dry Land Drowning

*April 22, 1915*—Platoons of the Third Saxon Pioneer Corps moved up the revetted communications trenches in the heart of Houthulst Forêt and took up positions between Poelcapelle and Steenstraate where they faced the Ypres salient that curved out of Mont Kemmel and arched over to Pilckem Ridge. The weary Prussian Guard that had held the line for two weeks, stood back and allowed the Pioneers to take over those strange, gray steel canisters that had been placed against the firesteps.

"What is it you have there, Heinrich?" a curious infantryman inquired.

"I would not know. I just have a key that opens the valves— that, and this ridiculous thing I am supposed to strap over my mouth and nose. When my officer blows a whistle, I just open a valve. That is all."

"You open a valve and put on that face mask? Why? Is it dangerous?"

But before Heinrich could answer, every piece of artillery in the German back area opened up and shells whistled across the Ypres salient for fifteen minutes. Heinrich applied his metal key and awaited his officer's signal.

*Time: 5:15 P.M.* Until the German batteries broke the mellow spring afternoon quiet, the birds were beginning their evensong in the scraggy debris that lay before Langemarck and Zonnebeke. There were a few early scents of the season in the air, and men imprisoned in the trenches defending Ypres looked up at the sky and wondered; some thought of home and cottage gardens; some thought of the peace of the North African deserts; some pondered on life in the British Midlands, while still others beamed their memories across a vast ocean to a province called Ontario in the Dominion of Canada.

The Allied front at this point was held by the French 87th Territorial Division and the 45th Algerian Division. To their south, Canadian regiments, newly formed in Alberta and Ontario, wore the new shoulder patch of the Canadian 1st Division. Farther to the south the British 27th and 28th Divisions were responsible, and below that the British 5th Division linked up to the Franco-Belgian border.

A tall Senegalese sentry of the 87th leaned against the sandbags above his firestep as the enemy barrage went over. He knew that the minute it stopped, the rugged men who wore such strange metal helmets might come charging through the passages in the barbed wire to kill. It had happened to others, and it would be well to keep alert.

Then the artillery stopped and the Algerians shuffled out of their bays, shelters, and dugouts. Now they would come—those *Alleymen.* They always came when the guns stopped. The tall sentry checked his magazine and made certain his sword-bayonet was locked on properly.

But this time no enemy soldiers came charging through. In a few minutes they could hear the birds again. Then the sweet song halted and the French Territorials crouched, tense for an attack, but nothing happened. A light trickle of fog began to twist just beyond the enemy barbed wire, but it was spring and getting late in the afternoon. The Senegalese had seen fog before in these inhospitable fields of Flanders.

The trickle of greenish mist seemed to come up in spurts, then grouped in small columns and formed bulbous ghosts that edged across no man's land. A gentle northeast wind urged these vaporous figures along and gradually they spread and formed what seemed a wall of greenish-white steam. It wasn't smoke and it certainly wasn't fog. This couldn't be the foul waste from artillery fire. What was it?

The tall sentry sniffed and turned to appeal to his captain. Now the cloud came rolling on like a great juggernaut of dirty dough. It moved silently over the barbed wire, over the shell-holes, over the battered parapet. What was it?

"*Capitaine! Capitaine!*" the sentry screamed and rammed a massive hand over his mouth and nose. "*Capitaine!* It is a devil smell. Devil . . ." He tottered and fell to the bottom of the trench, and fourteen Territorials trampled him deeper in the mud in their haste to escape from the all-enveloping cloud that burned into their lungs.

Understandably, they panicked, and clambered up the trench wall and ran away. No order, no ingrained discipline, no basic human courage could keep them there. Who could blame them? No drillmaster on the barrack squares of their garrison towns had told them of a deadly fog.

The two French divisions withdrew in wild disorder and left a hole two miles wide in the line. The men who had held it were running away, clutching at their throats and screaming until no further sound came. Rifles, bayonets, ammunition, and machine guns were abandoned as they tried to get where some clean air might douse the fire in their lungs.

*Time:* 5:35 P.M.—A group of British officers in area-consultation behind the Canadian front were disturbed to see a torrent of terrified humanity pouring rearward. They watched with professional interest first, and then with military resentment.

"What goes on here?"

"It's those French Territorials! Where do they think they are going?"

"Aren't they from that division that's supposed to be in up near Langemarck?"

A staff major stared and then caught a whiff of pungent air. "Whew! What's that ripe pong about them? Don't the blighters ever wash?"

"They can't pull out of the line like that," a British captain grumbled. "They'll leave the Canadian flank wide open." He had never heard of poison gas.

The British officers tried to glean some explanation, but the Algerians only screamed, staggered, clutched at their throats, and pointed backward toward their deserted lines.

"We'd better rush into Ypres and get someone on the wire," a puzzled Guards colonel concluded.

By the time they had made their way across the war-torn fields and within sight of the Menin Gate the sun was lowering in the west beyond the North Sea. Ypres already was battle-scarred. The great Cloth Hall was roofless and ravaged by flames from burned timbers, but most of the commercial buildings were still standing, although battered by enemy bombardments.

The old city of Ypres (Wipers to the British Tommy) was the capital of Armageddon, a distinction it held from the beginning to the end of World War I, but on the afternoon of April 22, 1915, the green phantom of death slithered into the city and stalked its streets. The hairiest devil of war put the finger on Ypres and within a few weeks it was battered into a shapeless chaos of broken masonry, desolation, and, above all, had a distinctive odor of its own.

The first effect of the phantom came when a mass of French soldiers and Algerian colonial troops staggered across the fields. They were incoherent; wild panic blazed in their eyes, and there was a foul smell on them. They gasped for breath, vomited, and some crawled on their hands and knees until they sprawled into unconsciousness as they struggled against the wicked power that constricted their throats and scoured their lungs.

In an *estaminet* nearby a group of the Durham Light Infantry was singing,

> "*Wot cheer me old brown son,*
> *How are Yer?*
> *What cheer me old brown son,*
> *How are yer?*"

No one took much notice of the stricken Frenchmen. Who could understand the French? But the songs died away when a group of fear-racked troops wearing Canadian, English, Irish, and Scottish regimental badges straggled through the streets. This mob came on in a slow, uneven procession. Some faltered and rolled into the gutters, a few coughed as their desperate fingers tore open their jackets and shirts to ease the pressure in their chests. Their throats strained and heaved. A few tried to speak, but only a bubbling sound, hissing and uneven as though their lungs were perforated, could be heard. One or two tried to shriek, but it ended only in a high delirious cry. Some of the stricken were already quiet, their stiffened hands clutched at the collars of their coats. A few were painfully contorted.

"What the bloody 'ell goes on?" a Durham trooper croaked.

As the choking men tottered on, a few halted bravely, worked the bolts of their rifles and fired—at nothing! A few more tried to add to this pathetic musketry, but they twisted and fell into limp heaps. They stared, gurgled, and pointed at the whitish cloud that moved inexorably toward them.

A section of Canadians had linked arms and were plodding on, heads down, hacking and coughing. A trail of rifles, entrenching tools, haversacks, and mess kits were left behind—the flotsam of a military tragedy. Another section crawled to its knees, gave a last bold try and fired a clip of .303 into the taunting white vapor that curled into such fantastic forms. A few more men fell, groaning honest Anglo-Saxon oaths—the last words they uttered.

*Time:* 5:45 P.M.—Then came what possibly was the most ridiculously sensible command in military history. A young Englishman, attached temporarily to a Canadian regiment, made the same plea over and over. Today, he lies unknown, as do so many true heroes. His name has not been carved on the Ypres Memorial that stands at the Menin Gate.

"Try it, men," he begged. "Please try it . . . Damn it! That's an order! Urinate . . . er . . . piddle into your handkerchiefs. It'll make a filter. A sort of mask . . . cut the irritant, whatever it is."

Over and over, he ran up and down his thin khaki line making his revolting plea. A few took his advice—and lived. That gallant few went back to their slots above Zonnebeke and made a counterattack. Those gallant—or crazy—Canadians actually went back to brave that vapor. A few did. Not too many.

The unknown Englishman had been a chemist in civil life and knew that urine contains ammonia, and ammonia was the answer to those toxic vapors. But under panic men lose more than common understanding, they lose basic intelligence. Vocabulary means little to a man whose lungs and throat have been seared; nothing to a man who no longer can whisper.

"What does the bloody fool mean—urinate?"

"Irritant, be damned! The blasted stuff is tearing my guts out!"

Some men, encumbered with the false pride of environment, could make no sense of the order, and what was worse, it was degrading!

"Does he expect me to piddle in my handkerchief and then slap the mess against my face? He must be balmy. It's indecent. No decent man would do a thing like that."

The decent men coughed out their lungs, the indecent, somehow, lived. When the decent stared at those who obeyed the revolting order, they thought their trench pals had gone mad. "Coo! I never thought I'd live to see you do a thing like that, 'Arry!"

*Time:* 5:55 P.M.—The devilish death cloud crept on, moved along by that hellish zepyhr. By the time it rolled through the gates of Ypres it had a distinct tang of violets. Violets? Of course, it was springtime, there could be violets out there in Flanders fields.

The shop girls along the Grande Place hurried to the *pavé* and raised their perky nostrils, their eyes shining with the delicacy of the perfume. They sniffed and clapped their hands. What a dainty war! What a change from the dank of swamps, the fetid odor of the gutters, the tang of cordite. Well . . . it was *something* like violets. The girls smelled again and then gasped. They screamed and lurched as they ran, and then fell clutching at their throats. Someone remarked later, "It must have been like dry-land drowning."

More retreating troops staggered in uneven files along the cobbled streets of Ypres, coughing and hacking like men in the terminal ward of a consumptive hospital. They groaned and wept, weaving on, uncertain, trip-wired, and gasping. They used their rifles like staves, and one and all pleaded for the mercy of the breath of life. No one gave any orders now. The unknown young Englishman had taken his trusting few back to the line. Today, no one knows what became of him, or how long his "piddling" few hung on and put the stopper on the German advance.

Civilians, staring out of their casements, were finally enticed outside by the fantastic sights, and foolishly mixed with the troops, and by the time they realized that some silent death was stalking their streets, it was almost impossible to get back into their homes. The Germans were now dropping high-explosive shells into their battered city, and only a few reached the safety of their cellars where most of them died under the avalanche of roofing and masonry. Many burrowed into the big street culverts where they stayed for three days and nights, wallowing in their own filth.

*Time: 6:10* P.M.—At German brigade headquarters in front of Staden, a general was on the field telephone. "And how goes it, Colonel?"

"Perfectly! The wind has held and the gas has spread over the whole front. A wonderful result."

"Then you have, of course, moved up to take the deserted positions. That you have done. May I have your new co-ordinates?" the general demanded.

"Well, sir, we have sent investigating patrols in, but the gas is still in the enemy trenches. It would be impossible to get in and consolidate. We had better wait until the formula dissipates."

"You mean to say, that with this success of our new weapon you have failed to take advantage of the enemy withdrawal? Why haven't you ordered a full-scale attack over the affected front?"

"But, sir, we have no reserves to make such an attack. We have used most of our artillery ammunition, and until the gas dissipates in the enemy lines, we cannot occupy them. Our infantry forces do not have suitable masks. They were issued only to the Pioneers who were in charge of the gas canisters."

The German general uttered a full-souled oath. "Just as I explained to our corps commander. This poison gas is of no use. It gives us a bad name. It has only a temporary effect. We have wasted its surprise element. The enemy will soon devise some sort of gas mask and may even employ poison gas against us."

To which the colonel added: "You are right, General, and we must remember we have given the enemy a tip. The prevailing winds across Flanders are westerly or southwesterly. All in his favor. We should have waited and used it in gas shells."

This is the story of the first poison-gas attack made by the Germans. It was a terrifying experience, but a military failure. The Germans, who could not believe that it would be so successful, had no reserves and could not capitalize on their initial success. Although they faced no opposition and were able to advance about four miles, they could not maintain that advantage. The failure was brought about by the lack of foresight and full appreciation of the new weapon.

The attack took the Allies by surprise, although the French had reason to believe that such a weapon might be used. History discloses that shortly after the battle for Neuve-Chapelle, or some six weeks before the gas attack was made, the French had captured two German soldiers, who, hoping to gain preferred treatment, revealed that a new form of attack was being prepared, and offered detailed accounts telling how a number of gas cylinders had been set up in the trenches, and explained the method of discharging the vapors. The French looked on this as an interesting development, but failed to advise the British of the ominous possibility.

Later, a more definite warning was uncovered when, on April 18, a German deserter wandered into the lines of the French 11th Division opposite Langemarck. This renegade repeated the story of "tubes of asphyxiating gas" set up in batteries of twenty tubes along every thirty yards of front, and to substaniate his story produced a crude respirator that was issued to safeguard the cylinder handlers and attackers.

Then a tragic series of high-level omissions ensued. A General Ferry, a French divisional commander, was gravely impressed and advised the French division on his left, and made certain that British and Canadian divisions in the same sector were apprised of the situation. General Ferry also warned his corps commander, a General Balfourier, and to make sure this poison-gas threat came to the notice of staff headquarters, he informed General Joffre's liaison officer who was visiting the sector.

Up to this point General Ferry had done his best, but General Balfourier considered him to be a gullible fool and refused to take Ferry's advice to shell the enemy trenches where the gas cylinders had been set up. When Ferry next suggested that the number of men in the Allied front line be reduced to cut possible casualties, Balfourier was ready to demote him.

Marshal Joffre's liaison officer reacted in much the same way, at first dismissing the threat, and then reproving General Ferry for ignoring military procedure in warning the British directly, and for suggesting that men in the front line be withdrawn for safety, a move quite contrary to Joffre's doctrine. Although justified in his actions, General Ferry was punished by removal for being right and acting in a co-operative manner.

A new commander, a General Putz, who took over the left of the salient from General Balfourier, was not inclined to believe the poison-gas story, either, although new warnings came next from the Belgian front farther north. General Putz mentioned the tale offhandedly to a British liaison officer, but did not think it worth mentioning to his own troops who waited in ignorance until suffocation overtook them.

To be exact, the British did take some vague measures. Aircraft reconnaissance was made over the area, but the observers failed to note anything unusual, so British General Herbert C. O. Plumer passed the warning on to his divisional commanders "for what it is worth." No precautions against gas were suggested or ordered, and within a few days the warning was forgotten. After all, it did seem like an "ungentlemanly novelty," even when on April 17—five days before the first German gas attack was made —a German wireless communiqué stated: "*Yesterday, east of Ypres, the British employed shells and bombs of asphyxiating gas.*" They were practicing the art of getting in the first verbal blow.

Next came the sinking of the *Lusitania* on May 7, and the German periodical *Die Welt* rhapsodized with "Clad in virtue and in peerless nobility of character, unassailed by insidious enemies, either within or without, girded about by the benign influences of *Kultur,* the German, whether soldier or civilian, pursues his destined way, fearless and serene."

## First Amphibious Operations

In the spring of 1915 the military heads of the British War Office began to consider plans for opening a campaign on another front, although their army was far from strong enough to conduct a war in France. There were volunteers aplenty, but the training of capable officers was completely bogged down. Britain was fighting a parliamentary war; a campaign carried out by amateur strategists, guided and controlled by political ministers. A War Council had been established some months after the war had begun by the Prime Minister at that time Herbert

H. Asquith. This left the Committee of Imperial Defense inoperative. As Secretary of State for War, Lord Kitchener was for an all-out decision on the Western Front. The First Lord of the Admiralty, Winston Churchill, had some vague ideas of a military expedition to the Dardanelles. The Secretary of State for India was advocating a campaign in Mesopotamia. Lloyd George, at the time Chancellor of the Exchequer, wanted to withdraw the British Army from France and send it to some mysterious Mediterranean theatre, and the Secretary for the Colonies was building up attention on several "small wars" going on in Africa. This is a general summation of the British military picture, when a telegram received from the British Ambassador at Petrograd (now Leningrad) explained the critical position of the Russians in the Caucasus, a situation that had passed, by then.

As a result, Lloyd George suggested a campaign to be aimed against the Austrians, using Salonika, Greece, as a base. The War Council wanted to strike at Germany through Turkey, and argued that if the Black Sea could be reopened, 350,000 tons of shipping would be released. But Lord Kitchener topped everything by stating that Britain would "make a demonstration against the Turks" that would distract the enemy pressure. To this Lord John Fisher, First Sea Lord of the Admiralty, suggested a strong attack on Turkey in a combined operation that was to involve the Army, Navy, and units of the Royal Naval Air Service, to say nothing of aid by Bulgarians, Serbs, and Greeks. Winston Churchill became fascinated by this over-all idea, and almost overnight absorbed every tactical detail; information he could spout at length at any given time. It was this amazing familiarity with a plan not yet fully conceived or authorized that in later months drew down on him the full blame for the grim failure at Gallipoli.

There never was such a muddle. At one time Lord Fisher believed the Dardenelles could be forced with a number of old battleships and that once they were through, Constantinople (now Istanbul) must fall. Allied aid could then be sent to

Russia with the ease of a cross-Channel packet system. Churchill soon took up this enthusiasm, but Vice-Admiral Sir Sackville
H. Carden, in command of the British Mediterranean squadron,
dreaded such an operation, and when an abortive attempt was
made, he was ill and had to be replaced by Vice-Admiral Sir
John Michael de Robeck.

After listening to the glowing explanations of Churchill, Lord
Kitchener suddenly decided on a naval-military expedition,
but before available troops could be assembled a lone Royal
Navy-French Navy force attempted to break into the Dardanelles.

This endeavor was under way by mid-March. The *Queen
Elizabeth* aimed her fifteen-inch guns on the Turkish batteries
along the Narrows and had no trouble in silencing them, but
when this mixed fleet attempted to move into enemy waters, it
encountered a minefield that should have been cleared. One by
one, the big battleships met disaster. The French *Bouvet* was
struck first, then the British *Irresistible* and *Ocean* had great
holes blown in their bottoms and all three ships went down
almost immediately. *Inflexible* and the French *Gaulois* were
hit, but both of them limped to the island of Tenedos where
temporary repairs could be made. *Suffren* was mined, but was
able to stay in action.

Meanwhile, two British divisions were being ordered to Egypt
to join two from New Zealand and Australia. Two divisions of
the Royal Naval Divisions were also available, but there were
no maps of the area, and General Sir Ian S. M. Hamilton, who
had been placed in charge of the military operation, had been
given no plan of action. In contrast, the Turkish Army was under
command of General Otto Liman von Sanders, an astute German officer who, with six divisions, immediately set up a plan
of defense. General Liman, as he was known, had no aircraft,
but he needed none since he commanded the heights that overlooked the Allied lineup. A few airplanes were available to
General Hamilton, but they had arrived in crates and had to
be assembled, and suitable landing ground had to be prepared

to accommodate them. Some flying was attempted, but brought small reward.

British troops, shipped out from England, arrived without their equipment. Guns, wagons, limbers, horses, harness, and general supplies were loaded haphazardly; when the horses arrived there was no harness or fodder for them; wagons and guns were on other ships; ammunition and spare parts were aboard others. The whole lot had to be run into Alexandria, Egypt, offloaded and reloaded for combat operations.

Once the attack was under way, all forces seemed to operate independently. Some swarmed ashore with no trouble—and then sat in the balmy sunshine awaiting the arrival of the others. Some were cut to ribbons as they stormed up the enemy beaches, but those already ashore did nothing to relieve them. An old collier, *River Clyde*, was equipped as a floating Trojan horse with hundreds of troops who were to be discharged down sally ports once the vessel had been grounded at V Beach— Sedd el Bahr—at the toe of the peninsula. This effort proved murderous, as the Turkish soldiers, huddling behind natural rock cover, picked off the Britishers as fast as they appeared on the gangways. At Y Beach, only four miles away, 2000 other British troops walked ashore without a shot being fired at them. These fortunates settled down, made and ate one meal, and when nothing happened, withdrew and re-embarked, instead of moving on to the key objective at Krithia.

Such a situation could scarcely occur today, but it must be remembered that this was 1915, not the 1940s. Communications were very limited. Radio was not a simple portable device, and because of lack of planning few Allied troops knew who might be on their flank, what uniforms they would be wearing, or what their general objective might be. On one occasion naval gunners aboard one British battleship put through requests: "Are we using cavalry in this operation? Who are the men wearing blue uniforms?"

Sacrifice and gallantry were wasted, but these grim qualities were there in rare values. Horror and heroism were displayed on both sides, and when the first vague details of the action were reported in London, Lord John Fisher resigned his Admiralty position after a wild outburst of temper. Churchill also went out when a new coalition government was formed on May 26.

On May 18 the Turkish troops made a mad attack for no apparent reason, and in the ensuing fight more than 10,000 of them were wiped out. The Royal Navy, particularly its submarines, continued the fight and unbelievable heroism was displayed as its primitive undersea vessels repeatedly dared the mined Narrows to get at Turkish shipping.

After a breather in which a truce was made to permit both sides to bury their dead, new plans were drawn and the British made another attempt to capture the peninsula. More landings and hand-to-hand fighting piled up the casualties. Again, the plans were not clearly understood or carried out. Both sides staged amateurish blunders. What troops got ashore had no idea what to do after dry ground was under their feet. Once their men were ashore, British commanders were unable to respond, and every effort was wasted.

When General Sir Charles C. Monro was sent out from France to replace General Hamilton and report on the Gallipoli situation, he recommended an immediate evacuation. This created a resounding furor throughout Great Britain and even Lord Kitchener joined in it, although he had advocated such a move a short time before. And it was not until he himself visited the narrow beaches and saw the hopeless carnage that he agreed the situation was beyond rescue, and recommended that most of the peninsula be abandoned. He did hope, however, to keep a foothold at Helles at the base of the peninsula— for the time being at least.

Arthur James Balfour, who succeeded Winston Churchill as First Lord of the Admiralty, pressed for a renewed attack on the Narrows, and Commodore Sir Roger J. B. Keyes, chief of staff of the Eastern Mediterranean squadron, who later won the V.C. at Zeebrugge, also demanded that the Narrows be assaulted once more, but wiser and more restrained minds had their day and a full evacuation was finally agreed on.

More than six months had been wasted in this questionable venture, and by November 27 a terrific blizzard swept over the peninsula for seventy-two hours. Hundreds of men died of exposure. There were five thousand cases of frostbite, two hundred men were drowned, and numberless wounded frozen to death.

This terrible storm hastened the evacuation. After much political intrigue and wrangling in the War Committee, General Monro was finally allowed to carry out his original plan. All Allied troops were withdrawn by January 9, 1916, without a single soldier being lost, but of the 410,000 British, and 70,000 French troops that had landed on the peninsula, 252,000 had been killed, wounded, captured, or died of disease. Turkey had sacrificed 218,000 men, of whom 68,000 were killed. The Allied booty left behind required nearly two years to gather in.

On looking back, most students of military tactics now agree that the Dardanelles-Gallipoli campaign was not a blunder in concept, or even a reckless gamble. It is now accepted as a very imaginative design with potentialities beyond appraisal. In its strictly military aspect it could have had enormous influence. It was the greatest amphibious operation known until then, but took place, unfortunately, when nearly all plans and equipment were in the experimental stage. Submarines and aircraft were scarcely out of their cocoons, and the use of heavy naval artillery against shore targets was in its infancy. The maneuvering of small boats against a hostile shore, the land mine, and many other devices were new and novel.

Modern amphibious operations were devised and perfected from the lessons learned at Gallipoli. There could have been no Dunkirk, Normandy, or island-hopping successes in the Pacific without a long study of the Dardanelles campaign. A large number of Gallipoli commanders lived to see some vindication. Sir Roger Keyes served as director of combined operations in World War II, and a spruce young captain of thirty-three, Clement Attlee, survived to become Prime Minister

of Great Britain. Rupert Brooke, poet and young officer in the
Royal Naval Division, died and was buried on the island of
Skyros in the Aegean Sea by a group of his friends, one of whom
was Bernard Cyril Freyberg, later awarded the V.C. and the
D.S.O. four times. Sir Bernard served with distinction through
World War II, and was governor general of New Zealand from
1946–52. General Hamilton never served again, but his book
*Gallipoli Diary* justified his actions at the Dardanelles. He died
in 1947 at the age of ninety-four, still loved and respected by
his fellow compatriots.

# CHAPTER III

*Patriotism Was Not Enough . . . Secret War Against America . . . Defeat on Defeat . . . Serbia Goes Down.*

## Patriotism Was Not Enough

The martyring of Nurse Cavell was one of the most stupid mistakes committed by the Germans in the Great War. This Englishwoman was serving as head nurse in a Brussels hospital in 1914, and she engaged in an underground system that helped a handful of British, French, and Belgian soldiers to escape and fight again. Her case has been long forgotten, but it aroused widespread indignation when she was executed in 1915. She died bravely, and if her heroism proved nothing else, it did point up German barbarism, since the line of her defense was, "I helped them for fear they would be shot if I didn't."

Edith Louisa Cavell was born in Swardeston, Norfolk, in 1865 and was fifty years old when a volley of firing-party bullets ended her humanitarian career. She began her nursing service at the London Hospital in 1895, and by 1907 was made first matron of the Berkendael Medical Institute in Brussels which became a Red Cross hospital at the outbreak of the war. She cared for many wounded German soldiers here, and she also had trained German nurses who were now serving in their own country. From November 1914 to the summer of the following year numbers of wounded and abandoned British, French, and Belgian soldiers were hidden from the enemy by Prince Reginald de Croy at his château near Mons. From there, those who could walk, were secreted in a few private homes in Brussels—

one of which was the residence of Nurse Cavell—where the military refugees were given money, food, suitable clothing, and guided to the Dutch frontier. Some of their guides were obtained through a Philippe Baucq.

This operation had been watched by German officials, and in all probability renegade Belgians aided in the betrayal of this group. Nurse Cavell was arrested and imprisoned on August 5. She admitted freely having sheltered and helped to convoy to the front about two hundred British, French, and Belgian soldiers.

Miss Cavell was held incommunicado for nearly ten weeks, although Brand Whitlock and his staff at the United States Legation made every effort to see her and arrange to provide a defense. Maitre G. De Leval, Belgian Councilor to the American Legation, was assigned to the case, and he induced Maitre Sadi Kirschen, a member of the Brussels Bar to assume the defense of the Englishwoman. Kirschen made a formal application to see his client, but was told that according to German military law barristers defending prisoners before a military court were not allowed to see the prisoners prior to their trial.

De Leval had intended to sit in and observe the proceedings, but was persuaded to refrain with the explanation that such an appearance might prejudice the court. Kirschen displayed no aggressiveness and said that the Military Court in Brussels had always been fair, and that there was not the slightest chance of any miscarriage of justice, but he did not see his client until the opening day of the trial, October 7. Late the next day the trial was over, but no judgment was passed until a few days later.

The day before the trial opened Nurse Cavell willingly signed a statement acknowledging the charges made against her. She also added before the court that some of the British soldiers she had aided, had written and thanked her after their safe arrival in England. It was this last admission that sealed her doom.

During the trial she was asked why she had helped these

soldiers go to England, and she replied, "I thought that if I had not done so they would have been shot—by you Germans." She added that she was simply doing her duty to her country.

The German military public prosecutor stated that her argument might apply to her aid to British soldiers, but was not applicable to Belgians whom she had *induced* to cross the frontier, and who would have been free to remain in their own country without danger to their lives.

Kirschen is said to have made a very good plea and used all the arguments he could muster in her favor in the short time he had to prepare his brief. The military public prosecutor, however, asked the court to pass the death sentence on Miss Cavell and eight other prisoners of the thirty-five rounded up on this general charge. The court did not agree immediately, and judgment was postponed.

At the time no one believed that Miss Cavell would receive the death sentence, but officials of the American Legation prepared a petition for pardon. German officials, however, made matters very difficult; no member of the American Legation nor any Belgian legal official, selected by Brand Whitlock, was permitted to see the British woman. When rumors started to circulate that Miss Cavell and Philippe Baucq had been sentenced to death, the secretary of the American Legation, Hugh Gibson, accompanied by De Leval, and the Spanish Minister to Belgium, requested an interview with Baron von der Lancken, a German official; first, to find out whether the death sentence had been passed; and second, to make an appeal for clemency. Once Baron von der Lancken had admitted that Miss Cavell was to be executed early the next morning, the Legation group made a frantic effort to have the sentence postponed. They begged for a delay so that a plea of clemency could be forwarded to the military governor general.

They used every persuasive force, pointing out the horror of executing a woman, no matter what her offense, and adding that heretofore the death sentence had been imposed only for actual cases of espionage. Miss Cavell was not accused by the German authorities of anything so serious. Mr. Gibson called attention to the failure to comply with an earlier promise to inform the Legation of the sentence, and he urged that inasmuch as the offenses charged against Miss Cavell were long since accomplished and she had been in prison for some time, a delay in carrying out the sentence would entail no danger to the German cause. He closed by pointing out the fearful effect of a summary execution of this kind on public opinion, in Europe and abroad.

Baron von der Lancken washed his hands of all responsibility and said that the military governor was the supreme authority, and that an appeal from his decision could be carried only to the Emperor; the governor general having no authority to intervene in such cases. He did, however, telephone the military governor and then explained that the military governor had said that he had acted in the case of Miss Cavell only after mature deliberation, that the circumstances in her case were of such a character that he considered the death sentence imperative, and that in view of the circumstances in this case he must decline to accept any plea for clemency, or any representation in regard to the matter.

On the evening of October 11, 1915, Reverend H. Stirling Gahan, a British chaplain in Brussels, was admitted to the prison of Saint-Gilles where Miss Cavell was confined. He was astonished to find her calm and resigned, and she talked with him in that manner for more than an hour.

"I want my friends to know that I willingly give my life for my country. I have no fear nor shrinking. I have seen death so often that it is not strange or fearful to me."

And after a few minutes of reflection, she added: "I thank God for this ten weeks' of quiet before the end. Life has always been hurried and full of difficulty and this time of rest has been a great mercy. They have all been very kind to me here. But this I would say, standing as I do in view of God and eternity, I realize that patriotism is not enough. I must have no hatred or bitterness towards anyone."

The German military chaplain, who was with her at the end, said, "She was brave and bright to the last. She died like a heroine."

Dr. Alfred Zimmermann, German Under Secretary for Foreign Affairs, stated in an open interview given to the foreign press; "It was a pity that Miss Cavell had to be executed, but it was necessary. She was judged justly. We hope it will not be necessary to have any more executions. . . .

"There are moments in the life of nations where consideration for the existence of the individual is a crime against all. Such a moment was here. It was necessary once for all to put an end to the activities of our enemies, regardless of their motives; therefore the death penalty was executed so as to frighten off all those who, counting on preferential treatment for their sex, take part in undertakings punishable by death. Were special consideration shown to a woman, we should open the door wide to such activities on the part of women who are often more clever in such matters than the cleverest male spy. The man who is in a position of responsibility must do that, but, unconcerned about the world's judgment, he must follow the difficult path of duty."

A rational examination of the Nurse Cavell case must agree that from the legal point of view, the Germans had every right to execute the British nurse. She had admittedly assisted British and Belgian soldiers to escape and return to their own lines. She knew this was against the rules, but more important, she and her associates made the grim mistake of allowing Allied secret service organizations to use their channels through which to pass vital information. It was this that had brought about their undoing. However, grim as was the penalty, Germany made an even greater mistake in shooting Nurse Edith Cavell, for the sentence, once carried out, had a terrific reaction throughout the British Empire.

The recruiting stations were overwhelmed with thousands of new volunteers.

## Secret War Against America

From the opening guns of August when German troops marched through Belgium, another equally illegal form of warfare was waged in the United States, a war that was intended to keep America from entering the lists on the side of the Triple Alliance. This campaign included unjustified attacks by German U-boats on American shipping, the spending of large sums of money to create strikes, manufacturing disasters, and promoting wars with Mexico and Japan to prevent shipment of ammunition or other war materials. Money was also spent to create a public sentiment favorable to Germany's aims, and in one instance funds were furnished for the manufacture of time-fuse incendiary bombs that were to be hidden aboard American cargo ships bound for European ports.

This undercover activity was discovered as early as September 9, 1915, when it was learned that James Archibald, an American citizen, traveling on an American passport, was acting as a secret agent for Austria-Hungary, and conspiring to cripple legitimate industries of the United States.

Evidence was uncovered that proved that Konstantin Theodor Dumba, Austrian Ambassador in Washington, had hired Archibald to carry official dispatches through the Allied frontiers. He also acted as a writer of propaganda, and with all this proof at hand, United States Secretary of State Robert Lansing demanded Ambassador Dumba's recall.

The Austrian diplomat pointed out that thousands of natives of Bohemia, Moravia, Galicia, Dalmatia, Croatia, and Slavonia were working in the American steel industry, ignorant of the fact that they were making munitions to be used against their countrymen. He said that he had subsidized many newspapers, published in their native languages, "to bring this felonious situation to their attention." He explained further that the letters and dispatches carried by Mr. Archibald were nothing more than a proposal to call out these workmen from American munition plants and provide other employment for them.

Nothing was mentioned of the thousands of German nationals who willingly worked for high American wages, knowing that their products were being used by the Allies. Nor was reference made to the fact that able-bodied Belgians were being herded into forced-labor camps on starvation rations and scant wages to work on enemy military projects; or that on the outbreak of the war there were 250,000 Polish workmen in Germany who were forbidden to leave, were kept separated from their families, and forced to work for German employers who paid them whatever they chose. Some of the captive Poles were paid at the rate of seven cents a day.

Professor E. E. Sperry, an official spokesman for the United States, later elaborated on these practices by German and Austrian representatives in America. His findings, printed in official government publications, disclose how widespread these illegal actions had become. It was evident that Germany never intended to remain friendly to the United States, but had filled many communities, and even offices of the government with spies, and had set up criminal intrigues against our peace, national unity, industries, and commerce. The evidence disclosed, in fact, that many of Germany's spies had been working in America long before the war began. All this was confirmed in American courts of justice where papers, records, telegrams, letters, and the financial data involving the hired agents who had worked against this country, were put in evidence.

The chief of Germany's agents was Count Johann-Heinrich von Bernstorff, German Ambassador to the United States. The Austrian Ambassador Dumba was his chief coadjutor and able adviser. Other lieutenants were Captain Franz von Papen, military attaché, Captain Karl Boy-Ed, Germany's naval attaché at Washington, Dr. Heinrich Albert, commercial attaché, and Wolf von Igel who also had diplomatic status. Supporting this central group were many of the consuls and a rank and file of threadbare servitors who carried out the plans of the General Staff in Berlin. Franz von Rintelen was a free-lance operator who had a separate supply of funds at his disposal.

The chief purpose of this undercover corps was to prevent the export of military supplies from the United States. The British Navy had driven German shipping from the seas, and her huge accumulation of munitions and the ability to manufacture more were threatened as the passing months brought an increasing volume of American products to the Allies.

One way to cut off this supply was to strike at American factories, and special military accounts were opened and made available for these "war necessities." These credits were used to an unlimited extent for the purpose of destroying factories, workshops, military camps, and the most important centers of military and civilian supplies. Labor troubles were to be incited, and measures taken to damage engines and machinery of manufacturing plants, and for the destruction of vessels carrying war material to the Allied countries. Special agents were to supply the German saboteurs with the necessary means for effecting explosions and fires, as well as with a list of people in the country willing to work on these destructive plans.

A German employment bureau set up its central office in New York City as early as 1915. Branches were also discovered in Philadelphia, Bridgeport, Cincinnati, Pittsburgh, Cleveland, and Chicago. These agencies pretended that their purpose was to afford employment for German and Austrian subjects who voluntarily had left positions in factories that were supplying the Allies. A later inspection of their files showed that coercion and intimidation were used to drive employees from munition factories. Through the foreign press, the Austrian government circulated a proclamation that threatened, with a penalty of ten to twenty years imprisonment, all subjects who, after working in such plants, ever returned to their native land.

In all about six thousand Austrians and Germans left American plants, many of them skilled engineers and machinists. Later on, Franz von Rintelen organized his Labor's National Peace Council in April 1915, and attempted to use the strike as another weapon. This council began its operations with the following resolution:

> Resolved, By the representatives of labor in Peace Congress assembled in the City of Washington, that an organization be and is hereby established, to be known as Labor's National Peace Council, having for its purpose the establishment and maintenance of peace universal by all honorable means.

One notable effort was made in an interview that Rintelen had with the president of the International Longshoremen's Union. The German agent agreed to pay strikers ten dollars a week while they were idle, and bragged that he could command the $1,035,000 necessary for such a purpose. Although he spent $10,000 trying to promote this project, the longshoremen refused to go on strike. Before he was through Rintelen expended $468,000 with nothing to show for his effort but a few newspaper articles that attacked President Woodrow Wilson. Whatever strikes did take place were the result of other causes, not Rintelen's German money.

Many American politicians relied on the German-American vote, and some of these gentlemen were approached to adopt pro-German policies. One German organization, known as the American Embargo Conference, was established to prevent the export of munitions. This conference distributed to voters 5,000,000 prepaid telegrams with an identical message that demanded an embargo on munitions. Many of these telegrams inundated Congressmen in Washington, and it is said that the telegraph companies in Chicago alone were paid $20,000 for these German-inspired messages. In addition, thousands of pamphlets and circular letters were distributed, and some money was earmarked for Irish organizations in the United States, but whether any such funds were available, has not been certified. Many Irishmen, however, worked for the German cause.

From all accounts, Rintelen's chief objective was to promote a war between the United States and Mexico on the assumption that such a conflict would absorb all the munitions that Ameri-

can factories could turn out. Rintelen even went so far as to
attempt to bring back General Victoriano Huerta who had been
exiled in Europe after his failure to win United States' support
for his regime in Mexico. At the same time, other German agents
within Mexico itself had been working up a powerful anti-Ameri-
can campaign, and used the argument that the United States
was impotent, unable to prepare for war, and that Japan was
its enemy. They also tried to create hostility to the United
States by asserting that it had aims of controlling or conquering
Mexico.

This feature in Germany's secret war came to a conclusion
with the famous Zimmermann telegram to the German Ambassador in Mexico, Heinrich von Eckhardt. Intercepted and
decoded by British agents, it read:

BERLIN, JANUARY 19, 1917

ON THE FIRST OF FEBRUARY WE INTEND TO BEGIN SUBMARINE WAR-
FARE UNRESTRICTED. IN SPITE OF THIS, IT IS OUR INTENTION TO
ENDEAVOR TO KEEP NEUTRAL THE UNITED STATES OF AMERICA. IF
THIS ATTEMPT IS NOT SUCCESSFUL, WE PROPOSE AN ALLIANCE ON
THE FOLLOWING BASIS WITH MEXICO: THAT WE SHALL MAKE WAR
TOGETHER AND TOGETHER MAKE PEACE. WE SHALL GIVE GENERAL
FINANCIAL SUPPORT, AND IT IS UNDERSTOOD THAT MEXICO IS TO
RECONQUER THE LOST TERRITORY IN NEW MEXICO, TEXAS, AND
ARIZONA. THE DETAILS ARE LEFT TO YOU FOR SETTLEMENT. YOU
ARE INSTRUCTED TO INFORM THE PRESIDENT OF MEXICO OF THE
ABOVE IN THE GREATEST CONFIDENCE AS SOON AS IT IS CERTAIN
THAT THERE WILL BE AN OUTBREAK OF WAR WITH THE UNITED
STATES, AND SUGGEST THAT THE PRESIDENT OF MEXICO, ON HIS OWN
INITIATIVE, SHOULD COMMUNICATE WITH JAPAN SUGGESTING AD-
HERENCE AT ONCE TO THIS PLAN; AT THE SAME TIME, OFFER TO
MEDIATE BETWEEN GERMANY AND JAPAN. [Japan had declared
war on Germany on August 23, 1914.] PLEASE CALL TO THE
ATTENTION OF THE PRESIDENT OF MEXICO THAT THE EMPLOY-
MENT OF RUTHLESS SUBMARINE WARFARE NOW PROMISES TO
COMPEL ENGLAND TO MAKE PEACE IN A FEW MONTHS.

ZIMMERMANN

It was the disclosure of this telegram, more than anything else, that compelled President Wilson to call for a declaration of war against Germany.

When strikes failed to close American munition plants, large sums of money were expended on plans to destroy war cargoes in the course of shipment. Captain von Papen and Wolf von Igel had charge of this project. A German chemist, living in Hoboken, Dr. Walter T. Scheele, was assigned the task of developing an incendiary bomb that could be hidden in munitions cargoes and timed to explode a few days after the steamer had left its American port. Ten thousand dollars was furnished to establish a factory to manufacture Scheele's bombs, and a Captain Wolpert, a Captain Bode, and a Captain Steinberg were in charge of their distribution. Many of these were placed in cases of merchandise, and some were hidden in the coal bunkers where they smoldered until a serious fire erupted.

About four hundred of these devices were manufactured, and fires resulting from them occurred on thirty-three ships that sailed from New York. A Jeremiah O'Leary carried a number to New Orleans and assumed charge of their deposit in that port. Four unexploded bombs were found on board a ship at Marseilles, and from the evidence gathered, indictments were issued for Rintelen, Bode, Steinberg, Scheele, and eight others. Scheele, Steinberg, and a man named Schimmel fled the country. Scheele, who was given one thousand dollars for just such an emergency, was found hiding in Cuba in April 1918.

Variations of these plots were conducted all over the country. In one instance, at Detroit, sticks of dynamite that were painted to resemble coal were carried in a launch and moved close to a coal barge. The guards were vigilant, however, and the dynamite never got aboard oceangoing steamers. Other infernal machines were hidden in Thermos bottles. One group of German agents even went into Canada and tried to put these incendiary bombs aboard ships belonging to Great Britain, France, Japan, and Russia. Many attacks on Canadian railroads, harbors, and military establishments were attempted by groups financed by Rintelen or Count von Bernstorff.

When the war broke out in 1914, large numbers of German reservists were living in the United States. Naturally, they were called up through their nearby legations, and in order to avoid capture on their way home, many adopted false names so as to obtain American passports. This particular intrigue is interesting, since passports were not used between the United States and the British Empire. I moved about freely without one in 1914, and my father, who followed me that same year, arrived in Great Britain without one, and returned to New York City a few weeks later without such a document. Germany, Russia, and most other European countries had established this identity system, however, and it is presumed that these German reservists had obtained some form of an American identity card to protect them when passing through any of the belligerent countries.

At any rate, it is recorded that Captain von Papen had been provided with a large supply of counterfeit passports that were issued from the German consulate in New York City. German consuls in other cities, such as Chicago and St. Paul, obtained these forged papers for the reservists in their areas. But the British broke up this ring when they captured a Dr. Starck who had attempted to return to Germany with a forged American passport. How many reservists reached the Fatherland is difficult to ascertain.

A number of German agents used forged papers for illegal passages to Germany for unneutral purposes, and in several instances German spies, sent to operate in Great Britain, worked under the protection of these false papers. Gess D. Berko, a former Austrian who had become an American citizen, returned to Austria with a passport that had been stolen by Stephen Csiszàr, an attaché of the Austrian-Hungarian Consulate in New York City. Another American, E. G. Woodford, was sent to Europe by German officials and paid $550 to take certain documents to Berlin, while traveling on an American passport. Richard P. Stegler a German national in America, was sent to Europe to spy for Karl Boy-Ed, while also using an American passport.

When Stegler was trapped, Captain Boy-Ed was protected from prosecution by his diplomatic immunity.

As these infringements were uncovered, the German government eventually, in December 1915, issued the following official document:

> The German Government has naturally never knowingly accepted the support of any person, groups of persons, society or organizations seeking to promote the cause of Germany in the United States by illegal acts, by counsel of violence, by contravention of law, or by any means whatever that could offend the American people in the pride of their own authority.

## Defeat on Defeat

The year 1915 provided a history that was to presage the program of defeats and setbacks that marked the Hitler war a quarter of a century later. After General August von Mackensen's Prussian battering ram had driven the Russians out of Galicia, the commander in chief of the German Eastern Front, General von Hindenburg, decided to make the most of the impetus and attempt to shatter Russian power for all time. While the Czar's forces were still reeling, the burly Prussian struck southward into Poland while General von Mackensen marched north from Galicia. Hindenburg hoped with this pincer movement to bottle up and defeat the main Russian armies in Warsaw.

A chain of strong fortresses made up the chief Russian defenses, the better known being Riga on the Baltic coast. Kovno and Grodno on the Niemen River in part separated Russia and East Prussia; Ossowiec and Lomza defended Poland from East Prussia; and Novogeorgievsk (Modlin) directly in front of Warsaw guarded the confluence of the important rivers, the Vistula and the Bug. Farther south on the Wieprz and Vistula Rivers stood Ivangorod (Deblin). This most southern fortress fell first, and then Warsaw itself went down under the Prussian attack.

Unable to catch their breath, the Russians' line was broken next at Lomza, and then Kovno where the defense was so weak its commander was accused of conspiracy with the enemy, and immediately recalled in public disgrace. At Ossowiec and Novogeorgievsk the defenders made a gallant stand and, although finally overrun, gave other Russian forces a chance to escape the German trap. The main Russian armies fell back to a second line, bolstered by Brest Litovsk, east of the Polish capital of Warsaw. But this line of defense soon buckled, and the high point of German victory in the east came on August 26.

Princess Catherine Radziwill, a well-known writer of that era, wrote a compelling account of this German push in which she pointed out that the loss of Kovno left a far deeper impression on the Russian people than the fall of Warsaw:

"I do not know what impression the fall of Kovno may have produced abroad. Here the consternation surpasses anything I have ever seen before . . . The pessimists who prophesied that no good could ever result from the Grand Duke [Nicholas] being in supreme military command, rejoice to see their prognostications verified, but even they forebear from indulging in the usual 'I told you so,' dear to the human heart. The situation is felt to be far too serious for vain boasting. The one thing that dominates is the knowledge that not only have we been beaten, but also that we did not defend ourselves as we should have done."

In a frantic and costly effort to relieve the pressure on the crumbling Russian front, the British and French made a number of heavy trench-warfare attacks all along the Western Front. Individual thrusts, all resulting in dreadful casualties, were made here and there, any one of which would have been considered a major battle in any previous war, but in this carnage, they were just bewildering names in the daily communiqués.

The French attack in Champagne during September coincided with the British attack on Loos. These combined efforts proved to be organized murder. Marshal Joffre, determined to drive the Germans out of France, was able to gather in only a

few enemy-held strong points and prepare them for future counterattacks. This offensive began with a tremendous artillery barrage, for by now field guns were said to stand wheel to wheel
from Ostend to the Swiss border, a catch phrase rather than an
actuality, but by the autumn of 1915 there were considerable
artillery ammunition and guns available. Once the batteries began, the roar and glare of shells, so marked in contrast to the
*rat-a-tat-tat* of rifles and machine guns, caused the Germans to
divert sixteen reserve divisions to the French front.

By this time a new shortage of shells put a halt to the Allied
artillery display, leaving the enemy in doubt as to what was under way, and his interest returned to the Russian front where
General von Hindenburg was attempting to move on Riga, with
the motive of eventually driving his enemy in confusion across
the Pripet Marshes. It was during this period of indecision that
the Allied generals, Joffre and Haig, decided to strike. Marshal
Joffre's official orders were generally vague and his commanders
had little conception of what his actual intentions were. His
mind seethed with ideas of strategic importance, but his actions
indicated that he was planning nothing more than a continuation
of his pointless "nibbling" policy.

On the British front two armies under Haig and Plumer were
holding a battle area fifty miles wide, while Joffre's forces of
eight army corps were responsible for only twenty miles. In the
center of this French sector, Champagne, portions of the French
Fourth and Fifth Armies assaulted the German positions between Souain and Missiges, while in Artois half a dozen divisions of the French Tenth Army co-operated with the British
IV Army Corps in its thrust toward Lens.

This was to be Neuve-Chapelle all over again for the British;
their big guns were limited to 90 rounds of ammunition and the
field guns to 150 over twenty-four hours. General Haig had
hoped to employ chlorine gas, and 5000 cylinders (about 150
tons) had been moved into the trenches. On the day originally
set for the attack, September 15, the wind was perfect, but with

Joffre vacillating between making his main attack in the Artois
sector, or thrusting from Champagne, a new date, September 25,
had to be accepted.

From all accounts General Haig was not in complete accord on
the Loos attack, but he had put considerable hope in his gas
canisters to limit his casualties. When the day of the move approached, the meteorological reports left him with many doubts.
At six o'clock the night before the wind was on the border line
between favorable and unfavorable. Three hours later it promised to co-operate, upon which the British general planned a
full-scale offensive to be opened with the gas cloud early the
next morning. At 5:50 A.M., zero hour for the chlorine, the wind
played various pranks. On one division's front it moved according to plan, on another it died down to nothing, and on a third,
held by General Henry Sinclair Horne's 2nd Division, it swung
around to the northeast. The officer in charge of the cylinders
refused to turn on the tanks, but General Horne decided that
"the program must be carried out whatever the conditions."

As a result of General Horne's senseless decision many British
soldiers were knocked out by their own gas, and those who could
stagger forward walked into heavy machine-gun fire directed by
German gunners who had not been affected by the vapors. General Horne then demanded a new assault which was abandoned
only when his brigade commanders protested against this useless
sacrifice.

Regardless of the direction of the wind, the situation was much
the same all along this British front. Once more, the defense was
stronger than the attack, and when openings were forced there
were no reserves to widen the gap. All this was the responsibility of General French who later wrote an untruthful dispatch
stating that reserves *were* available to General Haig, but that he
had never called on them. A bitter quarrel resulted, and General
Haig appealed to Lord Kitchener, and eventual conferences at
the War Office led to General French's being withdrawn, and
General Haig selected to take his place.

The French had some early success in the Champagne sector, since their opponents were mystified by the various activities and were unprepared for the enthusiastic charge of the poilu. The French brigades created havoc among the enemy and had no trouble clearing out the field works, dugouts, and trenches that their artillery had demolished. They stormed on from these front-line redoubts to reserve areas, with both colonials and regular infantry of the line moving ahead like clockwork. Some mounted troops even had important roles in the attack.

The attack was resumed on the second day, September 26, and the Germans made no real attempt to hold their first line, but withdrew slowly and awaited the arrival of their reserves. Here and there the line was breached, but the attackers were generally drawn in and annihilated by concentrated fire of artillery. When it was obvious that every yard advanced, now had to be paid for in serious casualties, the attack was called off to "cut our losses," to take what profit had been gained. By early October the French had advanced on a front of fifteen miles for an average of a mile and a half. They claimed to have taken 25,000 prisoners, 150 heavy guns, and considerable booty in munitions and small arms. How much of the combined Loos-Champagne thrust was a victory is still in doubt; the Germans had lost very little, and this Allied pressure had come too late to have any effect on the situation in Russia, as Russia was doomed to fall to revolution, and the Germans were not deterred in their new Balkan plans. Loos could only be added to Neuve-Chapelle, Suvla Bay, and other Allied setbacks.

As newcomers in the war, the Italians had a few weeks of comparative success when they swarmed over the enemy frontier north of Verona and west of Gorizia to take Cortina, but nowhere penetrated Austrian territory more than twenty miles beyond the enemy's fortifications. As soon as they came within range of heavy artillery sheltered behind permanent earthworks, they were forced to take to the earth, and the Italian campaign of 1915 thereafter continued to be another variation of trench warfare.

## Serbia Goes Down

With some last-ditch stands, the Russian armies finally halted the German drive by November 15; the enemy had been driven back in several places, and it was apparent that Hindenburg had reached the limit to which he could safely advance. The Grand Duke Nicholas had been transferred to the Caucasus on September 5 to take over the Turkish front, and in a dramatic gesture the Czar assumed the Grand Duke's place at the head of the Russian armies. The emperor, of course, did not take actual command, for he was not an experienced soldier, but his presence at General Staff meetings stiffened the discipline, and the questionable characters who had done so much to betray their fighting countrymen no longer could operate openly.

Russian resistance seemed to strengthen after Czar Nicholas II's proclamation of October 23. The Germans, once flush with victory, were now entering the real Russia where, as one Hungarian officer explained, "Every tree was an islet standing out in the gloomy marshland, and shallow lakes which extend for mile after mile. The roads were inundated by water which had risen high owing to the floods of rain; and from the miserable cottages, which at intervals were partly submerged along the roadways, strange-looking men with long beards and matted hair—mostly woodcutters and others earning a precarious living from the products of the surrounding wilderness—crept out to stare with amazement at the Austrian and German cavalrymen."

For a time Russia was saved by her marshland, and the fighting line now extended from Riga, which had withstood all assaults, to Dvinsk, a strongly fortified city on the Dvina River, and then ran to Pinsk, east of Brest Litovsk, and continued on to Rovno in the south where a number of Russian successes were staged.

How long the Czar could have held out, if internal strife and revolution had not betrayed him, can long be debated, but by the middle of October, convinced that Germany would win the war, Bulgaria joined the Central Powers. It was apparent that she had little choice, but her political leaders plunged eagerly into the partnership of greed and conquest. Germany compelled Turkey to surrender some property immediately to Bulgaria, and then promised her complete rule over Serbia. The Allies were in no position to compete with these political dealings.

Bulgaria had bitter reason for animosity toward the other Balkan states, particularly Serbia, since they all had conspired against her in the Second Balkan War of 1913. Ferdinand I, King of Bulgaria, now suggested that he rule all the Balkans as the Viceroy of Germany.

Serbia was doomed. The Allies did their best by sending an army to Salonika, the nearest seaport in the Aegean Sea, but Bulgaria controlled the inland route that led from Salonika toward Serbia. In the meantime a combined German-Austrian attack was launched to overwhelm hard-pressed Serbia, and no matter what heroism the Allies displayed, they could not fight their way through the mountain passes that were held by the Bulgarians. Serbia was crushed and once more disrepute was the reward of the Triple Alliance. No wonder the Balkans believed that Germany could not lose the war.

By early November the Central Powers had matters all their own way, and the trench warfare in the west could not obliterate the importance of Germany's success in the east. In fact, an empire of mid-Europe had been established; a German railroad ran all the way from Berlin to Constantinople; Austria-Hungary had been humbled into complete obedience; Turkey, under Enver Pasha, was a German satellite and tool, and Bulgaria had placed itself under complete Prussian domination.

Now the enemy was proclaiming the completion of a railroad from Berlin to Baghdad, but this final link was never to be forged. Other enthusiasts proposed that a train might run from Antwerp to Constantinople, but the fates were fickle, and the Allies shed torrents of blood in France and Flanders to undermine this extravagant Prussian dream. How confident Germany was that her arms would be rewarded with triumph, will be noted in the Manifesto of the Intellectuals, a petition drawn up by a number of leading German professors, diplomats, and high government officials for presentation to the German Imperial Chancellor.

This amazing document, prepared in the summer of 1915, gave full details of a peace treaty. *Kultur* was to take precedence over the barbarians of the east and the west. Heavy indemnities were to be imposed on France, Belgium, Russia, and Great Britain. Germany was to acquire the Channel coast, and all French business undertakings were to be transferred to German ownership.

Belgium was to be held with a firm hand, and all Flemish people "emancipated from the artificial tie to French culture, and returned to their Teutonic affinities." The Belgians were to have no political influence in the new empire of mid-Europe, and all important business was to be transferred to German ownership.

Because of the large population of Russia, it was decided that Germany could hold her ground only by a strong boundary wall, and as a further buttress against the rising tide of Russian population, all measures to maintain a healthy increase in the German birth rate were to be taken. Any Russian agricultural land would be ceded to Germany for colonization. A land-grab made up the greater part of the manifesto in relation to Russia. England—meaning Great Britain—was to be relieved of all European markets, was to give up all her African colonies, and be deprived of all means of dominating the world's sea lanes. The European Channel ports were to be in German hands, and the chain of British naval bases all over the world were to be weakened by a corresponding acquisition of German bases. She was to be deprived of her control of Egypt, and surrender her control of the Suez Canal. Then, because of Britain's influence on the governments and press of the world, Germany would destroy her monopoly of the cable service and press agencies. She would "dominate" and exploit the world "like the English," and her aim would be to safeguard her own special needs, and then act like pathmakers and leaders of Europe, respecting and securing the "free self-development" of the peoples.

All this Germany would do when she had won the war.

# CHAPTER IV

*The War's Darkest Moment . . . They Shall Not Pass . . .*
*Blood Bath of the Somme . . . Tanks Are Trumps . . .*
*The Legend of Albert . . . Escadrille Americaine.*

## The War's Darkest Moment

The advent of 1916 introduced the gloomiest period of the war—at least from the Allied point of view. The National Conscription Act was a shock to Britain's pride. Gallipoli was being evacuated, and General Sir Charles Townshend was besieged at Kut after suffering a wicked repulse at Ctesiphon. The Sinn Feiners in Ireland were promising trouble, and there was a serious labor situation along the River Clyde. German mastery was everywhere, and with the new year the Teutonic threat seemed grimmer than ever. Neither side would give in to the black exhaustion, although it seemed that no one could win. War had been shorn of its pageantry, the toll was heavy, and there was little opportunity for heroism or glory in the trenches.

With each succeeding week of this deadly if spasmodic warfare, it was obvious that the conflict would become a war of supplies. This was most noticeable in the increase of field and heavy artillery. The production and expenditure of high-explosive and gas shells was fantastic. Trench mortars and rifle grenades cost a large fortune, while the materials needed for the improvement and repair of roads, railroads, bridges, water supplies, communications, and the inventory of bombproof shelters, dugouts, duckboards, and sandbags rocketed beyond normal imagination.

Both sides had drawn heavily on manpower and the ranks already were filled with downy-cheeked youths and men of middle age. Their factories, forests, mines, and workers had all been channeled into the war effort. What materials were lacking, were bought from the neutrals, and the bills were paid with money provided by loans. Everyone's future was mortgaged to buy victory, for no other outcome could be conceived.

Nevertheless, the major powers realized that the war had to be won on the Western Front, and although second-guessers have since discovered half a dozen doors that might have afforded paths around the quagmire of trench warfare, such enlightened viewpoints were not available to the commanders of that day.

It must be admitted that Allied efforts to win the war on the Western Front had till now been handicapped by the lack of Franco-British co-ordination, a point often brought up, but with no rational explanation offered. General Joffre had done his best, but because of her traditions and pride in her historic regiments, Great Britain found service integration difficult. It was one thing to cross the Channel and fight for France and Belgium, but quite another to take orders from a foreign general, even though the foreigner already was commanding an army at least twice the size of that under General Haig. America posed something of the same problem a year or so later, but in that instance her attitude was based on General John J. Pershing's determination to keep his forces intact, and have Americans fight only under their own flag. The European code of national unity has no symbol comparable to the Stars and Stripes.

Great Britain's continued refusal to co-operate fully has often been charged as the chief reason for the war dragging on with great loss and waste. This may be true, but almost all German leaders considered her to be the arch enemy and soul of resistance. And whatever her military worth along the Western Front, she did fulfill her traditional role by maintaining the largest navy in the world, and keeping the seas free for her allies. How great a part the Royal Navy contributed to the continuing pressure and the ultimate victory will be presented in a later chapter. But even more dramatic, if not as important militarily, was the fact that Great Britain was building up the greatest air force in the world. It was this effort with its victories and sacrifices that the rest of the world has not appreciated fully, and to this day the attainments of the old Royal Flying Corps have seldom been presented honestly—particularly in the United States.

## They Shall Not Pass

The year 1916 saw the savage German attacks on the French forts at Verdun. Never before had such a tornado of ammunition or such an avalanche of men been hurled with such wanton prodigality. Insane with desperation, the enemy forced the French back, yard by yard, until the whole world wondered how much longer the human barrier could resist. Was Prussianism to conquer? Was France to go down, as had Belgium, Poland, and Serbia?

Success seemed to be in the hands of the attackers until a clarion cry rose from the throats of the French troops. "They shall not pass!" This defiance raised the curtain on one of the most dramatic periods in the war, and the free world held its breath until the determined poilus made good their word.

Germany intended to stage her chief operation of the year at Verdun, and planned to shatter France, as she had Russia, with such a concentration of artillery there could be no resistance of any kind. With France thus eliminated it was presumed that the armies of Great Britain would quickly be driven back to their island retreat. "Little Willie," the Crown Prince of Germany, was to be placed at the head of the Teutonic forces so that he might become a Hohenzollern hero to be worshiped, and prepared for his leadership in the Fatherland.

Verdun lies on the Meuse River, which here winds in easy loops through a network of hills. The first attacks were made well to the east of the river, and in five days the Prussians had surged halfway to the old town and were close to the

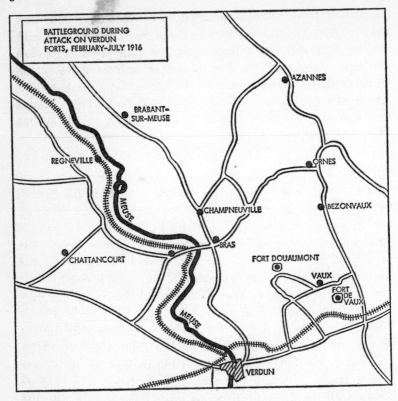

BATTLEGROUND DURING
ATTACK ON VERDUN
FORTS, FEBRUARY–JULY 1916

defenses around Forts Douaumont and Vaux. From that point on French resistance stiffened, and the Crown Prince lost his chance to become a national hero.

The main drive for Verdun opened on February 21, although preliminary bombardment had been made some time before. The defenders were battered for three days with a gigantic concentration of shellfire, and German infantry had little difficulty in advancing. Only 12,000 French troops were in the front line, but heavier reserves were concentrated some distance in the rear. Although the men in the advance trenches mowed down the oncomers in serried rows, German artillery put up a barrier of steel and concussion that prevented French reserves from moving up.

Because of this situation the Germans made some advance and by February 25 the famed Brandenburg Infantry Regiment stormed into Fort Douaumont. Here legend takes over. Allied reporters claimed that the French, staging a fake retreat, lured them in and then when the weary Brandenburgers had settled down and removed much of their equipment, the poilus stormed back and captured the lot. The German version indicated that only a few men of this regiment were taken.

A more astounding version is that a German Sergeant Kunze, patrolling a wood with a small force of ten men, spotted Fort Douaumont ahead. Being a venturesome soul, although his orders limited him to a search of the wood, the sergeant decided to investigate the fort's defenses. His small force first came upon a swatch of barbed wire and with no trouble at all cut its way through in clear daylight. No one inside the fort fired a shot, so the group moved on through a barrier of spiked railings. Still no one questioned their visit, so the eleven-man force moved inside, and Sergeant Kunze, pushing a revolving gun to one side, burst in on a gun crew that was supposed to be manning a 155-mm. weapon, and captured them at pistol point.

The astonished Frenchmen were herded deeper into the fortress until they suddenly darted into a chamber that was filled with French soldiers. Sergeant Kunze quickly sized up the situation, slammed and bolted the door and held the redoubt until a number of German officers sauntered in to take over. All this is said to have taken exactly forty-five minutes, and could have cost France some 100,000 men. Whether or not Sergeant Kunze received a reward or promotion for this feat, is not known, but since the Kaiser carefully eliminated any reference to Verdun from his memoirs, it is quite possible that Sergeant Kunze suffered the same fate.

Another legend comes from the dispatches of Lord Northcliffe (Alfred Charles William Harmsworth), British newspaper tycoon, who witnessed the whole battle. He explained in his report that Verdun lies in one of the coldest and most misty sectors of that line. Changes in temperature are abrupt and frequent. At one point the French and German trenches were built up with their parapets just above shallow ditches. These earthworks, composed of sticks, sandbags, mud, and general debris, were cemented together by the low temperatures. At one point these breastworks were so close the men on either side could hear the others talking.

During the battle, a rapid thaw set in one day and both parapets melted and collapsed. The defenders on each side were left with most of their bodies exposed, a situation that presented only two possibilities; each could wipe out the other, or some sort of temporary truce could be agreed on while new parapets were erected.

In this report we are given another variation of the 1914 Christmas truce. Without conferring, and wasting no time with unofficial negotiation, both sides turned their backs so as not to look at their enemies, and carefully rebuilt their parapets without a shot being fired.

It was in such inclement weather that the Germans undertook the attack against the French strongholds at Verdun. Besides the concentration of shellfire, all troops concerned had to bear up against a gruesome tableau in which men who had been wounded were left in fantastic positions and later found frozen to death.

Once the full force of the enemy attack was comprehended, the French troops were ordered to make a strategic withdrawal, particularly from the Waville Wood where they ran the risk of being surrounded. Some of the troops protested the order and demanded to be permitted to make a stand, and if necessary, die there. It was soon evident, however, that evacuation was wiser and an organized withdrawal was carried out, but only after a fearful defense of Herbebois where more than 3000 Germans charged in waves, only to be mowed down, until the dead and wounded formed a high parapet of bodies. Hundreds of others were scattered about the assault zone. This gallant stand stopped the enemy rush and allowed some French reserves to be moved up.

Fort Douaumont provided several such ghastly spectacles. As the Prussians advanced to take the stronghold, French artillery mowed them down from ranges of less than three hundred yards. In one instance a force of Bavarians, wearing French greatcoats, crawled up to the defenders' lines and, shouting French military commands, attempted to induce the poilus to withdraw across an open area. This deceit failed, and the French, instead, charged out of their trenches and engaged the Germans in a wild hand-to-hand conflict that left dead and wounded all over the battleground.

Still, the German infantry crashed on, although their artillery had slackened, and French machine guns added their wild chorus to the snarl of the seventy-fives, but against these continued defense efforts, the German assault died down gradually.

This awesome savagery continued until April 11 when there was a breathing spell. Battered, dazed, and bewildered by the unexpected resistance, the Germans used the pause to reorganize and make new plans. Their losses had been prohibitive, and their morale was low. Unable to produce a better plan in the interlude, the German General Staff started a new series of assaults in May. This campaign, just as bloody and reckless, lasted two more months, but again the French refused to retreat or surrender.

A desperate assault was directed at Dead Man's Hill on the Meuse River on May 20, and to this was added more fighting around the old Fort Douaumont area. Slowly, and at terrible cost, the Germans finally gained possession of these two heights. By June they turned their attention to Fort Vaux where again they attacked with wild frenzy and gained some ground at tremendous cost. In July they made attacks on the villages of Fleury and Thiaumont, which proved to be the high point of their advance. Here objectives were taken and retaken, day after day, and Thiaumont, by then a mere crater in the ground, was said to have changed hands twenty-one times. The French finally retook it and held it until the end of the war.

But the great sacrifices the French had made at Verdun gave

the Allies time to build up their resources and strengthen their situations elsewhere. In fact, General Joffre hoped they would be able to employ all their resources simultaneously in a more efficient manner. By August of that year it appeared that Russia might do better than hold her own, for she was now using her forces with some effect in Galicia, Volhynia, and Armenia. Reaping the reward of conscription, Britain was building up her armies in France and Flanders, and it was believed that Germany had come to the end of her resources, and that only by superhuman efforts was her railroad transportation facilities and transport command able to keep her reserves moving from front to front.

Joffre was convinced that the Allies had turned the corner and were heading for victory. It must be added that by now a small handful of officials in Germany realized that their war had been lost.

### Blood Bath of the Somme

At the Marne, and again at Verdun, France had made a prime effort to hurl back the aggressor. She had taken the brunt of battle for almost two years, sacrificing her sons and finest regiments in a vain effort to break the enemy line. At Verdun in particular she suffered the full impact of the German offensive. By the spring of 1916 her armies still crouched exhausted, but defiant. She had accounted for the loss of 600,000 Germans, but most of all she needed a rest to gather her military wits and restore some strength to her infantry columns.

Till now the British Army had been capable of little more than defensive actions, and what minor attacks had been made, only punched out small salients. Britain was learning this new science of slaughter, but the Old Contemptibles and Territorials who had borne the brunt, had bought the time required to build the New Army. Why Germany permitted this period of grace, instead of concentrating on and annihilating the BEF before it could be built into a major force is puzzling, but again, the German General Staff proved to be as inept as its opposite numbers.

By June 1, 1916, Britain had 600,000 well-trained infantry-men in France and Flanders, and in addition there were more than sufficient reserves. The munitions workers had produced thousands of big and medium guns—twelve-inch 9.2s, eight-inch 4.2s, and long muzzled sixty-pounders of great range and power. More important, Britain's Royal Flying Corps, now the elite corps of the services, was ready and willing. Despite the postwar assertion that they were Fokker fodder, the records disclose that the new fighter pilots were beating the enemy at his own game. True, the Germans had the much-publicized fixed-gun Fokker fighter, but the R.F.C. was well equipped with the D.H.2, a pusher biplane of smart performance that also fired a front gun—without the complex interrupter gear mechanism. These, and the several new two-seater fighters, now fitted with front-firing guns for the pilot, and a nippy Scarff-mounting weapon for the gunner, were creating havoc with the German squadrons. The new aerial gunners, in particular, were reaping a harvest, a situation that was to force the Germans to adopt the flying circus concept. During the Battle of the Somme the British airmen literally drove the Boelcke squadrons from the sky.

The British now had transport, plenty of it, and hundreds of men who never before had handled anything more complex than a horse-drawn milk wagon, were tooling massive trucks, lorries, ambulances, and road-building equipment. They also had hundreds of new canvas shelters, all marked with a large Red Cross, for an anticipated Big Push was being prepared, and those already wounded or disabled were being moved out of hospital beds and returned to blighty. Meaning home to British soldiers the term had been adopted earlier by troops serving in India from the Hindustani word *bilāyati,* which means foreign. Army nomenclature in those days was full of Hindustani terms, but only blighty seems to have survived.

The troops as a whole were not perturbed by the prospect of a new offensive, and they looked forward to it with keen anticipation. Many of them hoped that once a breakthrough was made, trench warfare would be over, and the war could then be carried on in the traditional manner. The cynicism of the postwar years had not as yet sullied the countenance of these young men.

"If we can only get them out in the open," they all said.

But only the Royal Flying Corps knew how deep the enemy had carried his earthworks, a vast maze of trenches and barbed wire, in some areas thirty miles deep. Only the R.F.C. and the General Staff knew, but dared not tell.

The cream of the Empire was on hand, eager and ready. Hundreds of new British regiments were camped on the pastoral fields of the Somme. Even Ireland was represented by the 16th Division from Dublin and the 36th from Ulster. Scots there were, flaunting their kilts once more, after the 1915–16 winter of mud and frozen slots that made "trews" more serviceable. The Canadians were there, singing, "I want to go back . . . down on the farm . . . far away from harm . . . with a milk pail on my arm." There were the pink-cheeked, well-mannered New Zealanders, and suddenly, to our amazement, the Australians wearing their big hats, straight from the debacle of the Dardanelles. Giant men, boastful, sun-tanned, and fearless, moving with the natural carelessness of the wide open spaces.

The British effort had to be carried on without the guidance of Lord Kitchener who had been lost at sea when H.M.S. *Hampshire* was sunk while on its way to Russia. Early in May 1916, conditions in Russia were critical, and the Czar had invited the British military leader to visit Petrograd with the idea of turning over to British command certain sectors of the Russian front, along with Russian troops.

The Royal Navy arranged to take Lord Kitchener from Scapa Flow in the Orkney Islands off Scotland, to Archangel (Arkhangelsk) in northern Russia. On June 5, after visiting Admiral John R. Jellicoe aboard his flagship, Kitchener transferred to the *Hampshire* which had been prepared for his comfort and communications convenience. The Battle of Jutland had been fought only a few days before, but the British warship, a cruiser, was sent on this mission unescorted and through a channel between the Orkneys and the Shetlands that had not been swept of mines. Why this arrangement was ever made is not clear, but shortly after getting under way, the *Hampshire* struck a mine and went down. Practically all hands, including Lord Kitchener, went down with her. Thus, when Britain's armies took on their first great offensive, their leader was no more, but Sir William Robertson, his chief of staff, was a reputable organizer, and no doubt did as well as could be expected. He had risen from the ranks and was to become a field marshal, so he must have had valuable qualities.

Apart from the urgent need to relieve the pressure at Verdun, this British contribution to the common task was overdue. The Somme, where the two armies joined near Hardecourt, provided a situation in which for the first time the Allies could set up something approaching a unity of command. Thus, it was hoped that on a front twenty-five miles long, the German line could be rolled back toward the Belgian coast, which would not only assure the safety of the Channel ports, but make the German position in the south untenable.

The men in charge of the artillery sneered at the mention of enemy wire and trench defenses. They now had sufficient shells to wipe out any artificial opposition, so they thought. But there were many natural barriers in the rolling downs of the Bapaume Ridge where the Germans had dug in their vast underground chambers that no artillery could destroy. And it was these defenses, more than any other single cause, that defeated the British thrust toward Gommecourt and Serre.

General Haig's plan perhaps lacked elasticity, for in this Somme offensive he held no such fantastic hopes that marked his attack at Loos. He was now a cautious man who had learned a grim lesson. He expected no rapid breakthrough, and had decided that if matters were to go against him, he would switch his reserve army toward Ypres. This was the only alternate plan on his map, and when he found himself plagued with a mixture of success and failure, his inflexible mind could not adapt to these unexpected conditions.

Haig had hoped to break the enemy line first between Maricourt and Serre, and then to take the high ground between Bapaume and Ginchy, while the French would seize the area flanking Sailly and Rancourt. If all these plans materialized, he would then wheel to the left and ram the German flank back as far as Arras, and to capitalize on this he even had some cavalry forces available to complete the breakthrough in his best Boer War style. In addition to these major thrusts, he added a number of subsidiary assaults, feints, and probes that might take the British through to the Cambrai-Douai line.

Shortly before the jump-off, the French warned that they were in no condition to give any valuable aid, but Haig went ahead. After all, he had 5000 artillery pieces, a gun set along every twenty yards of the front, so General Sir Henry S. Rawlinson's Fourth Army of eighteen divisions was sent off to open the attack on July 1. Within a few hours Sir Douglas saw that a general breakthrough was out of the question, and in a later report he said that all he had hoped to accomplish was to wear down the Germans and have them weakened for a final blow in 1917. General John E. B. Seely in command of a brigade of Canadian cavalry stated, however, that his orders read, "to gallop right through Cambrai, encircle it, and cut the railway lines to the east."

The morning of the attack was a scorcher, and by seven o' clock the Germans were well aware of what was to transpire, and they greeted the attackers stolidly. Once the British infantry clambered out of the slots, it was mowed down like grain. No man's land was soon carpeted with their bodies, and still the enemy front line had not been reached. What artillery barrage had been sent over had done small damage, for the experienced Germans ducked low in their deep chambers, and the instant the barrage ceased, hauled their guns and mortars back to where they could be used.

The British battalions attacked in four to eight waves, not

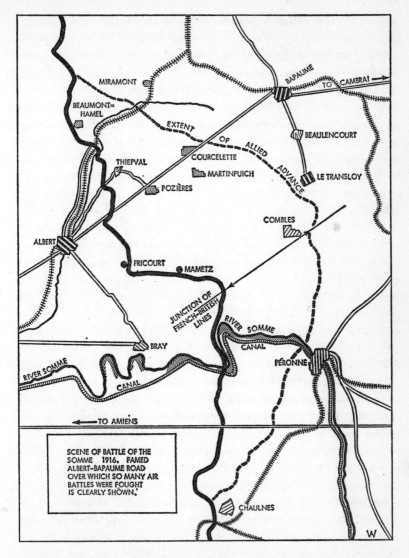

SCENE OF BATTLE OF THE
SOMME 1916. FAMED
ALBERT-BAPAUME ROAD
OVER WHICH SO MANY AIR
BATTLES WERE FOUGHT
IS CLEARLY SHOWN.

more than one hundred yards apart, moving almost shoulder to
shoulder in well-dressed alignment at a slow walk with their
rifles at the "port." By nightfall most battalions were scarcely
one hundred strong. The few who survived gradually formed

small groups under a leader and continued their advance in short rushes or by primitive crawling tactics. These few often moved on for considerable distances, but enemy machine guns continued to exact a frightful toll.

The French, who finally joined the attack, had little trouble south of the British line and gained their objectives, thanks to a heavier artillery barrage, and the fact that the forces of the enemy were less strong along their front. Also, the French attack had been a surprise since only a British assault was expected.

The degree of success along the British front varied. Most objectives were reached, but at what a cost! July 1, 1916, saw the greatest one-day British loss of the war; 57,470, of whom 19,240 were killed, or died of their wounds. German losses were somewhat lighter, but still quite heavy, and one division immediately south of the Somme had suffered a loss of 5148 men when relieved the next day, and another lost 4187 on July 5. Only 1989 German prisoners were taken, but this epic heroism had proved the moral quality of Britain's New Army. These civilian soldiers bore a percentage of losses such as no professional army of the past wars had suffered, and still they were not broken. But what they fought for was not to be attained until one year later in the Battle of Cambrai.

This Battle of the Somme, which soon turned into a series of probing attacks, continued for more than two weeks, but no great success was achieved. General Haig, another of Great Britain's pious leaders, added to one of his dispatches, "I feel that every step of my plan has been taken with Divine help." Behind the Front, high commanders were writing rosy reports that pictured great numbers of prisoners, but refrained from mentioning the heavy casualties. Where opportunities for advances were offered, no one made a move, but the troops were ordered to continue their attacks "uniformly" so that in some areas they had little opposition, but in others walked into infernos of automatic fire.

By July 14 one particular opportunity presented itself, and a portion of Rawlinson's army made a night approach, following a short, hurricane bombardment. This resulted in a successful storming of a second position, but no attempt was made to exploit the situation. Haig then ordered another series of what came to be known as "attrition" thrusts, that in turn became more and more expensive; so much so that by July 23 the British general had to stage another major attack to cover up all previous mistakes and account for some of the losses.

And so the battle of the Somme went along, week after week, with no particular success, except in official communiqués. Still more attacks and more thrusts were planned and made until by the middle of September there was some hope of getting all the way through to Bapaume. There were few reserves left, only a handful of very tired troops, but it was believed that any success at this time would bring the Germans to terms. Haig still hoped to gamble on a breakthrough and it was at this point that he remembered Colonel Swinton's fantastic idea of a war machine, a land destroyer that would break down the enemy barbed wire, straddle his trenches, and smash his machine-gun nests.

In desperation he called on help from Britain's new Tank Corps, at the time known as Heavy Section, Machine Gun Corps. In fact, it was General Rawlinson, who long had derided the idea, who suggested this appeal for help, and it was these two officers who first ordered the new weapon into action.

## Tanks Are Trumps

To return to September 1915 when Swinton's Mark I tank was just emerging from its natal bed. As explained before it weighed 30 tons, had a speed of 3.7 mph and could travel a distance of 12 miles on its tank of 53 gallons of fuel. It required four men to steer and drive it, and the gunners sat on metal bicycle saddles, and vision was obtained by prismatic glass peepholes built into a short periscope. This was discarded later owing to the danger of shattered glass, and polished metal mirrors were substituted.

An experimental test area had been set up at Wembley Park,

west of London, and prototypes were trucked in from Lincoln and secluded there under a small circus tent. Military officials then worked out the armament requirements, the thickness of the armor, and figured out how to incorporate the six-pounder gun. By December 1915 the Mark I was as perfect as it ever would be; all it needed was a name.

As secretary to the technical committee, Colonel Swinton was asked to furnish some term that would aid in keeping the production of this juggernaut a secret. The men working on the project had called it a "box of tricks," "shove-'apenny," and the "thingum-a-jig."

That Christmas Eve Swinton pondered on the matter. He recalled that up to now the machine was boxlike in structure, and from that he worked out variants through to "container," which he rejected, as he did "receptacle," "reservoir," and "cistern." Finally he thought of the monosyllable "tank," and the word seemed to fit perfectly.

That holiday eve, one of the glummest of the war, he wrote his regular report, using the word tank for the first time. Nine months later the word echoed around the world, and was incorporated eventually into the language of every nation possessing a military vocabulary.

On January 18, 1916, the first complete tank moved under its own power and carried out all the required maneuvers. Its guns were fired successfully from the sponsons, or turrets, and the first field test was made in a simulated war area composed of trenches, shellholes, duck puddles, and barbed wire entanglements. Again, considerable success was attained, and despite the secrecy, some information did filter out, and the military officials in France sent out an impassioned plea for at least forty of the new machines. Word has gotten around that they *actually* could negotiate trenches, and crawl over barbed wire while trained gunners battered the enemy with cannon and machine-gun fire. Needless to say, the new vehicle's capabilities lost nothing in the telling.

When the first Mark I tank arrived at the Bisley training area in England, and the volunteers realized what they had signed on for, there were several amusing reactions. About half of them wanted to bolt the service immediately, some refused to believe the "bloody thing" would move, but many were delighted with the crazy project and anticipated a "hilarious picnic." This final reaction spread all over town, and in a short while Colonel Swinton found he was heading a very popular service, and was overwhelmed with volunteers.

The first tank establishment consisted of six companies, each company composed of twenty-five tanks and their crews. An original order for one hundred machines had been increased to one hundred and fifty, and it was hoped that in time the section would have 184 officers and 1610 men.

As soon as General Haig made his appeal, the first few companies of tanks were moved across the Channel, as reports were deliberately circulated that the partly dismantled machines were water tanks for the troops in Palestine, or were snowplows for the Russian Army. Some were dubbed WITH CARE TO PETROGRAD in Russian letters twelve inches high on both sides of the machines.

When the first companies arrived in France, many military men, not members of the Heavy Section, looked on the invention as a new toy, and others had a tendency to place too much reliance on these few machines. After C Company arrived in France and set up training exercises at Yvrench, it was expected to give frequent displays for the benefit of the troops at rest.

Although neither the men nor the tanks were ready for combat, Haig was determined to send a number into action as soon as possible. Swinton pleaded for more time and training, adding that few members of his crew had been in France and not many had an idea what a trench system looked like; they were far from proficient with their weapons; there were steering problems to overcome; ventilation inside the landships was inadequate, and he already was losing men through nausea and mild dementia brought on by the foul conditions within the machines.

None of these arguments was given consideration, and plans were made hurriedly to send the tanks into action during the middle of September. No special reconnaissance was made of the target area by tank officials; what orders were finally drawn were canceled a few hours before the actual attack was made, and new ones issued—verbally. D Company was rushed from England and had but two days in the area before it went into action for the first time. A Company did not reach France until the morning of the first tank attack.

In the early, haze-swept morning of September 15, 1916, the art of ground warfare was revolutionized. World War I that had already introduced a new element of battle and given wings to young men of valor, saw the first direct move to lift the carnage from the mud and slots of the trenches.

That morning still lingers in the memory of thousands of ex-servicemen now living. Few of them can forget it. The German infantry, protected by barbed wire in the area of The Loop near Bray on the Somme, were contemplating the tranquillity of the British lines opposite. They probably contrasted their security in the Hindenburg line with the hazardous lot of their comrades struggling in the shell-churned mudholes around Ypres to the north. A few may have pondered on the pertinacity of the Tommies who had so engulfed themselves in the mud of Flanders, they could not consider an assault before the winter set in to solidify a foot-sure battleground.

The first faint warning came when on-duty sentries, huddling against their parapets, sensed a distant growl of internal combustion engines. Their immediate reaction was to peer up into the low-hanging mist—but what madman would be flying an airplane under such conditions, what young fool would risk entanglement with the steel cables looping down from the kite balloons?

The *clank, clank, clank* of pistons and the grumble of heavy mechanism continued. The sentries peered left and right. One or two tried to recall whether any narrow-gauge railroad snaked through this vicinity. Some wondered about the boldness of British supply-truck drivers. A Prussian *oberleutnant* insisted that it was the vagary of the atmospherics that carried sounds so far; when the sun came up and the mist lifted, the sounds of mechanized activity would dissolve.

But the rhythmic resonance of unseen engines intensified. The thunder increased and rolled its basso profundo along the whole sector. The German sentries eased off the safety catches of their Mauser rifles; the machine-gun teams stroked the loaded canvas belts of their Parabellum guns; the rocket signal corporals rubbed their quick-match brassards to make certain the abrasive surfaces were dry—just in case.

One or two disturbed sentries called down the dugout steps, seeking assurance from higher ranks, but by the time they had crawled back to peer through the cross-hatched designs of the barbed wire, the thunderous dread was upon them. A number of fearsome machines, moving on clanking treads, and shaking grotesque tails, clambered over the protective wire, crushed the parapets, and prepared to leapfrog the trenches.

One or two machine gunners opened fire, but their copper-jacketed slugs bounced impotently off the great slabs of metal and fortlike turrets that covered these charging monsters. From the sides of the land dreadnoughts six-pounder guns coughed, and blasted MG pits to bloody craters. Light machine guns swept the German trenches like steel flails, whipping everything that lived to the slimy duckboards below. What few *Landwehr* troops remained at their posts were transfixed by these lozenge-shaped war machines that screamed their challenge, hosed their gunfire, and went lumbering on their way.

Twenty-four hours later the German High Command issued a memorable communiqué: *The enemy in the latest fighting have employed new engines of war as cruel as* [they are] *effective.*

Thirty-two of these ungainly machines ravaged the German back areas for more than an hour. Nothing like this had been seen or recorded since the legendary armored elephants of Kublai Khan, or the infamous war chariots of the old Egyptian campaigns. The war tank had been centuries in development.

This attack was not a complete success. The crews had been trained hurriedly, and no tactics for the use of tanks had been devised. Although adequate against rifle-caliber fire, the armor was not tough enough to withstand field-gun shells from the back areas. The machine developed unexpected mechanical trouble, and one important disadvantage was the gravity fuel system, since supply was cut off when the tank was ditched nose down—as frequently happened. It was then necessary to hand-feed the carburetors with gasoline drawn from the fuel tanks into small cans.

The first use of this secret engine of war was premature, but in some respects necessary, and the tactical mistakes became the target of military second-guessers the world over. These experts, who had not even visualized a tank, argued that Britain had lost the chance of a great military surprise, but gave not one iota of credit to those who had designed the weapon. In fact the name of Colonel Ernest D. Swinton is difficult to find in modern history of armored warfare. It should be understood, also, that the man who conceived and fought for the development of the tank, had no say in how or when it was first used.

## The Legend of Albert

Strangely enough, the long-drawn-out Battle of the Somme produced one of the beautiful stories of the war—the legend of Albert Cathedral. This old industrial town that stood on the Ancre overlooking a delightful waterfall was severely shelled throughout the carnage, and during one bombardment the colored stone statue of the Virgin that graced the tower of the Church of Notre Dame-Brebières was almost destroyed. A shell struck the upper portion of the tower and the steel supports, carrying the weight of the figure, instead of giving way, were bent over so that the Virgin, still holding the Christ child in her outstretched arms, hung precariously over the rubble in the street.

After the battle subsided a British YMCA hut was set up nearby and we used to wander through and gaze up with understandable curiosity and concern at the dangling figure, probably wondering what modern miracle held her there. Most of us predicted that one day something would give and the heavy stone statue would crash into the roadway.

Over the following months there were all sorts of ponderings and speculation, and as some of the former residents came back to poke about in the ruins searching for property and possessions we would talk to them. It was pathetic to see them claw through the piles of bricks and shattered timbers trying to restore a room or two, or set up some shelter from where they could begin the long toil of rehabilitation. It was then that the subject of the damaged church and hapless position of the Virgin was touched on.

"That is a token," one old codger told us. "You wait and see, *soldat*. Some day the Virgin she will come down and then the war will end."

"If she ever clambers down from that mess, anything is likely to happen." We presumed that the anguished figure dangling from the top of the church tower would come miraculously to life and would be seen descending the brick sides of the battered edifice.

"I'd like to be here when that happens," one of us reflected, and we talked of the old man's prediction with some anticipation, but none of us realized how true his words would be. We just hoped we would still be alive to witness the phenomenon.

Then on November 10, 1918, a stray shell from the German lines struck Albert Cathedral again—and the Virgin came down. Not as we had pictured in our minds, perhaps, but down she came.

The next day, November 11, 1918, the Germans signed the Armistice, and World War I was over.

## Escadrille Americaine

From the beginning of the war, American isolationists, President Wilson, and the bold-faced maneuverings of German and Irish factions kept the skirts of Miss Liberty free of the mud and blood of the European conflict. The war was three thousand miles away, and regardless of its rights or wrongs, it had little emotional impact on the bulk of the American population. The broad coverage of the Hearst press was openly hostile to the British cause and political expediency at the various levels played both ends to the middle.

At least that is how America appeared to us who were fighting in France—opinions gleaned from newspapers and letters sent across the Atlantic by our friends and relatives. But here and there many Americans were concerned with the Allied cause. True, some of them were sons and daughters of French or British emigrants and their sympathies were understandable. During the early months of the war many of them found various routes and pretexts to join French or British services. Many Americans with varying depths of British backgrounds crossed the border and joined Canadian regiments, or paid their own passage to Great Britain to enlist with the Army or Navy. Few of these were farsighted enough to volunteer for the infant flying services.

Although great numbers of German reservists who were living in the United States at the time were spirited out by various ruses, there is no record of any American citizens volunteering to fight with the Germans. Joseph "Fritz" Wehner of Boston did work with a German Red Cross organization in Berlin, furnishing comfort to German wounded before America entered the war, but Wehner later served with distinction in the U. S. Aviation Service, and was killed in action while flying in France.

One outstanding group of Americans who volunteered to fight for the Allies were, in most instances, already in France or Britain at the outbreak of the war. These men, together with a few more who had immediately offered their services to French or British consular officials in the United States, became the cadre of what was known at first as the Escadrille Américaine, an all-American squadron of fighter pilots who for many months flew with and for the French. It was this Lafayette Escadrille-to-be, that furnished the experienced nucleus of what became the U. S. Aviation Service in France.

These idealistic volunteers wove a tapestry of heroism with which few standard war stories or action novels can compare. No chapter in the story of the professional soldier can be more stirring than that of the handful of winged Galahads who first represented America on the Western Front. They came from mansion and tenement, and from every section of the country. They volunteered from all walks of life. One was a third-rate boxer, another an Ivy League collegian who actually had learned to fly before the war—and had to learn all over again.

Many plainly were unfit for military service, but all were attuned spiritually for the defense of their civilization. Some were writers, poets, architects, medical men, and artists. Some were out-and-out adventurers, but all were men who, once they had an idea, did something about it. The motives that inspired their beliefs and guided their footsteps were many and varied, but practically all had one instinct in common; an unconscious idealism and manly courage, backed by an abundant measure of sacrifice that seems ridiculous in these materialistic days.

Before their enlistments they had no conception of modern warfare. Fatigue, frustration, and defeat became their daily lot, but they could laugh in the face of adversity, because humor, recreation, and romance enlivened and leavened their trials.

In the beginning not many of these men had even dreamed of meeting an enemy in aerial combat. The airplane was less than a dozen years old, and the prospects of mile-high battle had not been envisioned. Most of these volunteers went into action with rifle and bayonet, but when the entrenching tool became a vital military implement, when barbed wire took as great a toll as high explosive, it was natural that their eyes should be raised to the blue skies and golden sunshine that promised surcease from the hopeless mire. It was as simple as that, and many of these men sought their goal above the ground, rather than in the murky tunnels beneath.

This handful was the true cadre of the first American aviation service to go into battle, but many of these men who made their mark on the history of the Lafayette Escadrille, were first blooded in the trenches of the Marne, or before Verdun.

The original roll of American volunteers lists many recognizable types; Victor Chapman, Alan Seeger, Henry Farnsworth, idealists of a most admirable kind. Who can argue whether Seeger, a well-known poet of the war, had a right to leave his home and family to die with six dumdum bullets in his chest? Chapman was the first American to go down in an air battle. He was a brilliant student of architecture, and from the realistic point of view had no especial reason to take up the gauntlet. Farnsworth never saw an airplane; he did not live long enough; but was killed by a bullet in his spine just as his infantry company reached a shell-torn objective.

Dr. David E. Wheeler, who served first as a surgeon near the Front, was so aroused by what he saw, he tore off his surgical mask, stripped himself of his gown, and fought as a private in the Foreign Legion. Ivan Nock, an American who held a lucrative post in a Peruvian silver mine thousands of miles from the rumble of the big guns, was so troubled by the turn of events, he went to France, volunteered, and was killed in action.

Edmond Genêt, the great-great-grandson and namesake of Citizen Genêt whom the revolutionary government in France sent to the United States in 1792 as its first minister, volunteered at the age of eighteen, and after many months as an infantryman, flew for France. Young Genêt died in an air action, the first American to be killed *after* the United States declared war on Germany. Brooke Bonnell and Joseph Lydon both left legs, but no regrets, on the battlefield. Jack Casey volunteered just to repay France for the hospitality he had enjoyed as an art student in Paris. After finishing college, Frederick Zinn went to Europe for a summer holiday, and stayed on to fight the common enemy.

He spent nearly two years in the trenches, transferred later to the French Aviation and was posted to a French squadron with which he served with distinction. Eventually, he was commissioned in and served with the United States Air Service.

Dennis Dowd, a native New Yorker, played his Foreign Legion role to the hilt, following a pattern that might have been drawn by Percival Christopher Wren. When a pretty girl refused to marry him, Dennis gave up his job, took his heartbreak abroad and joined the Foreign Legion. After a year of active service at the front, he also transferred to the French Aviation, and was killed in a flying accident while completing his final training.

Many of these altruistic men began as volunteer ambulance drivers, serving with the American Field Service, an organization that attracted those who wished to serve without risking the loss of their citizenship. It was while driving on these missions of mercy that dozens of them saw the full significance of the French cause, and were determined to contribute more of themselves. Most of them enlisted in the Foreign Legion, which, in many instances led to appointments in the French Aviation.

This was a very complicated conflict, but these volunteers did not huddle behind the old chestnut "Why should I get involved? I haven't the slightest idea what this war is about." They were not puzzled by its causes and effects, the right or wrong. They had no illusions that this was a capitalistic war, a pointless carnage subsidized by the merchants of death, the armament barons, or a sordid political readjustment to deal with the balance of power.

They applied no "Old Country" prejudices or religious strictures. They *knew* what they were fighting for, and did not require a psychological warfare officer to interpret the causes. They willingly discarded the comfort of a high standard of living for a foreign uniform, for it mattered little under which Allied flag they fought. They had a goal, a determination to retain all the human decencies laid down by their forebears. The guide rails of their ancestry were straight and clear, leading to the highest ideal of modern civilization.

# CHAPTER V

*The Italian Success ... Revolution Finishes Russia ...*
*Mixup in the Mediterranean ... Defense of Suez ...*
*More Valor at Verdun.*

## The Italian Success

Having had some success in repulsing heavy Austrian assaults from the Alps, the Italian forces were apparently ready by midsummer of 1916 to assume an offensive of their own. The Italian commander in chief, General Luigi Cadorna, had been preparing a major attack designed to sweep across the northeastern frontiers of Italy and drive the Austrians from their solid positions in the mountains bordering the Isonzo River, where his forces had been held in check by smaller groups of the enemy who fought from these almost impregnable defenses.

General Cadorna's initial attack was launched on August 6, and thundered forward with amazing dash. In three days his eager and enthusiastic troops swept aside every Austrian defense and captured Gorizia, chief city in the Isonzo Valley. This was the most brilliant and spectacular success of the whole Italian campaign.

Small forces of Austrians had made a few halfhearted expeditions along the Trentino front, a section of Austrian territory in the Southern Tirol largely inhabited by people of Italian descent, but after some minor successes scored by the lavish use of available artillery and other war material, these thrusts were blunted, and Italian counterattacks drove back the Austrians to the mountains.

General Cadorna continued his pressure on the Trentino front, chiefly as a diversion, but under cover of various passes and convenient fog, he moved large forces of troops to the Julian sector and by the first week of August was ready to strike.

The capture of the bridgehead of Gorizia was of prime importance in his desire to move far into Austrian territory. This focal point was wedged in deeply behind mountain positions that been strengthened further by every device of Alpine warfare. Rock barriers were built up, tunnels bored, and heavy guns hauled up to commanding positions. The Austrian Fifth Army, under General Svetozar Borojevic von Bojna, had Mount Sabotino at their command, from which high ridges ran south to Oslavia and the Podgora plateau. On the farther side of the Isonzo River was the craggy San Marco and the great bastion of Carso, which jutted out into Mount San Michele and was cleft by the long ravine of the Vallone.

General Cadorna threw 100,000 men into this sector, and his first attack was a simple feint ten miles south of Gorizia against Austrian positions at Monfalcone where he hoped his adversary would think that he would move to turn the great mountain block on that side of the Carso. A severe artillery barrage was laid down, an assault made, and a few enemy troops captured. The Austrians were taken in by this ruse and moved many regiments to prepare for a counterattack.

Instead, General Cadorna put on a one-day artillery barrage against the Sabotino block and the height of San Michele. His batteries and trench howitzers set up a concentration of fire on a wide target that had been well patrolled, and also photographed by Italian airmen. These glossy charts proved invaluable, for every range was marked in to the yard. The Austrian front line was soon battered to rubble; all shelters, observation posts, and communications centers were taken out, and with this completed, Italian infantry moved forward, fanned out, and captured position after position behind a creeping barrage of artillery.

They poured over every obstacle on the Austrian rampart between Sabotino and the Gorizia bridgehead. One column under Colonel (later General) Pietro Badoglio took by brilliant assault the heights of Oslavia which protected the town from the west. The Italian infantry then broke through the open country below and forced their way to the southern spurs of Podgora and the Isonzo and reached the bank of the river. On the Gorizian Carso another breakthrough overran a strong system of trenches and the assault thundered on toward San Martino. To add to this victorious thrust, a force of Bersaglieri cyclists struck at Monfalcone again, where a key position was taken and held.

After Sabotino and San Michele were seized, the Italians had three days of hard fighting to clear out trenches and mop up the support heights that maintained the last defenses of Gorizia. Once again their artillery was an important feature, and by August 10 the path was wide open and the Duke of Aosta (General Emanuele Filiberto), entered Gorizia at the head of the Italian Third Army.

The capture of Gorizia was one of the greatest feats in Italian military history. General Cadorna became a world-renowned hero, for his brilliantly handled troops had taken 18,758 prisoners, 30 large-caliber guns, 92 machine guns, 12,225 rifles, and untold quantities of ammunition. The City of Violets now belonged to Italy.

Unfortunately, however, Gorizia proved to be but a single forward step. Beyond it towered mountain range after mountain range. Trieste, the great Austro-Italian city, Cadorna's ultimate goal, was only twenty miles beyond his outposts, but almost every foot of the way would demand a costly battle against great natural barriers. This left the Italians no choice but to fight on all summer without ever getting far past Gorizia. At best, they compelled the Austrians to transfer many troops from the Russian front, but that was all.

Thus the Isonzo battle, like the even greater struggles of Verdun and the Somme, was indecisive, a vast, mass grave, another long and bloody stride toward the utter exhaustion of humanity.

### Revolution Finishes Russia

The death of Rasputin was a colorful event in the history of Russia in World War I, but how much this man contributed to the eventual revolution is difficult to assess. We are told that Rasputin opposed Russia's entry into the war, since he was living in high style in the royal family and court circles. Whether his murder triggered new political disturbances of any importance is hard to define. Playing the part of a holy man, and having mysterious influence on several of the Czarina's children, he moved through the various court circles, maintaining a fakir's role that has been presented as important, or comic, depending on the viewpoint of the historian. It is true that he did make suggestions concerning political appointees, basing his opinions on his personal contacts with the Almighty, and his advices were passed on by the Czarina to her husband who was serving at the front. None of these appointments appears to have made much difference in the grim military situation, but since Rasputin was a favorite of the royal family, there was understandable rejoicing when he was so crudely eliminated, and it is said that the Kaiser saw a new hope of getting Russia out of the war.

With continued setbacks in the field, and little hope of aid from the Allies, the seething revolution broke out in the open. All the splinter reform parties were howling for a change of government. Leaflets were distributed, and the workers urged to rise against the ruling class. Aleksandr Kerenski made a violent speech in the Duma, exposing Russia's complete exhaustion, and said the moment had come to liquidate the war. Czar Nicholas II was warned that a revolution was imminent, but he took no notice of the advice. But whether he was cautioned that his and his family's lives were in danger is a question. It has been declared by some authorities that they were advised to flee quietly to Great Britain, and that arrangements actually were made to carry out this trip.

By March 1917 matters had reached a critical stage. Bread was rationed, strikes broke out in heavy industry, and Russian

women took up the cause and made public demonstrations. Street
fighting was recorded, but nothing was organized, and those willing to hurl themselves into the ordeal had no idea how to face
such a situation. The revolution was not of great immediate impact; on the contrary it moved with the sluggishness of a con-
suming disease. The Petrograd garrison had 160,000 soldiers and
3500 uniformed police, all well-armed with rifles, machine guns,
and full field equipment. Few of these men, however, were professional soldiers with ingrained loyalty to a king and since most
of them were citizen soldiers, lately taken from industrial
benches, it was difficult for these uniformed men to turn on their
fellow workers when the uprising began to move.

The Romanov rule was destroyed with little resistance. A
message from the president of the Duma, explaining the situation, and demanding his abdication, was received by Czar
Nicholas II while he was at front-line military headquarters. He
submitted to this with dignity and composure, and after considering the fact that his son, the Czarevitch Alexis, would never be
strong enough to ascend the throne, he named Grand Duke
Michael in his place. But the Grand Duke refused to accept the
crown unless it was awarded him by the will of the people.

The British government again offered sanctuary to the royal
family, but the provisional government in Petrograd refused permission for them to leave the country, and sent the family to
Tobolsk beyond the Ural Mountains where they lived in primitive conditions under heavy guard.

In the meantime the political opportunist, Nikolai Lenin, who
had been living in Switzerland, was permitted by the German
government to cross through Germany and return to Russia
where he seized control of the moderate provisional government
under Kerenski, and the Bolsheviks gained full power. Russia
was at last out of the war, and her evil men were free to nurture
the seeds of international communism.

In April 1918, Citizen Romanov and his family were removed
to Ekaterinburg (Sverdlovsk) in the Ural Mountains where the

industrial population was strongly Soviet and openly hostile. They were confined in a local merchant's house and lived on military rations, eating out of a common cooking pot.

On June 12 Grand Duke Michael was shot, and, on receiving reports that a Czech Legion that was anti-Bolshevik was approaching Ekaterinburg, and after several bungled attempts had been made to rescue the royal family, the officials in Ekaterinburg decided to wipe out the Romanovs.

The ex-Czar and his family were told on the night of July 16, 1918, that they were to be moved again and should gather in the cellar of the house for final instructions. Nicholas had to carry his twelve-year-old son who was very ill. The rest of the family begged for chairs to sit on as they awaited the supposed instructions; instead the new commander of their guard, a Captain Yurovsky, entered with a band of armed civilians and read out the sentence of execution. Some soldiers also entered, and the Russian royal family was lined up against a wall. As the Czar stepped forward to make a statement, Yurovsky shot him in the head. The civilians then opened with a wild fusillade until the whole family was wiped out. The sick boy, Alexis, did not die immediately and had to be dispatched with a burst of fire from Yurovsky's revolver. Princess Anastasia, the youngest daughter, also showed signs of life and is said to have been dispatched by bayonet. Ten years later a Mrs. Anastasia Tschaikovsky appeared and claimed publicly that she was Princess Anastasia, youngest daughter of the Czar. She said she had been rescued from the massacre by two Soviet soldiers, but her claim was never authenticated. For years the world had been told that the bodies of the whole family had been taken out of the cellar to a deserted mine shaft where vitriol was poured on them, and fires lit to destroy them completely.

On July 25, 1918, Ekaterinburg was captured by the Czechs, and the Bolsheviks routed out of the area for a time. Some authorities in Moscow have stated since that twenty-eight of the assassins were arrested and five executed.

## Mixup in the Mediterranean

Practically all European states had been drawn into the conflict by late summer of 1916. Greece, which had acted neutral for some time, was involved eventually and added more problems to the Allied cause. At the beginning of the war the people of Greece were strongly pro-Ally, but her young king, Constantine I, who was pro-German held a tight rein. The royal family of Greece had been built with German princes, and for three generations ex-Germans had sat on the throne. Constantine was a Greek but he had been educated and militarily trained in Germany and had married a sister of the Kaiser. The Queen, like the German Czarina of Russia, cared more for the land of her birth than for her adopted one.

It has been learned since that the two Greek rulers not only gave moral support to the German cause, but carried out secret communications that furnished important information about their plans and needs. At one time "Tino," as he was known to the German court, gave his word of honor that no Greek soldier would ever aid the Allies, but so many of his people desired to join the Allied cause, Constantine was forced to discard his country's constitution, and rule as a dictator.

When Serbia went down, the Greeks saw a like fate for themselves, and the Allies made much of the psychological situation, putting pressure where it would have the most effect, namely commercial. In the end the King seemed to have his way, but in May 1916 he ordered his soldiers to surrender the Greek fort of Rupel to the Bulgarians. Rupel was a valuable strategic point to the Germans, and a menace to the gathering Allied army in Salonika. Many Greek patriots were aroused by this surrender, and denounced their king. Serious rioting ensued as the people who had always thought of their ruler as Greek, suddenly remembered he had been pro-German.

More concessions to the Bulgarians roused this patriotic group to revolution and a provisional government was formed in Salonika where it ruled until the end of the war. Constantine re-

mained in power in Athens, however, and he next surrendered
a seaport to Bulgaria, an act that so aroused the people that all
of eastern Greece joined the new government. Realizing that his
last claim over his subjects was slipping away, Constantine finally
resigned his crown and authority and departed for Switzerland;
taking with him a sum of $15,000,000 which he had secretly
borrowed from Germany following the surrender of Fort Rupel.
He had also attempted to get an additional loan of $25,000,000
from the Allies, but was unsuccessful in this deal.

Constantine lived for three years in seclusion in Switzerland
and, following a plebiscite in November 1920, he returned to
Athens. On January 11, 1923, he died from hemorrhage of the
brain, at Palermo.

Romania was next. Tricked by a number of halfhearted promises given by Russia, she soon fell under the malevolence of the
Kaiser's Germany. Russia had promised Romania considerable
support, which carried the impression that her northern border
was secure. She also had sworn to support Romanian neutrality
and indicated that Bulgaria would not make a hostile move
against her. Believing that Germany had been bled white in the
battles before Verdun and along the Somme, and would be
incapable of continuing her aid to Austria, and with all these
interlocking misunderstandings, Romania was encouraged to
send her troops across her northern border for an invasion of
the Hungarian province of Transylvania.

This was all Germany needed as an excuse for a new thrust.
Hindenburg's smartest aide, August von Mackensen, was raised
to a field marshal and sent secretly into Bulgaria, and with a few
German troops, backed by a horde of Bulgars and Turks, he
attacked the Romanian southern border. To counter this, units
of the Romanian Army were withdrawn from the Transylvania
front.

No sooner had this northern force been so weakened, than a
new German army appeared in Hungary, and the Romanians
were defeated at Hatzeg (Hateg). While the unfortunate Roma-

nians tried to clarify this situation, another German force was moving through eastern Transylvania and pressing between the Romanian Army and its own frontier to seize the critical mountain passes and cut vital communications. The trapped army just managed to escape with grim losses in its effort to return and defend its homeland.

By October the Germans had begun a savage invasion from the north and Mackensen's main army was advancing from the south. Romania's only seaport, Constantsa, fell on October 22, but this only stiffened the home defense, and some Russian troops were sent in to render aid. Then, in November, General von Falkenhayn, leading the German army in the north, scored a decisive victory at Târgu-Jiu, a success that enabled him to swing straight across Romania and unite with Mackensen's forces. When they reached the Danube, Romania's defeat was certain. Her western areas were occupied, and with German forces moving toward her capital of Bucharest from every direction but the northeast, her future was bleak. There was no help from Russia, and where was the hoped-for aid from the Allies at Salonika?

Salonika? Here was the most unrealistic situation of the whole war, a ludicrous political and military complication. Great Britain had a strong garrison in Salonika, chiefly a token force, not necessarily to fight. It was hoped at one time that this Allied concentration would take some of the pressure off Verdun, but the best that can be said for these half-forgotten forces in Macedonia, is that they contributed to the security of the Suez Canal.

Romania had now suffered 200,000 war casualties, of which 50,000 were killed. Despite this loss the country did not capitulate, but reorganized what forces it had left and moved into the northeastern section of the country, first for refuge, and then to make a final stand. With some supplies from Russia they dug in, hung on to one quarter of their country, and kept the invaders out. In fact, these Romanians saved the Eastern Front, for all through 1917 this harassed little army resisted until Mackensen's offensive was broken. Their cavalry fought as mounted troops

or infantry; they dug trenches and set up machine-gun posts.
Every form of delaying action known was tried, and eventually
the enemy advance was halted.

## Defense of Suez

The British had concentrated on the defense of the Suez Canal
from early in 1916, a difficult undertaking since it involved considerable water supplies, military roads across the sands, pontoon
bridges across the canal, the extension of existing railroads, and
large-scale military defense and entrenchments. Although, as
matters turned out, this danger was not serious, the work, nevertheless, was necessary.

Faulty intelligence had presumed that great forces of Turkish
troops would be sent across Sinai to capture Egypt and disrupt
British concentrations in that area. To counter this, General Sir
Archibald Murray proposed that all troops be taken out of Egypt
proper and sent into the Sinai Peninsula, a move that he thought
would afford a better and cheaper defense of the canal. There
was some pointless shuffling of available divisions for a time,
some of which were sent to France, and some to Mesopotamia,
leaving General Murray with only four Territorial divisions that
fortunately included several British Yeomanry regiments and the
Australian-New Zealand Mounted Division.

With this conglomerate force General Murray undertook the
defense of the Suez Canal by moving into Sinai. While his engineer troops were laying a railroad line east of the canal, work
that had to be covered by fighting forces, the Turks made a
sudden attack, striking at a few Yeomanry detachments at two
oases located twenty-five and thirty-two miles east of the canal.
Three of these Territorial squadrons were wiped out, but the
progress of the railroad was held up for only a few days.

Yeomanry are actually mounted-infantry forces. They are
formed as regular cavalry, but can operate equally well mounted,
as on foot. These volunteers, raised and trained in peacetime,
were developed during the Boer War where their particular role
was appreciated. In World War I Yeomanry forces were neither

fish nor fowl; while unable to play any vital role, their troopers
had to assume the dual responsibilities of both cavalrymen and
infantrymen. The regular infantryman can shift for himself, and
has only his own comfort to worry about after he had done his
day's fighting. The Yeomanry trooper must first care for his horse
and its saddlery, for in the British Army a horse is not expendable. If there is available shelter, it goes to the mount, not the
mounted man. Only after both horse and equipment have been
cared for—usually a two-hour chore—may a trooper tend to his
own comfort and requirements.

General Murray had decided to defend Suez in the sector
between El Arish and Kossaima (Qusaima), since all level
routes that attacking forces would use passed through there.
This proposed battleground was about one hundred miles east
of the canal and close to the Palestine frontier. Although Murray
commanded skilled engineering forces in the laying down of a
railroad, a pipeline, and a light motor road, the work was carried
out in a slipshod, lackadaisical manner. The Egyptian fellahin
employed in labor gangs so enjoyed this new work he sang all
day long, quite content to toil at his own pace.

During this felicitous proceeding, a strong Turkish force of
15,000 men, commanded by the German Baron Kress von Kressenstein, and supported by machine-gun companies and batteries
of field artillery, had started to move. The desert was in the full
blaze of midsummer heat, but Kressenstein risked the weather,
the slim water supply, and headed straight for the railhead at
Rumani, a point five miles northwest of the Qatia oasis where
one of the most colorful battles of the war was fought.

The Turkish force attacked with zest and gallantry on August 4, 1916. General Murray's left was protected by the
Bardawîl Lagoon, and it was reasonable for him to assume that
General von Kressenstein would attempt to turn his right flank.
So he revised an old Boer War tactic by preparing a false flank
that hid the extension in the dunes, and held a mounted reserve
to threaten the attacker's flank. This ruse was successful up to
a point, but there was delay in striking the critical blow, and the

main body of the Turks escaped the trap. They were defeated, however, losing six thousand men to a thousand British casualties. But the Turks, as always, displayed courage and unusual endurance in retreating skillfully in the terrible heat and with a shortage of water that hampered the men and horses of the pursuing force.

During the defense of the Suez Canal and the Red Sea, the British also faced the problem of Turkey's attempt to set the Mohammedan world against the Allies by proclaiming a holy war. An Arab revolt in the Hejaz, a kingdom along the Red Sea coast of West Arabia and now part of Saudi Arabia, promised a large reward for the British. In fact, by June 1916, a small Turkish garrison near Medina was overpowered by the Arabs who were aided by Egyptian mountain batteries. The following September another Turkish station at Taif, south of Mecca, surrendered with three thousand men. In December the combined Egyptian Expeditonary Force attacked a Turkish outpost twenty-five miles southeast of El Arish where the whole garrison was overwhelmed, with only a handful of men escaping.

With this new success by the end of the year, General Murray had his defense plans complete, and the canal was unquestionably safe, but the pressure was to be continued for political reasons.

Lloyd George, who had succeeded Lord Kitchener as Secretary of State for War, was distraught by the cost of the Somme, and he was sage enough to know that with some luck, Turkey might be removed from the enemy front by success in Palestine—a strategic victory that might be gained at small cost and with a psychological reaction the world over. However, General Sir William R. Robertson, commander of the Imperial General Staff, wanted to finish the war on the Western Front, and had tried for a long time to withdraw British troops from Macedonia. Although he preferred Palestine, if any action was to be taken in the Near East, he hesitated to send more troops there, even though "slow and stodgy" Murray asked for at least two more divisions if he was expected to cross the frontier. In London, Rob-

ertson and Lloyd George each pretended to bow to the will of
the other, and this byplay resulted in a weak and vague policy.
Murray was left with a primary mission, known as the Defense
of Egypt, an ambiguous term that was to be construed as the
defense of the Mesopotamian oilfields.

## More Valor at Verdun

The giant German attack on Verdun slackened in July and
August, and, with the colors of autumn, the wholesale murder
had subsided with both sides in complete exhaustion. There had
been little gained, and little lost on this battlefield that was no
larger than a modern city park.

When the British opened the Somme offensive the Germans
were forced to withdraw artillery from Verdun and spread it
thin to halt the Tommies, a move that encouraged the French
to plan counterattacks that would regain Forts Douaumont and
Vaux. General Robert Georges Nivelle was given command, and
on October 24 he launched a sudden and most successful attack, but abrupt as it was, it was not unexpected since the enemy knew the French would make the most of the Somme situation to regain losses they had suffered previously.

After a violent artillery assault, the French stormed down
from the heights of Haudiomont, streamed over the crests of
Fleury, and from Vaux-Chapitre toward Damloup. The Germans
had twenty-eight infantry battalions and ten reserve battalions
in the Douaumont-Vaux sector, supported by 130 artillery batteries, against which General Nivelle launched three divisions
with an additional infantry regiment covering each wing.

Within two days the German position, including their third
line, was in French hands. Fort Douaumont, now afire from the
artillery barrage, had been evacuated long before the French
troops started their attack. Fort Vaux held out until November 2.
The Germans moved back to "prepared positions" and were un-
molested while the French repaired the roads that had been so
destroyed by shellfire. No artillery could be moved forward un-

til well into December, and no new attack could start until December 12.

Now the goal was the line Bezonvaux Forest, over Chambrettes, Louvemont, Vacherauville. Four French divisions began the assault, and after several bloody encounters, reached their goal on December 18, ending the Verdun carnage. The Germans had no stomach or motive for continuing the attacks, and all heavier activities were held down through the winter. Verdun did not enter the war lists again until March 1917.

With the end of this tragic battle came the harrowing summation; of all the ground gained in those nine months of struggle, the enemy retained on the east bank of the Meuse only the advanced positions that had been held by the French on February 21, 1916. On the west bank, however, the Germans still held firmly the important ground taken in the fighting of April and May, including Dead Man's Hill and Hill 304. With observation posts on the Côte de Talou they could hamper French communications and disturb the garrison within Verdun.

Therefore, when Petain was made C-in-C the following summer, he ordered a third offensive that drove the Germans off both dominating hills, and retook the ground south of Forges Brook, the Côte de Talou, and the villages of Samogneux and Champneuville on the east bank of the Meuse, together with Hill 304. This success re-established the old situation, completing the task of restoring the Verdun position from which the French had been thrust during the grim days of February 1916, and as it turned out, laying the foundations for an American offensive in September and October 1918.

We know now that had France failed at Verdun, the war might have been lost, since she held the enemy there while Britain prepared for the Somme offensive. In this respect Verdun was only less important than the Battle of the Marne itself. Verdun was a national epic of endurance and tenacious military virtues.

# CHAPTER VI

*Germany Defies America . . . The Fall of Baghdad . . .
The United States Declares War . . . Canucks at Vimy
Ridge . . . The Blowup at Messines . . . In Flanders
Fields . . . The Phantom Piper of Polygon Wood . . . The
Tanks at Cambrai . . . America's First Shot.*

## Germany Defies America

The year 1917 saw German behavior at its worst. All civilization suffered from Teutonic bestiality as its black breath spread over all Europe. The facts concerning Germany's treatment of war prisoners had been established clearly by the autumn of 1916, but protests by investigators from neutral nations made no impression on the Prussian tyrants. A quarter of a century later the same evil acts were repeated, but were then charged to the Nazis.

Most American investigators who had access to the details did not exaggerate the treatment accorded prisoners of war, but presented the best possible case for Germany, explaining that these crimes were not national, that the better class of Germans "supposed" that prisoners were well treated, that the guilt fell on only a few military commanders, and any complaints made by the Russian government were framed to excite her people against her foes by "painting their foes at their worst."

But the reports made by responsible British officers who had been captured and had escaped, or had been repatriated in a general prisoner exchange, could not be ignored. From the statements of a number of these men it was clear that the German government had taught its people to despise other races—especially the British—and this resulted in shocking mistreatment of prisoners of war.

Finally, there is evidence that the so-called upper classes, the nobility, the intellectual, and political groups repeatedly issued orders that prisoners of war should be treated harshly, and that those who became stockade nuisances should be executed. These orders resulted in overcrowding in transit, revolting sanitary arrangements, which spread disease through prison compounds, and cruel treatment for any captives who attempted to escape. The humane rules of the Hague Convention were deliberately ignored.

Perhaps these violations of the Hague Convention were the desperate reactions of a people who sensed that by now the battle was going against them. Germany had suffered two wicked reverses on the Western Front, and although Russia was out of the war, it was clear that the Allies had molded a determination to carry on, were eager to prepare more offenses, and expend ammunition in a manner never predicted before.

The submarine offensive had been abandoned the previous year partly because Germany's U-boats had received a serious beating from the Royal Navy, and partly because of America's demand that such warfare be discontinued, but early in 1917 Germany had a new force of more powerful submarines, and nourished a frantic hope that she could eventually starve Britain, as the British blockade was starving her.

The right or wrong of this type of warfare that attacked and sank every ship, neutral or belligerent, in European waters disturbed German leaders not one wit. There was no right but German might, and to the amazement of thinking men, the Germans presumed that the rest of the world would accept this dogma. When the decision to renew unrestricted submarine warfare was broached, the only doubt raised was how the United States would take it. Would America stand by its ultimatum of 1916 and go to war for a mere principle? Of course not. Only the impossible British were so unreasonable.

German consular officials in the United States reported that American merchants and manufacturers were doing very well supplying the Allies with food and war equipment. President Wilson had been re-elected on the slogan, "He kept us out of the war!" and it was obvious that the President would continue along this line. If by some complete change of face the United States did declare war, few of her people would volunteer to fight, and their government, being democratic, would not force them to enlist. America would never be more than a token partner, supplying the means to fight. Great Britain was the arch enemy. If Britain could be starved out, the war would be won quickly.

Content with this wishful reasoning, the German High Command announced on January 3, 1917, a new submarine campaign of frightfulness and destruction, and determined at the same time to restrain its land campaign to simple defensive operations, thus saving battle-weary troops for the time when Britain would be exhausted and willing to abandon all Europe to Germany.

When the British launched new attacks against the old line early in February, they found that it was lightly held, but they suffered some casualties from the string of machine-gun nests that had been left. It was in this sector that the attackers came upon crews who had been chained to their machine-gun tripods, a precaution that forced the German gunners to hang on until they were overwhelmed. The new enemy line eventually ran from the city of Arras on the north to Saint-Quentin on the south, and the Tommies prepared to concentrate on Arras while their French partners agreed to launch another attack south of Saint-Quentin along the Aisne River. These hastily planned thrusts resulted in small success, but to the north an epic battle was fought that brought the first great honor to Canadian forces.

### The Fall of Baghdad

Still smarting from the debacle at Kut-el-Amara and its humiliating effect on the Allied cause in Asia, Great Britain reorganized her eastern flank for another thrust. General Sir Frederick Stanley Maude was given the command, and he began by improving his lines of communication, and selected Basra as the base of operations. Field railroads were constructed between Basra and the operating army, and the flotilla on the Tigris was better equipped, and increased in size.

Moving methodically, General Maude attacked from two sides while the river gunboats aided in the pressure, and captured Kut by February 23, 1917. The Turkish troops were so shaken by this businesslike assault, they could not put up further resistance, and Maude's right wing, protected by a Russian group under a General Baratoff, stormed the last Turkish position in the angle formed by the junction of the Diyala and Tigris Rivers. When this post fell the Turkish forces were forced to evacuate Baghdad, and British troops entered the city March 11. A few squadrons of the Royal Flying Corps carried out valuable observation patrols throughout the assault, and a Gurkha battalion fought with savage determination.

This engagement before Baghdad is worth more than a passing mention. It was a historic event that since has been held up as a lasting tribute to the gallantry of British arms. Following an opening action at Lajj, the Turks fell back on Diyala after destroying the bridge that crossed the river where it joins the Tigris. The British continued their pursuit along the left bank, sending cavalry and two columns of infantry to work around the right bank. With these arrangements completed, General Maude decided to attack Baghdad from the west where the enemy line was weakest. Speed was essential, and the troops striking at Diyala had to make another crossing with little chance of surprise. The village sprawled over both banks of the stream which at that point is 120 yards wide. Houses, trees, nullah (ravine), and walled gardens made it impossible to lay out a road and grade ramps for pontoon crossing without disclosing the point of embarkation. So the original bridge site was selected, and here rare heroism was needed, for the first sections scrambling over the temporary crossing were cut down, as a bright moon made them shooting-gallery targets for Turkish sharpshooters and machine guns.

A second group got as far as the middle of the stream when a new fusillade, fired from the windows of the houses, cut down the men who were trying to cross on a pontoon, that was being rowed by five men, and carried ten infantrymen. A third almost reached the oposite bank, but some sort of bomb was dropped, and that pontoon sank with all its crew. But the Britishers continued to try their luck, as crew after crew pushed off to certain death, while farther down the river infantrymen were shocked to see battered pontoons floating by with their cargos of dead.

New companies volunteered, and more attempts were made, until there were no pontoons left, and another group decided to try to cross higher up, after hauling their boats almost a mile across country to the stream.

The attempt was continued on the second night with equal heroism, but by now artillery could register, and after a heavy barrage, a footing was gained, although machine guns still raked all pontoons that tried to cross. In one instance the crew of one boat floundered in the smoke and dust, unable to find a landing, and were cut down under heavy machine-gun fire. When a volunteer party attempted to cross to rescue these attackers, they were killed, as well as the men in the landing craft.

Eventually about sixty Tommies got over, and these men put on a Western Front Mills-bomb attack. Although heavily pressed on both flanks, they found themselves between two woods where they discovered a natural cover in the form of a bund—an artificial embankment—and here a group of Lancashire Tommies hung on through the night, all the next day, and the next night against repeated attacks. Twenty yards west of this bund was a small grove of mulberry and palm, but any pontoon heading for this little cover was greeted with heavy machine-gun fire. British artillery furnished some protection, but communications, carried out by shouting, often were interrupted.

On two nights the Turks climbed to the top of the bund, but

were driven back by the garrison, now reduced to forty men who remained cool and hung on valiantly. Ammunition was removed from the bandoliers of the dead, and when they were relieved, there was only one remaining clip of five rounds and one Mills bomb, but outside their bund lay more than one hundred Turkish dead. The crossing was completed finally, and cavalry and infantry worked their way around the right bank, threatening to cut off the Turkish forces. By midnight of the second night the defenders had withdrawn their machine guns but left individual riflemen to cover their withdrawal. A crossing farther upstream was a surprise, and passage here was made without loss of life. When the Turks realized their flank was being turned, they were forced into a general retirement.

By nine-thirty in the morning of March 10, the whole brigade had crossed, and the pursuit continued. After some short, bitter actions, the enemy evacuated his last trench line, and Baghdad was entered and taken on March 11.

Content with this spectacular success, and made wary by the General Townshend disaster, the British did not follow the Turkish forces into the mountainous regions farther north. Instead, they undertook the reconstruction of the whole captured region; in fact General Maude worked hard to improve living conditions in his area, but, ironically, died of cholera on November 18, 1917. For a time there was a report that he had been poisoned by a treacherous native in the pay of the enemy, but this rumor was never substantiated.

## The United States Declares War

At the first session of the Sixty-fifth Congress, held on April 2, 1917, a joint resolution declaring that a state of war existed between the Imperial German Government and the Government and the people of the United States was adopted. The Congress also made provision for the prosecution of the war. This was not approved by President Wilson until April 6, 1917, although the President had delivered a speech to the Joint Session on that previous date. In other words, the Chief Executive had asked for a declaration of war on April 2, but this was not formally carried out and announced until four days later.

He had said: "With a profound sense of the solemn and even tragical character of the step I am taking and of the grave responsibilities which it involves, but in unhesitating obedience to what I deem my constitutional duty, I advise that the Congress declare the recent course of the Imperial German Government to be in fact nothing less than war against the Government and people of the United States; that it formally accept the status of a belligerent which has been thrust upon it; and that it take immediate steps not only to put the country in a more thorough state of defense, but also to exert all its power and employ all its resources to bring the Government of the German Empire to terms and end the war."

The attitude of the German government had some verity; the war in Europe *was* keeping the factories of America humming, and those who worked in these plants were making more money than they had ever earned before. Many of them could see little reason for going to war. What moral fervor was manifest, was displayed along the Eastern seaboard, the area closest to the conflict, and their newspapers presented the war news in greater detail than did those of the Middle West or West Coast.

Another realistic viewpoint disclosed the fact that in April 1917 the United States had little to fight with. There were only 92,000 men in the Regular Army and a few understrength National Guard divisions. These forces had 285,000 rifles, and 550 pieces of artillery with which to wage war—and little else. A draft law was drawn up and passed by Congress on May 18 to fill out the ranks, but Registration Day was not until June 5, since 10,000,000 forms had to be printed and mailed to all able-bodied men of draft age—twenty-one to thirty years of age in 1917, and extended to eighteen to forty-five years in 1918.

By June 15 more than 9,000,000 American males had gone to their polling places to sign up. Of this number 4,800,000 served in the armed forces—4,000,000 in the Army, and 2,086,000 of them went overseas to Europe. Forty-two divisions were sent to France to fight a war that cost more than $1,000,000 an hour throughout 1917 and 1918. Of every one hundred men who served, ten were National Guardsmen, thirteen United States Army Regulars, and seventy-seven of the United States Army—civilians accepted by the draft.

The average American soldier who fought in France had six months' training in the United States, two months more in Europe, and before entering the line was given some practical experience for a month in a quiet sector.

Although not much in favor of aviation—in fact palpably ignorant of its application in war—General Pershing was disturbed by America's lack of an air arm. Of 65 officers and 1000 men in the Air Service Section of the Signal Corps, only 35 were pilots. Only five or six of this number had ever seen a *military* aircraft, and none had any technical experience with aircraft guns, bombs, cameras, bombsights, or bomb-dropping devices. There were about 55 training planes of various categories and conditions of usefulness, but none was equipped with modern weapons, and had no value for service at the Front. America could not have put one squadron in the field, although it was estimated that at least 300 squadrons would be needed, each to be composed of 24 officers, 180 men, and 18 airplanes, to say nothing of a large reserve of planes for replacement.

The French Minister for War, prodded by Colonel William Mitchell, who was already in France hoping to head an American air service, suggested that the United States adopt a program to build a flying corps of 4500 airplanes that would reach the Front by the summer of 1918. The program also included the training of 5000 pilots and 50,000 mechanics.

General Pershing, who had no idea that Colonel Mitchell had devised this prospective air arm, was shocked by this French suggestion and mistakenly took it to mean that the Allies were destitute of planes and personnel. Fortunately, British and

French airmen were more than holding their own against the German flying circus, but the program did become the hope and goal of American aviation.

Following the declaration of war it was thought that at first only a "token" force could be sent to Europe. The United States Navy was to help in the campaign against the U-boats, but at the time it seemed obvious that the Allies were more in need of financial credit, supplies, food, and small-arms ammunition, and when asked what they needed most both French and British military missions in Washington agreed that the above items, plus mechanical transport, would be most useful. They also suggested that any troops available could be brigaded with French and British divisions, but this point was misconstrued, and turned down. Prodded by a patriotic press, America said she wanted her sons to fight under their own flag. But what the Allied representatives had intended was that the first few American regiments to reach the war zone be put in French or British sectors for training with experienced troops, and on their withdrawal they would have valuable instructors with which to build an American training center in Europe. This logical point was ignored and outraged Americans decided that the French and British only wanted American troops to fill out their depleted ranks.

The loudest protestations were made by those who overlooked the fact that rookie American airmen were being absorbed into French and British squadrons for training and experience, although wet-nursing novice airmen over the line was a chore few veteran pilots cared to take on. In these instances, the newcomers soon learned the tactics under skillful guidance, and were valuable assets in American squadrons later on. Portions of the United States Navy also were eager to work under experienced British command until the many tricks of U-boat warfare had been learned.

At the height of this national vehemence General Hugh L. Scott, then U. S. Army Chief of Staff, suggested that all but a

small part of the Regular Army, the National Guard, and the
first 500,000 men of the draft be sent to Europe as rapidly as
they could be organized, clothed, and transported, since he
hoped to have them trained abroad with Allied weapons and
equipment. This was a sound idea, but when General John J.
Pershing was put in command of the new American Expeditionary Force, he feared his little army would be broken up
into fragments, and he therefore objected to this plan. He used
the popular cry that American divisions should fight under
their own command and flag; that he did not propose to be
left with a shadow army, filling a ceremonial role while "foreign"
generals won high glory handling his troops.

This flag consciousness puzzled Europeans at the time, since
flags were merely a decoration—none had been carried into
action for years, certainly not in trench warfare. But General
Pershing apparently thought the American flag would not
appear anywhere in the battle area if his AEF was distributed
through the divisions of the Allies. The problem, of course, was
an understandable national consciousness, as opposed to the
realistic attitude of the French and British.

Once America was committed to the war, national mobilization quickly knitted the whole nation. A Council of National
Defense had been formed as early as August 1916 in which
business and industry were well represented. Executives of
exceptional talent offered their services to the government for
"a dollar a year." A record-breaking shipbuilding program got
under way. As food administrator, Herbert C. Hoover multiplied
food production and prepared wide rationing procedures.
Edward R. Stettinius, Assistant Secretary of War, was in charge
of munitions production, and John J. Ryan assumed the responsibility of aircraft production. Patriotic civilians everywhere
guided the resources of the nation into the military and naval
forces that were to oppose Germany. Physicians over military
age set a fine example by signing up in the thousands. The
American Protective League, backed by lawyers and other legal

officials, rendered important service in exposing German propaganda, and handling the "slacker" and conscientious-objector groups. Bankers and financial men led the Liberty Loans and War Savings Stamps drives, and placed the resources of their institutions at the service of the government.

Women and children rallied to the cause, toiling in shops, fields, hospitals, and Red Cross offices with cheer and enthusiasm. When rationing, lightless nights, gasolineless Sundays, fuelless days, and limited transportation services were imposed, they were accepted with little complaint.

Congress was given a free hand in making appropriations, and the public approved without hesitation a program of taxation that in other times would have scuttled any political party proposing such long-term expenditures. Millions were voted in areas where thousands had been the rule. The spirit of the country was excellent.

### Canucks at Vimy Ridge

Canada's greatest victory in the war was fought on the slopes of Vimy Ridge. When it began on April 9, 1917, the United States had been in the war but three days, but as stated before many American volunteers had previously joined the Canadian or British Army. At this point it might be well to clear up a long-standing fallacy concerning Americans who went to Canada to join the Royal Flying Corps. In the years following the Armistice, they, or their families, often explained that they had joined the Royal Canadian Air Force. How this was done is a puzzle, since there was no such organization until about 1923. Late in 1918 some effort was made to form a Canadian aviation corps, but nothing concrete was forthcoming before the war ended.

However, legend has it that at Vimy Ridge an unnamed gallant American fighting with the Canadians, tied an American flag to his bayonet, and as he charged up Vimy Ridge his patriotic display was seen by his companions who cheered as they plunged on beside him. It is also said to have been the first American flag seen on the battle line.

But this story of the first appearance of the Stars and Stripes on the Western Front is probably apocryphal, as similiar instances were reported by various sources. It would not be unusual to find such a statement in any of the autobiographies written by these volunteers. The noted James Norman Hall, who first served with the 9th Battalion of the Royal Fusiliers from August 18 to December 1, 1915, claimed to have displayed an American flag at the front. Arthur Guy Empey, a New Jersey volunteer who wrote a book, *Over the Top,* was photographed in a British hospital, holding an American flag. He was recovering from a trench-raid wound at the time.

This standard claim may have first been made by some member of the Lafayette Escadrille; in fact several of them seem to have taken turns in asserting to have been the first to carry the American flag into action, and it is most likely that one of these stalwarts best deserves the honor.

As for myself, while serving as an aerial gunner with a British two-seater fighter squadron, I once displayed a small American flag from my gun mounting, possibly in the hope that some alert news photographer would notice it and project me into posterity via a glossy weekly. Instead, I was mildly reprimanded for this pointless display and advised to be satisfied with carrying the banner of neutrality in my map case. At the time, however, my pilot was taking me into action with a pair of feminine flimsy panties fluttering from a wing strut, a prize he had gained in a residence of questionable repute in Amiens, but while they lasted, I must admit our luck was inordinately good, so I refrained from forcing the issue between the pride of background and the gossamer glamour that proved to be such an invulnerable shield.

By early March of 1917 General Haig was so discouraged with the course of events, he considered resigning his post, but a message from King George V convinced him that such a decision would be disastrous, and a few days later another message from London, written in the King's boyish hand, announced: "I have decided to appoint you Field Marshal of my Army." Thus, when Britain's spring offensive moved off, Haig held the highest rank in the British Army, but despite this promotion he found himself pledged to support an offensive that was dictated by the French, whereas he would have preferred an action more fitting the British situation—he wanted to move against the Germans who were threatening the Belgian coastline.

Over the previous winter Haig had attempted halfheartedly to relieve the pressure on the French with some harassing operations, and at the same time set the stage for a major push in the spring in the Arras sector. Abominable weather had interfered to a great degree, and Haig was content to allow his troops to rest whenever possible and prepare for better weather and objectives that would be more rewarding. The ground conditions were impossible, and mechanical and horse-drawn transportation was practically slowed to a standstill. But over these months the Royal Flying Corps, at considerable risk and sacrifice, had compiled a new photographic war map and uncovered full details of Germany's new Hindenburg line. Blows that had begun in January had harried what was intended to be an orderly retreat, but by the end of March it was evident that the Germans were well entrenched in their new redoubts, and obviously intended to sit it out there while awaiting the outcome of the new U-boat program.

Another Easter dawn opened with a terrific bombardment, as hell broke out all along the Arras front. The famous cathedral, a wounded edifice of stone, marked the battle area, and nearby a pile that once had been the Town Hall added to the sad ruin of a city. None of us will ever forget that battered roadway that led out to the Cambrai highway, a thoroughfare to death or glory.

With the roar and flame of shellfire came additional thuds where mines went up west of Arras and marked the wide sweep from Vimy Ridge to Blangy southward. The low clouds were washed over by the scarlet of explosion, above which a few daring airmen tried to view the proceedings and make their patrol reports. Some records state that rain fell, others that a harsh hail-flecked snow descended as the first waves of troops started over. The minute the Tommies moved forward, the enemy retaliated by shelling Arras, then began sending up rocket signals of distress, indicating to British observers that the push was going well.

By the middle of the afternoon the Canadians had stormed up most of Vimy Ridge, with the exception of one high, strong post known as Hill 145, which was taken after nightfall. The artillery had ripped out most of the enemy wire, and the village of Thélus had been wiped off the map.

This majestic attack was actually begun in a snowstorm, with probing patrols moving through Farbus Wood until they could establish some outposts along the railroad embankment. It was here that some of the boldest work was carried out by Canadian forward observers who climbed to the top of Vimy Ridge the minute it had been captured and, disregarding the storm of their own batteries, hung on to direct important "shoots" against the enemy country ahead.

Through all this, British flying men, ignoring the German fighter formations, rode out the storm, and maintained artillery-spotting patrols, giving the Canadian sixty-pounders a field day. The RFC observers found moving trains, massed troops, enemy guns and limbers, and provided dozens of other valuable targets. The enemy loss was frightful, and before this complete action was over nearly 20,000 prisoners and 257 guns had been captured.

The Canucks advanced in three waves and followed the rolling barrage that slammed through snow flurries. The smoke and snow obscured their range of vision, but also lessened the accuracy of German riflemen and machine gunners. The troops on the extreme left met heavy opposition, but caught up when those of the center and right were halted by heavy hand-to-hand and bayonet fighting between the German first and second lines.

An unexpected dip in the ground caused a switch in direction, and for a short time the central objectives were ignored, and this left the troops on the flanks in a perilous position as they were enfiladed from the center defenses. In the middle of this temporary tieup a force of German soldiers that had been secluded in a series of caves, connected by tunnels, suddenly swept out to reoccupy their old front-line trenches, and opened fire on the Canadians' rear. It was here that Canadian valor showed at its finest as the Canucks reformed and turned on their enemies, fighting on, hour after hour, until every objective had been taken. By ten o'clock that night the whole ridge was in their hands, and the next few hours were spent in consolidating all positions and planning for any possible counterattack.

The Canadian effort at Vimy Ridge was possibly the big factor in the victory claimed in the Battle of Arras, and it was from this ridge that the enemy retreat went into high gear. Hill 145 gave considerable difficulty since it was defended by a large number of Germans who held a strong pocket with machine guns, but when this was eliminated, the ridge was clear, and dominated the plains that spread to Douai. A great barrier was thus removed from the British path, an impediment that had been fought for over many long, painful months.

After the abortive effort by British tanks the September before, the development of these war machines had been pressed with enthusiasm. The old Mark I model with its wagon-wheel tail was soon discarded, and one hundred improved versions, listed as Mark II and Mark III, were being turned out at the Foster & Sons plant. These machines were similar to the original design except that a transmission steering system had been incorporated in which guidance of the vehicle was effected by clutching or de-clutching either track. These tanks could traverse a ten-foot-wide trench, climb a twenty-two-degree slope, clamber over a wall four-feet six-inches high, but they still

moved at the same snail's pace of 3.7 mph. The male versions
carried two six-pounder guns and four machine guns. The female was fitted with six rifle-caliber guns, and general improvement in ventilation, entrance and exit doors, and a new fuel
system were built into all these designs. Now the fuel tank was
mounted outside and in the rear to reduce danger of fire within
the hull during battle action.

About ninety Mark II and Mark III tanks were assigned to
the British forces in the original plan for the Battle of Arras,
but only sixty were available, even though many of them were
drawn from the tank-training centers in England. Because of
this deficiency it was decided to use them for mopping-up
operations. Eight were attached to General Henry Horne's
First Army to work against the heights of Vimy Ridge. Forty
were given to General Edmund Allenby's Third Army—eight
of which were to work with the VIII Corps north of the Scarpe
River, thirty-two with the VI and VII Corps south of this
river—and the remaining twelve to General Hubert Gough's
Fifth Army which was to drive north toward Vis-en-Artois.
Thus, all tanks were assigned to particular units and given
specific missions, but no provisions were made for withholding
any reserves. Also, because of the scarcity of these landships, a
hurricane bombardment of 2,700,000 shells was fired that, although cutting most of the enemy wire, churned the attack area
into a quagmire—certainly no ground suitable for tank operations.

The complete Battle of Arras was fought from April 9 to May
5, and despite the initial success and the taking of vital objectives, the cost in British casualties was enormous; more than
132,000 British officers and men were reported killed, wounded,
or captured, and once more Colonel Swinton's grim appraisal of
trench warfare was substantiated.

The part taken by the tanks was slight, but colorful. This time
they were well handled, supply bases were established, but any
movement of materials forward from these dumps was difficult
since it had always to be hauled by hand. Later on, outmoded

Mark I machines were turned into combat-supply carriers. Tanks operating along the Tilloy-lez-Mofflaines, The Harp, Telegraph Hill line encountered a new form of enemy resistance when the Germans used a high-velocity "K" type of armor-piercing cartridge, and when the tanks returned, the British decided that future models would have to be protected by armor that would stop this high-velocity round.

The Battle of Arras showed that where the ground was suitable for maneuvering these vehicles, it was possible for them to make sharp, successful thrusts into enemy-held sectors. Under such conditions they were not sitting ducks for enemy artillery. Although the Germans may not as yet have had a completely suitable antitank gun, they could not stand their ground when they were opposed by well-handled tank forces. This operation also demonstrated that the training of all ranks had been conducted along practical lines.

## The Blowup at Messines

Trench warfare had prompted many men to cudgel their minds for new methods of operation, and in many instances their new concepts were nothing more than old, or variations of, ancient battle tactics. Once both sides settled down to a conflict that was carried on from a series of trenches and dugouts, it was soon evident that old-fashioned, siege-war techniques were necessary. Since neither side could attack across the open space between their front lines without dreadful losses, it was apparent that the one way open to each was to burrow under the other's trenches to place, and ignite, heavy explosive charges. Thus began a new, and somewhat private, war between rival sappers (engineers) that lasted for nearly three years—a terrifying, primitive, exhaustive war-within-a-war, the like of which may never be recorded again.

It has been mentioned that a number of mines were exploded during the Vimy Ridge assault, but many others had preceded these eruptions at Mont Saint-Eloi, Hill 60, and other sectors

with varying results. The concept had been adopted early in
the war by the British engineer and contractor, Sir John Norton
Griffiths, at the time a Member of Parliament. In his earlier
days he had held mining interests all over the British Empire,
and during these operations had noted a style of tunneling in
these outposts in which a man, resting his back against a cross-
shaped support, dug into the tunnel face with a short shovel
and heaved the loosened earth over his shoulder to another
worker who passed it on for removal. These men were known
as "clay pickers," or "workers at the cross," and with this system
could bore out long chambers in remarkably fast time.

Griffiths had seen the value of this type of warfare, and ad-
vertised for men who had had experience of this kind, but, as
had Colonel Swinton, he had difficulty in persuading the War
Office to take an interest in his idea. Lord Kitchener, however,
was fascinated and declared, "Get me ten thousand of these men
immediately."

Griffiths closed out his contracting firm, ignored his Parliamentary duties, and built up what was known as Royal Engineers Tunnelling companies. In fact, two such companies
were formed by February 1915, which was fortunate since the
Germans were already exploding mines under several sectors
of the British front, particularly in areas where new troops, or
Indian soldiers had just moved in.

The development of the "clay-picker" technique was weary-
ing and hampered with disappointments. Tunnels were started,
only to fill with water; tools furnished were useless for this particular work, and on occasion, after some advance had been
made, the sector was turned over to or taken over by the French.
Nothing of importance happened until March 1915 when a mine
was dug all the way under Hill 60, but before it could be deto-
nated, the Germans set one off on March 10 at Mont Saint-Eloi
that delayed the Hill 60 operation for a time and warned the
British that their enemy was further advanced in this work than
they had thought. The Mont Saint-Eloi blowup was a real disaster, but by April 10 the Hill 60 tunnel and galleries were ready

for the massive charges of gunpowder and guncotton, and by April 17 the explosives and igniter systems were in, and all was ready.

The whole charge took ten seconds to erupt, and then 300 feet of front was suddenly hurled into the air and scattered over 300 yards. One British Tommy who tried to get a first-instant look, peered over his parapet and was hit by a chunk of clay that decapitated him. Lumps of earth, sandbags, and enemy bodies went skyward. British bugles blared, and the Royal West Kents and a motley crew of engineers charged over with rifles and bayonets to complete that moment of carnage.

This operation left one hole about half an acre in size, and after considerable inspection it was learned that the Germans previously had prepared a mine in the same sector, already charged and fitted with an exploder—a mine that prisoners said was to be touched off two days later.

Hill 60 justified Griffiths' idea, and his tunneling companies were accepted as a new trench force and played many such roles before the war was over.

The Vimy Ridge show was aided, not only by a small force of tanks, but by Tunnelling Company 185 that had dug seven miles of fighting and communications galleries through the harsh chalk of the sector. A very elaborate system of tunnels, galleries, and working areas was hewn out of the Ypres clay between the area north of Hill 60 and Ploegsteert Wood, a distance of 15,000 yards, and this line linked nineteen major diggings, the chief of which was designed to destroy Wytschaete Ridge and the area south to Messines.

General Haig had wanted to drive the Germans out of Ostend and Zeebrugge, which would have given him a field over which to fight to turn the enemy flank, but the terrain was most unsuited to heavy operations since it was reclaimed marshland, crisscrossed with drainage ditches, an area no tank or heavy gun could negotiate. So his only hope was farther south, for east of Ypres was a narrow ridge that dominated the plain. The southern end known as the Messines Ridge might be taken in a single operation, and this Haig decided to attempt, so what has become known as the Battle of Messines, actually was begun months before when additional tunneling companies from New Zealand, Australia, and Canada joined the British ones that had been organized by Griffiths and the Royal Engineers. Whether Messines should have been incorporated into a wider and more ambitious push has been debated since, but the British field marshal had had too many disappointments and was understandably cautious.

The initial artillery bombardment began on May 21 and was intensified continually until June 2. About 2200 guns of all caliber were ranked up and poured on a continuous fire of explosive and steel. Then at 3:10 A.M., June 7, a series of igniter plungers were rammed down. A thunderous roar went out as these 19 mines, carrying 933,000 pounds of ammonal, then the strongest known explosive, erupted below Messines Ridge. Freak blowbacks of the blast knocked down men who were more than a mile away. Huge clods of clay as large as a motor truck flew skyward. One left a crater 430 feet wide from rim to rim. Shock waves flattened farmhouses 400 yards distant.

People in Dublin, five hundred miles away, heard the explosion. It was sensed in London by the men who had planned the stupendous mining exploit. It was impossible to learn how many enemy soldiers were killed in the blast, but when it was all over more than 10,000 were missing besides the known dead. Another 7354 were taken prisoner, but most of them were so dazed they had no idea where they were, what their names were, or what had happened.

British infantry, their ears ringing with the blast and concussion wave, went over the top expecting some opposition, but were able to advance unopposed, and by seven that morning Messines and Wytschaete were in their hands. In fact, the victory was so complete too many advancing soldiers crowded into this limited area, and German artillery took advantage of the temporary situation and lobbed dozens of shells into these groups.

The victory was complete, but was not exploited, and when General Haig requested authorization to widen this offensive on the Ypres front, the War Cabinet refused to co-operate. However, when Admiral Sir John R. Jellicoe presented the U-boat warfare figures and explained the sinkings—a situation that threatened all possibility of continuing the war into 1918—the War Cabinet finally gave General Haig permission to continue the complete Ypres offensive.

## In Flanders Fields

The Battle of Flanders, the third large offensive around Ypres, must be listed with the Somme as Britain's main efforts of the land war. This battle began in the summer of 1917 and continued until it bogged down during the middle of the following November. Weather, ill luck, and the mud and morass produced by the artillery pounding, contrived to defeat Douglas Haig's well-planned operation. Here, the British bore the full brunt of the war for more than six months. Russia was out of the conflict, the United States, from whom so much was expected, had not yet fired its first shot, France was totally exhausted by her efforts along the Aisne—portions of her Army were staging a mutiny— and Italy was setting up the big breakdown at Caporetto. Only Britain stood firm to hold off the massive German war machine. This British sacrifice of sacrifices, alone absorbed all the German strength and prevented Ludendorff from striking elsewhere, a point the German general admitted in his memoirs.

Haig's plan was ambitious. He would first capture the rest of the Messines-Wytschaete Ridge, and free Ypres by taking the grim Passchendaele Ridge that dominated the town and the surrounding area. General Gough was brought up to replace General Plumer who was considered to be a reliable, but not enterprising soldier. Any tactical success gained, was to be exploited to the full. For instance, if Passchendaele could be taken, long-range guns might reach out and cut the enemy's communications through Roulers and the submarine bases at Ostend and Zeebrugge.

General Haig asked the French to take over a portion of the British front to permit maximum pressure and reserves to be used on the Ypres front. This the French refused to do, but suggested that they take a small part in this Flanders operation. Haig dreaded the problems attending the handling of British, French, and Belgian troops in one compact sector, but thought it advisable to agree. The time taken in moving French troops, guns, and equipment delayed Haig's jump-off until July 31, thereby wasting many days of summer that would have been valuable, considering the dreadful weather experienced that August. Those who taunted Haig later with his decision to fight this battle, failed to appreciate that had no offensive been attempted, it is more than likely that Germany would have initiated one of her own—along a front of her own choosing.

The Third Battle of Ypres is better remembered by British Tommies as the Passchendaele show, a name proudly embroidered on many battle flags, but which since 1917 has stood for another example of military failure. Here was futility of purpose and effort. It achieved little except loss, and must be considered the climactic scene in the gloomy drama of British effort.

Once again, this campaign opened with a tremendous preliminary bombardment on July 22, and continued for ten days. At dawn of July 31 the infantry moved out and advanced on a fifteen-mile front as torrential rains added to their problems. Bixschoote, Saint-Julien, and Pilckem Ridge on the left were taken quickly, but along the vital Menin road the advance ran into difficulties. The rain pelted down day after day and held up the second phase of the planning; the available tanks were bogged down, and the infantrymen were equally handicapped.

The second thrust was started on August 16, and again the left flank moved up with ease through the valley of the Steenbeek and the ruins of Langemarck. However, on the right where some advance would have proved most profitable, the British were again knocked down like ninepins. Few prisoners or guns were captured and the old complaint of faulty staff work buzzed about General Gough's head. What satisfaction had been gained at Messines was being frittered away in the swampland beyond Ypres, but Haig and his generals continued to press on in areas where failure had already been experienced. In other words, they were employing the tactics of a battle where siege warfare better fitted. When the infantry did move up, their artillery was bogged down, and when the enemy counterattacked, there was no curtain fire to halt them.

The bad weather continued and all planning had to be held up until September 20. On that morning Britain's Second Army went over on a four-mile front and made excellent progress along the Menin road, with the artillery offering strong tactical support. Counterattacks were repulsed, and new assaults through September 26 gained possession of the main ridge east of Ypres which also gathered in Gheluvelt, Polygon Wood, and Brood-seinde, despite the rain that by now had turned the battlefield into a complete morass.

Squadrons of Royal Flying Corps braved the weather and furnished valuable visual, photographic, and artillery observation. In this period another 10,000 troops were captured, and it was noticed that the Germans were modifying their elastic tactics, and holding strong in their forward lines, only to be hammered to pulp by British artillery.

Had General Haig been content with this minor success, the campaign might have restored some prestige, and bolstered morale, but higher command decided to plod on over the few remaining weeks before winter set in, and thereby sacrificed all available reserves.

Between October 9–12 the British line advanced a trifle, and a combined push by the Fifth Army and the French on October 22 brought little reward. Four days later, the Second Army, moving through heavy rainfall, made another futile effort. The troops were exhausted trying to wade through the morass; mud

jammed rifles and machine guns and nullified the effect of shell
bursts. The Germans replied with doses of mustard gas, but by
November 4, when the 2nd Canadian Division finally occupied
the scar that once had been Passchendaele village, it was decided to halt this fruitless campaign. The British Army had
fought itself into a state of exhaustion, and when a high-ranking
officer of the general staff drove up to examine the scene of this
latest "victory," he burst into tears, exclaiming, "Good God! Did
we really send men to fight in that?"

Later that month General Haig turned to higher and drier
ground where the British staged a show that justified the new
tank warfare.

### The Phantom Piper of Polygon Wood

Reference to the capture of Polygon Wood revives the legend
of the phantom piper. Once more, the tale is credited to several
regiments and set against various fronts. Years ago when I wrote
the incident for a magazine, many readers on both sides of the
Atlantic responded with interesting reactions. Some said it took
place at High Wood, others stated that the phantom piper was
seen at Hill 60, but, of course, they were only claiming the story
for their particular regiment. For a time I was under the impression that it occurred at Hill 60 during the Ypres campaign
of 1915, but several of my correspondents convinced me that it
took place two years later at Polygon Wood. Most of them
agreed that it happened to the 42nd Royal Highland Regiment—
the Black Watch—and in studying their battle honors I find that
the Black Watch were not engaged at Hill 60 in the 1915 Ypres
battle, but they did fight at Polygon Wood in October 1917.

At any rate the story must be set against that cold, clammy
October when the 42nd was ordered to take Polygon Wood. No
poppies grew from that shell-scarred ground. Shrubs and flowers
had been replaced by entanglement stakes and lengths of thorny
barbed wire. Deep shellholes, sodden and green with stagnant
water, were everywhere. Discarded equipment, bully-beef tins,

and shattered ammunition boxes littered the ground in front of their parapet. Beyond that desert of debris rose the splintered shafts of what once had been trees.

To the men of the Black Watch this continued attack was a heartless campaign that numbed one and all. The old stories of the Ladies from Hell had long since been forgotten, and in some cases derided. Few of the Highlanders cared whether they lived or died, for no matter what they did, how well they fought, disaster usually crouched at the end of their onrush.

Zero hour approached and the early morning mists of that dreary autumn curled and drifted through the wire in front of them. The tapes laid down overnight to guide the Jocks through the pathways in their own barbed wire, unwound from the parapet and trailed off into the blank nothingness beyond. Here and there a few rifle bolts clicked as the kilted Scots made certain their magazines were loaded. There were a number of harsh hisses as bayonets were withdrawn from scabbards and fixed. Instinctively, a few felt for their fighting dirks tucked into their muddy hose tops. The sentries stared into the swirling mist, their tired eyes searching for any movement of enemy scouts on patrol. Others sat on the firesteps with dull expressions on their faces, and awaited the whistle blast that would send them over the sandbags again.

"Over the top an' the best o' luck, Mac!"

Up to this point our story portrays just another incident in a war that had churned its bloody way through thirty-nine months of horror and sacrifice. It had been repeated a hundred times from Ostend to the Vosges. It was always the same. A shrill command from a whistle, a frantic clambering up a muddy parapet, and the howling fear that comes to men when they charge across no man's land into a hail of enemy gunfire. From that time on it's a stew of unremembered seconds, climaxed with a bitter potion of death and glory as the only reward.

But on this October morning the 42nd Highlanders had an unusual experience to scrawl in their regimental records. While they waited, resting their weary backs against the trench wall,

1. Gun cupola of a Liége fort before heavy German artillery was brought out. These fortifications built to provide border defenses against conventional artillery attacks, held out long enough to inflict heavy casualties, but were unable to withstand the thunderous impact of 21-cm siege mortars and after several days of courageous stands, the Belgians had to surrender.    COLONEL G. B. JARRETT PHOTO

2. A Liége fort after a heavy bombardment. Some reports have it that a Zeppelin dropped a bomb which scored this hit, but it is believed that only the heavy siege mortars, brought up for the action, could have wreaked such havoc on these almost-impregnable cupolas. The delay suffered at Liége may have caused the Germans to revise their Schlieffen Plan, a decision that gave the Allies their great chance to score at the Marne.    COLONEL G. B. JARRETT PHOTO

3. Nurse Edith Cavell, British martyr who was shot by the Germans because she helped a number of Allied soldiers to escape into their own lines. She knew what she was doing and accepted the German court's decision without reservation. "Patriotism is not enough," she said before dying. "I helped them to escape, because I knew they would be shot if I didn't." Her sacrifice aroused Britain to a new effort and the recruiting stations were swamped with thousands of new volunteers. IMPERIAL WAR MUSEUM PHOTO

4. Another British martyr, Captain Charles Fryatt, seen standing on the gangplank of his ship S.S. *Brussels*. During March 1915 Fryatt boldly attempted to ram a German U-boat which had intercepted his vessel. More than a year later the *Brussels* was captured by a flotilla of German surface ships. Captain Fryatt was taken prisoner, jailed in Zeebrugge and later court-martialed in Bruges. Because he was not a member of a combatant force, he was found guilty of an aggressive act against *U-33*, and sent before a firing squad. By international law, he should have been held as an honorable prisoner of war. IMPERIAL WAR MUSEUM PHOTO

5.    During the Battle of the Somme, the tower of Albert Cathedral was struck by shellfire and the statue of the Virgin was left dangling from its battered supports where it hung for more than two years. French residents always believed that when the Virgin came down from her precarious position, the war would end. On the morning of November 10, 1918, a German shell again struck the cathedral and the statue fell into the street. The next day the Armistice was signed.    IMPERIAL WAR MUSEUM PHOTO

6.    The most superfluous service in World War I. Here, the author is shown as a cavalryman, complete with horse, sword, and bandolier of rifle ammunition. He was also trained in the use of the lance and the 1895 version of the Maxim gun; a weapon he never encountered once he arrived in France. It was from these ranks of wasted manpower that the dying services drew their most valued volunteers.

7. The first poison-gas attack in history. Here is shown how the cloud of chlorine gas, released from canisters set up in the front lines, was carried into the Allied lines by a prevailing wind. The defenders had no gas masks and were quickly driven out of their positions leaving a great gap in the line. The Germans, not realizing how effective this new weapon could be, had not provided reserves to take advantage of the situation, and its effect was nullified. COLONEL G. B. JARRETT PHOTO

8. The immortals of the Lafayette Escadrille. Seen here with their early Nieuport scouts are Lieutenant de Laage de Meux, French liaison officer; Choteau Johnson, Laurence Rumsey, James McConnell, Bill Thaw, Raoul Lufbery, Kiffin Rockwell, Didier Masson, Norman Prince, and Bert Hall. This photograph was taken in the Verdun sector in July 1916. PAUL A. ROCKWELL PHOTO

9.    The first time a tank was seen in action in any war. Here is "Clan Leslie" of C Company, Royal Tank Corps, moving up for the initial strike, September 15, 1916. This shows the size of the vehicle, the ungainly tail-wheels and the anti-grenade net erected above the control turrets. This model carried a crew of eight and was armed with two 6-pounder, quick-firing guns and four Hotch-kiss machine guns. In these models the armor was not proof against K-type, armor-piercing ammunition or artillery fire.    BRITISH INFORMATION SERVICES PHOTO

10.    One tank that didn't go to glory. This shows a Mark I tank which took part in the first tank attack at Flers on September 15, 1916. This one bogged down in difficult ground but remained in action, acting as a pillbox strong point, and aided in the planned advance. This shows the condition of the sector in which the first tank attack was staged.    BRITISH INFORMATION SERVICES PHOTO

11.   The gun that fired America's first shot in World War I. Left to right are Captain Idus R. McLendon, commanding Battery C, 6th Field Artillery; Sergeant Alexander Arch, Chief of the Section. The famous "first" was fired from this gun emplacement near the town of Bathélmont in the Lorraine sector, at 7 A.M., October 23, 1917.      U.S. SIGNAL CORPS PHOTO

12.   The indomitable Sergeant Alvin C. York, wearing his Distinguished Service Cross and the Croix de Guerre for killing 25 Germans, capturing 135 more, and cleaning out 35 enemy machine-gun nests. On his arrival home, Sergeant York was awarded the Congressional Medal of Honor.      NATIONAL ARCHIVES PHOTO

13. Major Charles W. Whittlesey (left), commander of the Lost Battalion of the 308th Infantry Regiment, which was trapped for several days in the Argonne Forest. On the right is Major Kenny of the 3rd Battalion, 307th Infantry which was the first to relieve Whittlesey's force. This was one of the classic stands by American troops in World War I.     U. S. SIGNAL CORPS PHOTO

14. Scene of the stand of the "Lost Battalion." This is the hillside near Charlevaux Mill, beneath which Major Charles Whittlesey's little force made its five-day stand under bitter fire and enemy encirclement. To attempt to crawl to these two puddles for water, meant possible death or capture.     U. S. SIGNAL CORPS PHOTO

15. The Paris Gun, often misnamed "Big Bertha," which could throw a 264-pound shell to hit a target seventy miles away. This weapon, still to be seen in the Krupp factory, had a barrel 120 feet long and a caliber of eight and one-quarter inches. The 3-inch steel balls on which the gun carriage rotated had been made in the U.S. for the Russian Purchasing Agency, and had obviously been captured by the Germans. Three hundred and sixty-seven shells were fired from seven of these guns, killing 250 people, wounding 640, and destroying property estimated at $10,000,000.    COLONEL G. B. JARRETT PHOTO

16. America's first contribution to the war effort was marked by the arrival of a flotilla of U.S. Navy destroyers, rushed across the Atlantic to join the Royal Navy in its antisubmarine operations. The first vessel to appear off Plymouth was greeted with the symbolic phrase: "The Return of the Mayflower," and this painting by B. F. Gribble depicts the memorable incident.
U.S. NAVY PHOTO

and watched their young officer as he peered into the indistinct face of his wristwatch, a new sound seeped into the clamor of the bombardment. It was toneless and without cadence at first, but it smoothed out gradually, and a hundred war-weary Scots stiffened as their ears caught the opening skirl of a bagpipe tune. Glengarry caps were pulled down to a more rakish angle—no Jock would wear the detested tin hat during a bayonet charge. The kilted men jerked to their feet, belts were taken in another notch, and seconds before the whistle blew hundreds of hobnailed boots were up on the firestep.

The sentries turned their heads slowly, trying to determine the direction of the sound. The skirl increased in tempo and the quick-step tune was recognized.

"Thot's a piper a-playin' 'The Hieland Laddie,'" one tall Jock whispered. "But how can that be? We left oor pipers back i' the billets."

"Ut's only wan piper," a sentry explained out of the side of his mouth. "He's a-marchin' oop an' doon beyon' the barbed wire, sor."

"Whist mon, ye're daft!" another Jock sneered.

The young officer no longer studied his watch; he was listening to the wail of the Black Watch quickstep, "The Highland Laddie." It was clear and distinct now as if the piper had finally filled his bag. The drones were taking it up, providing the fixed accompaniment to the fingered notes from the chanter.

The sentry turned with amazed eyes. "Ut's a pipe major, sor. A pipe major i' full dress. A dress tartan, sor, wi' a white tunic an' a proper bonnet—an' wi' buckles on his shoes!"

"An' Jerry's not shooting at him?" the officer gasped.

"Ah don't think they can see him," the sentry said in a husky whisper.

Someone blew the "Charge" whistle and the Jocks floundered to the top, scrambled through the gaps in their own wire, and then, sure enough, a massive pipe major strode back and forth across the width of their front, head up, chest out, his gay kilt swinging as he piped them on. The bagpipe wailed its warming tune of assurance, the Highlanders charged with new vigor, screaming their clan war cries, and plunged on through the German defenses.

They were met with enemy fire, but nothing stopped the Jocks. They stormed on, wiping out every machine-gun nest, every pocket of strength, every dugout that offered any resistance. They pounded up the slope to the edge of Polygon Wood, hacking, and clawing until the shell-torn copse was taken and its defenses consolidated.

Strangely enough, there were no serious casualties, but stranger still was the disappearance of the mysterious pipe major, for once the attack was over he was not seen again. Some said he had continued on, piping his march, until the mist swallowed him. Scottish scouts crept about the ravaged area for some time, seeking the giant pipe major, and a patrol was sent out that night, penetrating well into the enemy defenses, but no trace of him was found.

There was no explanation for it. What a regimental pipe major, garbed in the finest ceremonial equipment, was doing in no man's land could not be explained. Where he had come from and whither he had gone are still discussed in Scottish barracks from Holyrood Castle to John O' Groats. Everyone had seen him. Practically every man in the company could describe his dress uniform. Most certainly, all of them recognized their "Highland Laddie" regimental march.

One oldster in the regiment went so far as to swear he recognized the piper—the phantom pipe major was none other than Piper Geordie Findlater who had been honored with the Victoria Cross at the Battle of Dargai in the Northwest Province of India in 1897. But this statement was denounced loudly when it was recalled that Piper Findlater was a member of the Gordon Highlanders, whereas the Pipe Major of Polygon Wood had worn the dress tartan and equipment of the Black Watch.

But whoever he was, and wherever he came from, the ghostly pipe major certainly led the Jocks to victory at Polygon Wood.

Perhaps it all was imagined, just another war legend, but don't ever try to talk a Black Watch veteran out of his belief in the story.

All you'll get is, "Didn't the Jocks take Polygon Wood?"

## The Tanks at Cambrai

That same October while the British were suffering their trials in Flanders, the Italians fell victims to German propaganda, mass panic, and the belief that democracy was perishing. A violent attack along a fairly quiet front scattered detachments of Italy's Second Army, and permitted Austro-German forces to advance along the Julian front.

Through an ingenious plan, drawn up by the German Headquarters Staff, their 281st Division convinced the Italian soldiers opposite them that the war was about over, and they were to be betrayed and deserted by their allies. This was done by propaganda, printed in specially prepared newspapers that were dropped into the Italian trenches. In other instances Italian-speaking Germans made personal contact with Italian junior officers and explained this "situation" in complete detail. This plan had been used with varying success on the Russian front, but few Germans thought it would have such influence before Caporetto which lay near the great dams the Italians had built to control the flow of the Isonzo River.

With little contact with their rear areas, the bewildered Italians fraternized with clever German spies who convinced them that much anguish would be spared, and many lives saved, if the Italians and Austro-German forces would mutiny against their officers and refuse to fight any longer. Once this area of doubt had been set up, 100,000 of Germany's best troops seemingly moved out of nowhere, and suddenly attacked.

How much the moral breakdown contributed to the disaster is not easy to assess, but other Italian troops fought magnificently to halt the enemy breakthrough. The Duke of Aosta's Third Army saved the perilous position by superior discipline in the retreat from the Carso, and in turning to make a stand behind the Piave, where a furious battle that lasted for three weeks finally stopped the Teutonic drive. The assault that began with treachery at Caporetto was halted, and Italy was saved from the fate that had engulfed Russia. By November 7, 1917, Nikolai Lenin had led the Bolshevists and the faint-hearted Socialists into the maw of anarchy.

The heroics along the Piave and the shock of Russia's capitulation almost blotted out General Haig's frantic effort to save something from the Ypres sacrifice. Moving south from the bog and mire of Flanders, he prepared a new thrust in a dry, high area that extended from Bullecourt south to Villers-Guislain which lay opposite the important city of Cambrai, some seven miles behind the Hindenburg line.

This was intended as a surprise blow, a daring assault against the enemy-made barrier and support lines, more formidable than anything built previously along the Western Front. Enormous excavations of fantastic length and depth had been designed by skilled engineers and built by exploited slave and captive labor. Haig, however, conceived a plan by which he would dispense with a heavy preliminary bombardment, and substitute a full-powered tank attack. The Staff decided that the new Tank Corps was capable of breaking through the enemy front, and if sufficient infantry could be massed before this breach, a major opening could be forced through the Hindenburg line. The capture of Cambrai would be important, and the high ground around Bourlon might prove to be of great strategic value.

The battle was placed in the hands of General Julian H. G. Byng, one-time leader of the 3rd Cavalry Division and the Canadian Corps. Byng had taken Allenby's place at the head of the Third Army, and had some of the finest and most seasoned troops in the BEF under him. It was on the Cambrai front that the first wholehearted acclaim for Colonel Swinton's land destroyer was heard; where the tank finally was accepted as a vital military weapon.

Those who took any part in this battle may have had varied

viewpoints as to its outcome or the strategic value of the campaign, but few would dispute the fact that a complete tactical surprise was achieved on the opening day, November 19. The action was fought over terrain most suitable for tank operations. There was no preliminary bombardment, as stated before, but Haig permitted some counterbattery work, and a barrage of smoke and high explosive did open up the start of zero hour. There had been no particular change in aerial activity, no obvious relief of troops, and no registering shots made by the artillery.

Byng's forces, therefore, rolled promptly over the German positions, and by night of the first day had crossed the Escaut River at Masnières, and occupied a goodly portion of enemy ground. So satisfactory was this advance, all the church bells in London were rung in the sincere belief that victory was just a matter of weeks.

This success had been attained through the actions of four hundred tanks, commanded by General Sir Hugh Elles. These vehicles, that could cross wide trenches, moved with rare courage, although in many instances they had to carry fascines—great bundles of cable-bound brush weighing more than a ton apiece. The fascines were unloaded forward so as to fall into the enemy trench and fill a great portion of the gap.

The tanks were divided into sections of three machines, an advance guard tank and two infantry tanks; the guard vehicle was expected to protect the two infantry machines and the following infantry troops as they crossed the enemy wire and trenches. Since there were three systems of enemy trench to negotiate, and three tanks in each section, the following routine was carried out. The advance tank passed through the band of British wire entanglements, and, turning to the left without crossing the enemy's front line, used all the weapons that could be brought to bear from the right side of the hull. The first infantry tank approached the enemy front line, dropped its fascine, and crossed and also turned to the left. The second infantry tank crossed over the fascine dropped by the first, continued on to the enemy's second line, crossed over on its own fascine, and carried out the same maneuver. As soon as the second trench had been crossed by the last infantry tank, the advance guard tank moved around, crossed both trenches on the fascines already laid, and started for the third trench with its fascine ready for the final crossing.

It was this part of the planning that afforded the excellent co-operation between the tanks and the infantry. As a result, the Third Army quickly shattered the German defensive system. They had hoped to cut off the Germans in the sector south of the Sensée River and west of the Canal-du-Nord. The tanks set up the initial surprise, pinning down enemy fire, clearing up great swaths of barbed wire, and smashing pillboxes. In a few hours greater gains were made than those throughout the weeks of the Ypres-Passchendaele campaign. Everything worked according to plan before Cambrai, as long as each tank remained in action, but by attacking on such a wide front, instead of against se-lected targets, they finally were deprived of the chance to use their reserve tank forces properly.

Haig had hoped to complete this assault in forty-eight hours, but in that space of time Bourlon still resisted capture. A Ger-man battery that had not been reported by aerial reconnaissance wreaked havoc on one group of tanks, and at one point five of them were knocked out in as many minutes. As the hours passed, the troops wearied, and the tanks burned themselves out. The crews were exhausted, and when the vital opening had been made, Haig had no fresh reserves to move in, whereas a new German division was brought up, and made a gallant stand. They responded with a short hurricane bombardment, added gas and smoke shells, and set up an infiltrating assault. They trickled through weak points in the British line, swept over gun positions, and surged forward, threatening the recapture of Gouzeaucourt. Only the Guards Division and the 2nd Tank Bri-gade held them off. It was here that a brilliant offensive finally trickled out, a failure brought on chiefly—so it was said—by lack of training of junior officers, NCOs, and men. Sage consideration, however, would decide that the Cambrai battle, relying so much on mechanical vehicles, should have been planned for, and restricted to a limited time. All the success bought by the tanks was wantonly discarded when the battle was carried into extra days.

## America's First Shot

America's first shot in World War I was fired early in the morning of October 23, 1917, from a quiet sector near the town of Lunéville, not far from the province of Alsace from which General John J. Pershing's forebears had come. This historic spot was one kilometer due east of the town of Bathelémont and 300 meters northeast of the Bauzemont-Bathelémont road. The United States soldiers involved had, just the night before, been under a minor air attack that had been aimed at a French war munitions plant. No member of this United States 6th Field Artillery had been injured.

The battery had been moved by rail from Toul to within thirty miles of the front line and off-loaded at the town of Jarville, from where they rode along the highways in broad daylight, through battered villages, past houses without roofs, churches without steeples, and schools that were heaps of rubble. They were to be accommodated in the old town of Saint Nicolas du Port on the River Meurthe.

A French major in charge of the town was on hand to present the billeting schedule that showed where the guns were to be parked, the horses picketed, and where the artillerymen could set up their field kitchens, and perhaps snatch a few hours' sleep. But, as usual, most of these accommodations were on paper. There was no firewood for the field kitchens, and the accommodation for the men rougher than usual. The countryside was pastoral and rolling, but generally damp. Damp perhaps is an understatement; there was mud everywhere, the roads were bogged ruts, the gutters ran with streams of foul silt, and the adjoining fields were layered with muddy, wheel-gashed turf.

The next morning the battery pulled out and continued its march to the front, heading for the ruined village of Hoéville in the Lunéville sector. During this move the guns and caissons often had to pull off the road to allow truckloads of infantrymen to pass. These were some of the first Americans to be moved up into the war zone. Other trucks and wagons carried food and supplies. Ambulances went up empty, while others returned with their litters filled with French wounded. Now and then a YMCA truck, clattering with pots, pans, and portable stoves, went through into the reserve areas to furnish a few comforts to the men already employed on engineering projects.

When the battery reached the roads that were camouflaged with wire screens and curtained drapes, it knew it was getting uncomfortably close to the scene of action. Late that night, October 22, the guns of the 6th Field Artillery moved into their assigned positions. A light rain started to fall, making the roads sloppier than ever. Other guns boomed somewhere ahead, but infantrymen slogged forward under the cover of their ground sheets and shelter-halfs, as a stiff wind fluttered the skirts of their sodden overcoats.

It was well past midnight when the battery started to dig in and position their guns, and after their officers had checked their maps and time brackets, they realized that they were less than eight hundred yards from the German trenches, where it was understood that a number of Bavarian regiments were holding the line. Only a few muddy slots and swatches of wire entanglements separated them. There was no moon, but once the tattered drizzle-clouds had blown away, a few stars jeweled the sky. The mud was deep, but the spirits of these Americans were high, for each man sensed he was taking part in a historic occasion.

To these newcomers, the war seemed unreal in the darkness. A few shells arched across no man's land, dragging their eerie whine until a muffled explosion thumped out of some water-soaked spot to the rear. A few French poilus wandered into the section and watched the activity of their new comrades. One or two who spoke English shook hands and welcomed the artillery-men, for the Americans who had moved up that day were to replace war-weary French platoons and working parties. This was only a training session for the newcomers, an experience arranged to furnish a nucleus for the development of later con-tingents, but if they could afford only a few hours of rest and reserve, it would be more than helpful.

A rocket went up and plastered a blob of illumination against the clouds and revealed some fringy detail of the group ahead. The Frenchmen identified this flare and then told the Americans how to differentiate between the whine of a French shell and one fired by the Germans.

This intercourse was very interesting, but the gunners of the 6th Field Artillery had an important job to do. They set to and dug manfully, hacking out pits in which their pieces could be positioned in the quickest possible time. Each battery yearned for the honor of firing the first shot, and the winter, as it turned out, was Battery C. The men in this element, with almost super-human effort, had hauled a gun by ropes across a muddy, almost impassable meadow, and were so determined to get off America's first shot, they had refused to take out time for a meal.

They finally dragged the heavy weapon to an abandoned gun pit that had been built by the French, and as stated before, this position was two miles from the old international boundary line between French and German Lorraine, and one and one-half kilometers behind the French line then being taken over by American infantry.

The first shot was fired by Sergeant Alexander L. Arch at 6:10 on the morning of October 23, 1917, and was a 75-mm explosive shell ranged on a German battery of 150-mm guns located two kilometers behind the German front-line trenches. The position of the enemy battery on the map was a field one hundred meters west of the town called Xanrey. It was not a direct hit, but close enough to indicate some creditable gun-laying.

Captain Idus R. McLendon gave the command to fire,

Sergeant Lonnie Domonick cut the fuse, Corporal Osborne W. De Varila prepared the fuse for cutting, Sergeant Elward Warthen loaded the gun, and Corporal Robert E. Braley laid the piece for firing.

America finally was in the war.

# CHAPTER VII

*Germany Opens the "Kaiserbattle"* . . . *The Paris Gun* . . .
*With Backs to the Wall* . . . *America's First Battles* . . .
*The Trial of Château-Thierry* . . . *Germany's Blackest Day*
. . . *The Spectral Soccer Player.*

## Germany Opens the "Kaiserbattle"

In 1918, the fifth year of combat, the Great War rumbled toward its close. Although American manpower did not begin to have any influence until June of that year, American war production, food, military supplies, and its buoyancy and enthusiasm, contributed greatly to Germany's eventual downfall. The final decision came with swift, dramatic suddenness, for once the March push, sometimes known as the "Kaiserbattle," had been halted, American power asserted itself, and the great tidal wave of reversal was so stupendous, few people realized at the time what had been accomplished.

America's actual part through the last months of fighting has seldom been clearly understood, since few objective historians have attempted to present the checks and balances. Following the flush of triumph, many blindly overestimated her part, while others churlishly denied her the credit she deserved. Also, the long strain endured by other Allied nations was, to a great extent, forgotten by some bellicose patriots in the United States who claimed that the United States Army could have defeated Germany singlehanded.

The United States had had plenty of time to build up her armies and divisions, her troops were given six months or more of training under experienced leaders, and on them devolved the good fortune of striking what was considered by some as the final blow. But sober authorities have pointed out that this stroke was delivered against an antagonist already exhausted by many attacks. The American effort was timely, and gratefully received, but the doughboy did not have to suffer any major defeat. Whether his efforts turned the tide depends largely on one's point of view, but he certainly fought in a period when the Allies obviously were on the way to eventual victory. However, there was glory enough for all.

The strength of all the European powers was reaching a point of exhaustion by the spring of 1918, as four long years of continued fighting and labor to build tremendous war machines had carried them dangerously close to financial and manpower bankruptcy, to say nothing of actual starvation. This last point is not to be denied, since Germany was in a dreadful situation from the British Navy's blockade, and subsequent pages will give a clearer picture of this weapon and its effect on Germany's decision to capitulate. In fact, many sound minds have argued that it was the blockade from the sea that brought the final downfall.

Russia was out of the war, relieving Germany of all military effort in the east; Austria, though never a major factor, held Romania in check and threatened Italy which was still tottering from the disaster of the preceding months. In fact, for the first time since 1914, Germany could release all her forces against France and Britain. The question was, could these two allies withstand one final blow?

Germany had had to face the fact that her proposed spring offensive would be her final one, since this was the last time she could assemble rows of cannon, stacks of ammunition, and columns of "cannon fodder." General von Ludendorff made a stirring appeal for this contribution of men and munitions, an effort he knew would require at least 400,000 soldiers; but if Paris could be captured, France would be defeated and the British Army would be glad to scramble back across the Channel.

But there was one fly in the ointment. Although he had little respect for America as a military nation, General von Ludendorff wondered if she could send enough *competent* fighting men across the Atlantic and have them in the line in time to offset the reinforcements he now could draw from the Russian front. Great Britain was still strong in the air and on the sea, but he presumed that her armies had passed the zenith of their power. While General von Ludendorff pondered, President Wilson announced his famous Fourteen Points that raised the hopes of the Allies in clear, unequivocal words. The President made it unmistakable that America was fighting for a just peace for all the fighting nations; a stand France and Great Britain adopted, and overnight Woodrow Wilson was the acknowledged political leader of the Allied countries.

Germany also hoped for such a peace, but, obeying his soldier's instincts, Ludendorff decided to strike before America could put a military force on the Western Front. He made his move in what became known to the British as the Battle of Picardy, a bold thrust over a fifty-mile front in the region where the Battle of the Somme had been fought in 1916 when the Germans had been forced to retreat to their prepared Hindenburg line.

General von Ludendorff selected his battlefield well, for the British were not too strongly entrenched in this sector. The area between the Scarpe and the Oise Rivers had been taken over from the French, a relief gesture that was magnanimous in spirit, but far from realistic in purpose. General Haig had had to reduce the strength of his divisions from twelve to nine battalions, and Lloyd George was still keeping a great number of reserves in England, chiefly to prevent Haig from opening another offensive. Also, Haig had partly adopted the "flexible" front-line system in which forward trenches were lightly held while the "battle zone" some two miles behind was to be strengthened with pillboxes, machine-gun posts, and heavy wire defenses. The third, or reserve, zone was never completed, and mismanagement of the battle zone was penalized with losses and defeats.

General von Ludendorff turned loose forty-seven divisions against twenty-six available to General Haig, and after a shattering bombardment that opened at 4:40 A.M. on March 21 in which many gas shells were included, the Germans started to move forward. Dense fog added to the defenders' problems, for they were already compelled to wear gas masks, and whole parties of Germans passed through the British lines unnoticed. When the enemy's main body was encountered a stiff defense was put up, but was soon overpowered; the forward zone was overrun by nightfall as was much of the battle zone, and many British divisions were cut to pieces. Disaster was in the air as the Germans, under skilled generalship and clever tactics, appeared to be moving on to a major victory.

General Haig released four reserve divisions, and when the fog lifted British flying men roared out to put the brakes on the advance. In fact, it was the Royal Flying Corps that showed the greatest resistance, as any aircraft that could carry fragmentation bombs was sent into the air to deny the enemy the way. But the enemy plunged on, regardless of casualties, as they fought over territory they remembered well, and pushed back General Gough's Fifth Army for four miles.

The French to the south tried to rush in troops to fill a gap, but once in the line, and with their artillery dug in, they made no effort to counterattack, and again it was the low-flying Royal Flying Corps that kept the enemy from pouring through the open gaps. Although willing to move French troops into this area, General Henri Pétain was reluctant to risk too much action because he feared the enemy might attack along his front, using the thrust against the British as a diversionary move. In all probablity he was reserving his forces for a withdrawal to defend Paris, for he believed that if matters became critical, General Haig would fall back to defend the Channel ports and leave the road to Paris wide open.

This divergence of opinions and objectives resulted in a hurried French-British conference at Doullens, presided over by President Raymond Poincaré. The meeting was attended by Lord Alfred Milner, new Secretary of State for War, Sir Henry Wilson, the new C-in-C, General Haig and his general staff commander, as well as General Pétain, General Foch, and Louis Loucheur, France's Minister of Munitions. After a soul-searching conference, all concerned agreed that an over-all commander was necessary if the Germans were to be beaten. General Foch was selected and charged by both the British and French governments with the "co-ordination of the action of the Allied Armies on the Western Front." This was on March 26, and by April 3, the American Generals, John J. Pershing and Tasker H. Bliss, added their signatures to the document. General Foch was accorded the title of "General-in-Chief of the Allied Armies in France" on April 14.

Having been beaten back by overwhelming numbers, the British Army was soon separated from the strong forces before Arras to the north, but by determined fighting and some good fortune set up by the natural difficulties of the early spring season—and the condition of the bombarded roads—the Tommies delayed the German push, and saved themselves from being completely surrounded.

One disastrous-looking gap appeared in the front of the Fifth Army just south of Hamel where the enemy had a clear path for a sweep southwestward. There seemed to be no fighting troops to rush into this breach, but General Gough made a desperate appeal to hold this gap at any cost. To whom this appeal was addressed is a mystery; however, in this area a number of American engineers had been "on loan" for instruction purposes, and were brigaded temporarily with the Canadians and British. This was under the British Brigadier General Sanderson Carey, who had been on leave in England, and on his return searched for his old headquarters and learned of the tragic condition. A veteran of the Boer War, General Carey immediately rounded up anyone who could lift a rifle. He took cooks, bakers, road pioneers, truck drivers, and chauffeurs and had them hauled up to the line in anything on wheels. In one instance he discovered a storehouse of machine guns intended for a machine-gun school. These were taken out of their cases and a handful of Americans and Canadians were given a crash course in machine-gun operation, with NCOs reading from the instruction books as they churned up to the line.

This heroic detachment held the gap, which by then was more than a mile wide, for two days, and then their temporary commander collapsed with exhaustion. So General Carey took over and led this motley column through a number of attacks and counterattacks that left no time for sleeping or eating. They moved about like wraiths, firing belt after belt, chiefly for effect, and in this manner delayed the enemy for hours. Whenever the Germans probed to learn the strength of this opposition at any one point, General Carey would make a thrust elsewhere, and the Jerries would pull back in bewilderment. This ragtag outfit hung on for six days fighting like men possessed, and whenever the enemy gained some ground, Carey led a refreshed company against them and stalled the drive. They were still full of fight when they were relieved by a fresh battalion that marched up from the rear.

The push rolled on for several days; village after village was overrun, and south of Saint-Quentin the British line sagged ominously. General Gough then ordered a general retirement back to the line of the Somme, a decision that was made after an erroneous report indicated that the enemy was already across the Crozat Canal at Jussy and threatened his right flank. The Péronne bridgehead was abandoned next, and indifferent communications led to several more misunderstandings. Fortunately, General von Ludendorff made some mistakes, too, and missed several openings that had been offered, and his generals, who saw the glory road wide open, were ordered to hold their ground.

Early in April, General Ludendorff tried once more, but

his luck, and the discipline of his storm troops had run out. The Rock of Arras had splintered his lance, and he himself had been unable to mastermind his forces and take advantage of the many opportunities offered him. Thus, as pointed out by Liddell Hart, beneath the surface of military statistics and battlefield acreage of the defeat suffered in the March push, lay a psychological victory.

## The Paris Gun

An indication of the desperation of the German cause may be noted in the introduction of what could be called their secret weapon of World War I. It will be remembered that when the Allies successfully invaded the Normandy peninsula in 1944, Hitler hurriedly turned his V-1 buzz bombs against London and the southeast section of Britain. In 1918, two days after the big push of March opened, German artillery experts pulled the lanyard on a monster gun and shelled Paris, seventy-six miles away. This was followed by others of the same size at twenty-minute intervals that lasted for several hours. These shells had no particular military importance, but they did kill a number of civilians, mostly women and children.

This weapon, designed by a General Rohne, who was an artillery expert, was an assembled job in that the 15-inch barrels were composed of two parts, the main sections being 98 feet long, and the forward tubes 20 feet. The barrels were first bored out, and heavy, uniformly rifled tubes, 8.26 inches in diameter, were inserted. More than 40 feet of these tubes projected beyond the original muzzles, and added to this length of rifled tubing were muzzle sections 26 feet in length that were threaded to the ends of the projecting tubes. They were unrifled at this point, and probably were added to impart additional lineal velocity, or better to align the axis of the projectiles with that of the bore of the guns. About seven of these weapons were constructed, and their bombardment of Paris was timed to open with the German military attack of March 21.

After that first salvo, Paris was shelled again on Palm Sunday,

March 24, and the following Good Friday was marked by another savage bombardment. On this day when most of the churches were filled, one of the houses of worship was struck and 76 people were killed and 90 wounded. These long-range attacks continued almost daily until May.

In the meantime, Allied aviators had discovered some of these guns that were located behind Saint-Gobain Forest not far from La Fère. A few days later the positions of two others were found, and it was then discovered that three more gun emplacements were on the reverse slope of a wooded hill between the Laon-La Fère railroad and the Laon-La Fère road where they were sheltered by trees.

Whenever one of the big guns was fired, a number of 17-cm guns in the vicinity were fired simultaneously to cushion the sound of the larger explosion. When Allied airmen were seen approaching, the antiaircraft guns were brought into action, and volumes of smoke discharged to prevent any pinpoint observation. The long gun tube was not elevated until it was ready for firing, and the gun crews were sheltered in a bombproof dugout. The distance of these gun pits from the actual French line was six miles, and the French heavy guns capable of countering them were two miles farther back. Thus, in retaliation, they were firing over a range of eight miles—quite a distance for accurate aiming—but on March 26 a French shell struck one of the emplacements and put one of the big guns out of action. Other artillery shells and air bombs were contributed, but these inflicted little damage.

May 3, 1918, was a day of unusually clear visibility that permitted continuous observation and concentrated fire by French heavy guns, and most of the Paris guns were silenced until May 27 when a few more desultory shots were fired. General Rohne claimed that had these weapons been obtainable earlier they could have been trained on both Paris and London and might have forced peace on Germany's foes. The same hope was expressed concerning Hitler's V-1 and V-2 missiles sent against Great Britain late in World War II.

## With Backs to the Wall

Early in April General von Ludendorff made a new thrust against the British, this time in the Lys Valley just south of Ypres. During the winter this territory had been flooded to a large extent, but by spring the water had seeped out, leaving patches of marsh and treacherous footing that were horrors to foot soldiers. The northern sector afforded a gradual rise in the ground that was topped by strategic mounds at Kemmel and Cassel. Still looking over his shoulder, fearing the arrival of thousands of American troops, Ludendorff ordered the new attack for April 9, once he thought the Lys area provided substantial footing. This thrust continued until the last day of that month.

Making his plans in the hope that Haig would withdraw troops from Flanders to hold Saint-Quentin, Ludendorff sent his troops over the top along the line from Armentières to La Bassée, and although the sector was pock-marked and beaten to a morass by shellfire, they succeeded in breaking through a sector held by the 2nd Portuguese Division. Apparently these new allies panicked and fled from the battlefield, and when the British 51st and 50th Divisions tried to move up to dam this breach, they were hindered by these Portuguese and many shattered vehicles, and could not reach their positions. Some military sources indicate that the Portuguese had been in the line for a long stretch and were awaiting relief; at any rate it was their hurried departure that caused the initial breakthrough.

Despite the bad road conditions, the Lys was crossed at two points by nightfall, and after several days of hauling up supplies, the Germans took Estaires on April 10, and some ground was gained northwest of Armentières. Wytschaete was threatened, and the much-battered Messines again was in German hands.

It was at this point, on April 11, that General Haig issued his most famous Order of the Day, a historic document *intended only for his troops:*

There is no other course open to us but to fight it out.
Every position must be held to the last man; there must be
no retirement. With our backs to the wall, and believing
in the justice of our cause, each one of us must fight on to
the end. The safety of our homes and the freedom of man-
kind depend alike upon the conduct of each one of us at
this critical moment.

This simply was an order to all British troops, not an appeal
to the civilized nations. Haig was putting the situation clearly
as an incentive to make a stand, but the phrase "with our backs
to the wall" was picked up in many anti-British newspapers,
and by the Berlin Radio, and distorted into a frantic appeal
for immediate help from anyone! In many circles in Washington, it was expressed widely to justify America's entry into the
war, and over the following years was lifted out of context to
present evidence of Britain's hopeless position.

The circumstances on that particular sector were far from
satisfactory, but the Royal Navy still had its blockade noose
on German food supplies, the Royal Air Force—the recent
amalgamation of the Royal Flying Corps and the Royal Naval
Air Service—was pounding the Richthofen Circus to tumbling
wreckage, and German statesmen admitted later that their
armies were fighting only for a chance to glean a few meager
scraps from some future peace conference. It is interesting to
note that General Sir Arthur W. Currie, commanding Canadian troops, made a similar statement in an order to his forces,
but no mention of his appeal was ever made in the newspapers.
He even added: "You will advance or fall where you stand facing the enemy. You will not die, but step into immortality. Your
mothers will not lament your fate, but will have been proud to
have borne such sons. With God's help you shall achieve victory
once more."

The Germans continued their success, chiefly by force of numbers. They had 137 artillery batteries in the area, and their
infantry divisions outnumbered their enemies at least two to

one. They had to capture Mont Kemmel which had plagued them for months. They made diversionary thrusts against the French that always were repulsed, but after several days of assault by fresh troops withdrawn from Italy, Transylvania, and Albania, Kemmel was stormed and taken, a blow that shook Allied troops more than the war correspondents realized at the time.

Ludendorff next turned toward Cassel where, if success could be gained, the whole Anglo-Belgian front in Flanders would be turned and swung to the west. By now the Germans were seeing themselves in the all-important Channel ports, but it was here that Ludendorff made his final mistake. Instead of continuing his successful "infiltration" thrusts, searching for weak spots, encircling the stronger positions to cut them off from their bases, he resumed mass attacks and met bloody and costly failure. The British Army held long enough to be all but destroyed, but had snatched and held a great victory with immense courage. Even the Belgians who had not taken part in any major action since 1914 attacked from the Ypres-Staden railroad positions and ejected many German regiments from ground gained early in the battle. Seven French divisions were contributed by General Foch and these held reserve positions behind the British front in Flanders, and in several instances later took actual part in the front-line defense and counterattacks, assisting greatly in the heavy loss inflicted on the Germans.

When this great assault had run down, a General von Gaedke, a noted German military critic, explained that Ludendorff's failure to break through was to be found in the fact that the whole country as far as, and even beyond, Paris consisted of lines of trenches, one behind the other, and added that the Allies had used more barbed wire than in a whole year previously. General von Gaedke, of course, ignored the "previously prepared positions" to which the Germans had retreated after the Battle of the Somme.

In cold consideration, the Battle of the Lys was a failure. Some German reviewers have stated that strategically it was a worse failure than the March offensive. The German divisions that had been drawn from the Russian front received a severe shock when they faced the British, for the enemy to the east had not fought with such tenacity. No matter which side claimed "victory" both suffered about 350,000 casualties.

## America's First Battles

As had been long expected, the German Army began its March push with a drive over a fifty-mile front, but during this assault General Pershing's 1st, 2nd, and 42nd (Rainbow) Divisions were resting in a comparatively quiet sector on the French front. When the German push in the north posed such serious threats, Pershing offered to move any of these divisions into any available breach, but before this gesture could be put into operation, the German drive ran out of steam and the immediate danger was over. However, Major General Omar Bundy's 2nd Division was in a threatened area that faced some of the finest of the Kaiser's army.

Another big-gun shelling of Paris ushered in a new German thrust aimed at the French along the Chemin des Dames. The Cantigny sector was very active at this time, and unusually heavy artillery fire made any preparations for an attack difficult. Even while digging a jump-off area, straightening trenches, and moving forward any machine-gun emplacements, many casualties were suffered. However, the United States 26th Infantry under Colonel Hanson E. Ely, supported by French artillery and some small tanks, drew this assignment.

After a short artillery barrage, the U.S. infantry advanced on a front nearly a mile wide, and quickly captured the village of Cantigny and some adjacent heights. French heavies, flamethrowers, and aircraft had prepared much of the way, and the American doughboys, as they were known in that war, scrambled up from their slots, just as they had done in dozens of previous exercises. They held their formations and moved in perfect timing with the barrage creeping ahead of them. French tanks nosed in and out, back and forth, and the infantry made the most of the cover they offered.

The minute the shelling stopped on the lower end of Cantigny, the Americans were seen entering the town, still moving
in precise waves and artful rushes. Headquarters officers sat at
their telephones and took down the reports as they came
through. Every unit was accounted for, the number of prisoners taken, and the battle charts were kept up to the minute.
Headquarters then learned that the doughboys had passed
through Cantigny, while the second and third waves were mop-
ping up according to plan. Exactly on time, the Americans
reached their objective in front of the town with a loss of less
than one hundred men. Three hundred and fifty prisoners were
taken in this American unit's first actual offensive.

Everyone concerned felt that at last some of General
Pershing's troops were full-fledged soldiers. Even the wounded
were proud of their accomplishments, and confident that when
they had recovered they would once again fix bayonets and
take any sector they desired, and this indomitable spirit vital-
ized everyone.

While supply trains, ambulances, and more artillery support
moved up, the Germans set up their retaliation, and since they
knew every inch of the ground they had lost, they could zero
in hundreds of guns and pour out a combined bombardment
of shrapnel and poison gas. The old method of releasing tanks
of chlorine, and trusting a friendly breeze to carry the lethal
vapor into the enemy's areas seldom was used; now chlorine
and lachrymatory (gas that blinded temporarily) were usually
delivered by artillery fire.

A storm of eight-inch shells arched over from the Germans'
back sector and churned the ground captured by the Americans, forcing the doughboys to discard their rifles and use their
entrenching tools to dig in against this savage pounding that
went on for three days. More casualties were suffered, but
there was no retreating as they hung on to what they had
gained. The enemy counterattacked again and again, but French
artillery and American rifles and machine guns hammered him
back as fast as he climbed over his parapet. Cantigny received

the brunt of the heavy German guns and within a few days was as devastated as any town along the Ypres front, but the Americans had scored a definite victory.

## The Trial of Château-Thierry

Meanwhile another German offensive opened on May 27 in front of the Marne town of Château-Thierry when thirty fresh divisions were unleashed in what was a complete surprise attack, considering that only two months before the Germans had had to stop their March push owing to their terrible losses. This new attack was so sudden, the French did not have time to destroy important bridges over the Aisne and Vesle Rivers, and the Germans captured Soissons by May 31, and reached the Marne where apparently they halted to re-form and consolidate. This assault had carried them a distance of thirty miles and seemed headed unhindered for Paris. Not only that, the enemy had captured 60,000 prisoners, 650 guns, and 2000 machine guns, some aviation material, and vast quantities of ammunition and other supplies; in other words this was far from an orderly retirement, or a masterly strategic retreat. It was a rout.

At the height of this alarming situation General Pétain appealed to General Pershing for troops to take over the Château-Thierry sector, if only to slow the German drive. The United States 3rd Division, then in training at Chaumont, was the only one within reach of this particular sector, and was ordered to move north immediately.

On the afternoon of May 30, Major General Joseph T. Dickman, in command of the 3rd Division, ordered a motorized machine-gun battalion to move out ahead while the infantry and engineers entrained in railroad trucks that same night. Their supply trains moved over the roads aboard their own motor transport.

It was this 7th Machine-Gun Battalion that reached Château-Thierry first and went into action on the afternoon of May 31.

The gunners defended the river crossing and held the southern end of the town until more Americans could move in. All available weapons were in position by early morning, and one company held the main traffic bridge while another prevented the enemy from using the railroad crossing, and as this action was being fought, infantry of the division were moved into the French line as reinforcements, and covered a front ten miles in breadth.

The Germans attacked repeatedly on June 3–4 with hand grenades, machine guns, and shock troops, but failed to dislodge the newcomers, although dominating every height, patch of gorse, or wood. Every hill was crested with long-range artillery that could command each yard of territory, and the military situation was, and continued to be, critical. No Allied troops could be moved, no supplies transported, or defense work carried out in the daytime without drawing accurate enemy fire.

In order to improve their position the Marines opened an offensive, and took Bouresches with great spirit on June 6, and held it against several desperate counterattacks. They were only partly successful, however, in moving on to a more important objective to the north, namely, Belleau Wood, a forest nearly a mile square that was matted with dense undergrowth. It also was entrenched and held by elite German infantry whose machine-gun posts and trench mortars were well camouflaged and strongly supported by artillery. As fast as the Marines captured one machine-gun nest, they discovered that the same position was covered by another automatic-weapon post.

Knowing that they were on trial, the Marines refused to be denied, and despite heavy casualties gained a foothold in the wood that they never relinquished. Two subsequent assaults in the following week gained some ground, but again the cost was high, and the Leatherneck contingent had to be relieved by the 7th Infantry of the 3rd Division. When they had rested and their depleted ranks had been filled with replacements, the Marines returned and succeeded in capturing all of Belleau

Wood by June 29, taking more than one thousand prisoners and dozens of machine guns.

At the same time the United States 2nd Division was near Chaumont-en-Vexin, and was ordered to relieve Major General Robert L. Bullard's 1st Division at Cantigny, but on the night of May 31 the orders were changed, and, moving by trucks, the 2nd Division was rushed toward Meaux. Using this town as a jump-off point, the division started for Château-Thierry, making its way as best it could through crowds of civilian refugees and retreating French troops who gave the impression that nothing could stop the enemy drive. No one seemed to know the situation at the front, or what units, if any, were still fighting.

Making the best of circumstances, General Bundy first deployed his 2nd Division infantry and Marines across the highway leading to Paris near Lucy-le-Bocage, and gave support to two French divisions that withdrew through the American lines a short while later. This withdrawal was completed by June 4, and the Germans found they were attacking new, fresh troops who wore American uniforms. All these enemy assaults were repulsed, and by June 6 the 2nd Division began diversionary attacks that recaptured several important points and straightened out one or two salients.

This sudden and dramatic appearance of the U.S. 2nd and 3rd divisions, backing up the shattered Allied line, combined with the dash and spirit of the newcomers, must have brought encouragement to weary veterans who had been engaged in this type of warfare for nearly four years. Although it was the first full battle trial for the Americans, they fought like experienced soldiers, held their positions, and unquestionably stopped the German rush toward Paris, but more important their performance put the lie to enemy propaganda that had long downgraded the American effort. The Germans now had met Pershing's troops at Cantigny, Belleau Wood, and Château-Thierry, and the newcomers had carried the day everywhere.

*Germany's Blackest Day*

A distinct turn in the tide was met in France's victory, known as the Second Battle of the Marne, a success that raised General Foch to the rank of marshal. This campaign, it must be said, began with the American stand at Château-Thierry and extended until August 6 when the doughboys capped this climax with a drive that surged across the Vesle River. A series of defensive battles burst into a storm of aggressive attacks by July 18 when Foch unleashed General Charles M. E. Mangin's Tenth Army south of Soissons, and again the American 1st and 2nd Divisions had an important part. This assault was initiated without the usual artillery barrage, and the German line was overwhelmed by this unexpected swarm.

The Germans soon brought up reinforcements, and when Mangin's troops were stayed by the enemy's strength of numbers, General Jean M. J. Degoutte's Sixth Army, strengthened by troops from General Pershing's reserves, carried the fighting well into August, or until the dangerous Marne salient was wiped out.

Farther north the British began their historic drive for the Hindenburg line, a day that General von Ludendorff cited later as the "blackest day of the war." On August 8, 1918, the British opened their Battle of Amiens, and their drive to recover all they had lost the March before. It also supplemented the tremendous Franco-American drive begun almost a month previous.

The Battle of Amiens was a true "famous victory," in that it showed British arms at their best. It was brilliantly planned and fought; 16,000 prisoners were captured the first day, and 21,000 before the first rush was completed. These figures do not indicate how economical this attack was, or the excellence of its over-all strategy, but its initial penetration of from six to eight miles had a severe effect on German morale. Only twelve miles were gained ultimately, but this skillful thrust completely disorganized the German High Command. The Kaiser grumbled,

"I see that we must strike a balance. We are at the end of our resources. The war must be ended." Ludendorff thankfully agreed.

This victory was scored against Prince Rupprecht's army of 250,000 fresh troops, backed by reserves from the divisions of the Crown Prince of Bavaria. General Haig had to decide whether this opposition was strong enough to halt any new British advance, but once the attack was started, the enemy seemed unable to stop it, and the tide of the war turned in an astonishing manner. The initiative was completely in the hands of the British, and in addition to the number of prisoners, they also quickly took five hundred guns, and were in full stride to capture more.

This defeat, so shocking to German morale, created a great change in the minds of the Tommies, for to Mr. Atkins, taking territory seemed unimportant; he was more impressed with his own ability, and proof that he could get on with the war business, and acquire a quick victory. This climax came sooner than he could have hoped, as it is on record that Douglas Haig was making plans for the final campaign to be fought through the spring of 1919.

The Canadian Corps had a vital share in this victory, as did the United States 27th and 30th Divisions of the II Corps that had been working with British divisions through several probing operations. Later on, well into September, these American divisions together with the Australian Corps took part in the final assault on the Hindenburg line, particularly where the Saint-Quentin Canal passes through a tunnel under a ridge. Here Major General George W. Read's 30th Division skillfully broke through the main line of defense, taking all objectives, while Major General John F. O'Ryan's 27th Division rushed on impetuously until some of its elements had entered Gouy. Their spirit and aggressiveness were praised highly by British Army commanders under whom they served.

With the success that began on August 8, and timing their strokes with the Franco-American actions along the Marne, the

British continued their plunges until on August 26 the Canadians had the honor of breaking the Hindenburg line, and the complete clearing of that lengthy bastion was accomplished by September 29.

## The Spectral Soccer Player

Around this time another front-line legend was passed from regiment to regiment. The East Surreys have one that will not down, nor can any explanation for it be discovered. This tale has many of the features of the Pipe Major of Polygon Wood, but in this instance the central character was clearly identified.

The East Surrey infantrymen were awaiting an order to go over the top early in the Battle of Amiens. As the whistle sounded, and they clambered over the sandbag parapet, they were startled to see a man in soccer shorts and striped jersey bouncing a ball. As they darted through the gaps in the wire, the figure began to dribble the ball, and, ignoring the enemy gunfire, the East Surreys joined in the fun as they darted across no man's land.

The ball was passed back and forth, with the soccer player encouraging them on. Men who fell wounded, staggered to their feet somehow and again lunged for the ball, and when at last the East Surreys reached the German trenches where more deadly activity was required, the soccer player vanished, and no trace of him was ever found.

In this case, however, practically every man in the battalion recognized the specter as a star player who once had played for Croydon; a man named Weldon who in 1913 had won his International cap, meaning he had played for England against Scotland and Wales.

The unexplained point to this legend is that Weldon was killed in 1915 while serving with the noted Sportsman's Battalion. Nevertheless, whenever the East Surreys went over the top after that, their officers always tossed a new soccer ball into no man's land as the whistle blew.

*Success at Saint-Mihiel . . . Anguish of the Argonne . . .*
*Sergeant Alvin C. York . . . The Lost Battalion . . . Foul-*
*up at Sedan . . . Final Drive to Victory.*

## Success at Saint-Mihiel

Early in September the American forces began a drive that
was aimed to wipe out a hateful salient of high ground around
Saint-Mihiel that had thwarted every French attempt for several
years. Everyone knew this Yank attack had been in the making
for weeks since General Pershing had requested this particular
task, and Paris newspapers, possibly hoping to use the old taunt
of "I told you so," published his plans and intentions. There
was no need for a Mata Hari. Swiss newspapers picked up the
story, and German publications soon added the date and time
of jump-off. But even with this advance warning the enemy was
caught unaware.

The artillery opened with 3000 guns at one o'clock on the
morning of September 12, and roared for three hours. Then the
new, fully organized U. S. First Army, under the command of
General Pershing, climbed out of its trenches and advanced
deliberately across the pulverized ground. The creeping barrage
moved up, and as the first wave of Yanks disappeared in a
low-lying mist, the second and third waves followed.

But the salient was wide, and newcomers from New Jersey
and Delaware waited their turn to prove their worth. Only a
few months before these warriors had edited newspapers, paved
streets, sold fish, or picked fruits and vegetables on America's

farms. Gerneral Pershing, who stood on a hill just behind the jump-off line, knew that his military future was staked on what would happen here, but there was little he could do once his boys started across no man's land.

The Americans fought with skill and determination, and twenty-fours hours later two sharp, bayonet-tipped forceps cut into the side of the salient, met midway, and the bulk of the threatening fang was removed. No victory in the American effort was more complete or more successful than this operation that was wholly Pershing's. Both assaults were wildly successful as the entire area was caught in the pincerlike clutch. The defenders, 100,000 strong, made a hurried retreat as the two attacking forces pressed forward until they met at Vigneulles, located at the center of the base of the salient, pinching off 20,000 enemy troops, a few of whom escaped, but the majority surrendered willingly.

The import of this Saint-Mihiel battle is found in the statistics. On the opening day 16,000 prisoners and 443 guns were taken, but American losses were less than 8000 men killed, wounded, or missing. General Pershing's triumph brought the German-held Briey iron fields into a position where they were exposed to Allied attack both from Verdun and the new Woëvre front established by the Americans. Iron being an essential product in Germany's economic life, she could not continue the struggle without an unlimited source of the ore, and it was this fear that led Ludendorff to miscalculate the direction of the next American attack. He expected a thrust east of the Meuse within two weeks, and when Pershing moved toward the west, Ludendorff's reserves were trapped behind Briey, a situation that contributed to the initial success at the Argonne.

Armchair strategists have pointed out since, that once the Saint-Mihiel attack was well under way, the American forces were hampered by a serious breakdown in transport facilities. This was true, but the assault had been arranged with some hurried planning and an emergency army. A technically perfect job hardly could be expected. The lack of training and experience had to be made up for with sacrifices and courage—massed strength substituted for a finished effort. There was a scarcity of everything at Saint-Mihiel, but raw courage.

Saint-Mihiel was America's answer at the gathering of the Allied military staffs prior to the final battles of the war. It was not just another date in her history, it represented the result on which the respective governments had staked their hopes, the richly deserved reward of all who had collaborated for more than a year. Henceforward, the American forces were considered to be capable of undertaking any major operation.

## Anguish of the Argonne

The victory at Saint-Mihiel brought new responsibilities and an opportunity to have a leading role in a forthcoming Allied convergent attack, a thrust designed to bring the war to a close. But Saint-Mihiel also put a difficult burden on the newly organized American staff, since the First Army had but two weeks in which to mop up the battlefield, and then transfer its forces to another sector, take over new lines on a different front, and prepare to fight an even greater action.

There has been considerable discussion as to whether the Argonne Forest battle need have been fought. However, when General Pershing conferred with Marshal Foch in September concerning this great plan that carried the hopes of a successful converging attack by all Allied armies, he was given the choice of fighting in the Champagne sector or along the Meuse-Argonne. Why he selected the latter is not clear, since he admitted later, "The area between the Meuse River and the Argonne Forest was ideal for defensive fighting," meaning that it was the sector where the toughest opposition would be met.

Pershing also explained that when the over-all plan was discussed no one present even hinted that the end of the war was at hand, and when the general attack opened on September 26, Germany's first appeal for an armistice was only one week away—October 3. Prince Maximilian of Baden sent a message to

President Wilson stating that the German government was willing to accept the conditions set forth by the President in his message to Congress on January 8, 1918. Apparently after some discussion with other Allied leaders, President Wilson replied on October 23 that he could not now consider peace negotiations, only surrender. With that, the Germans begged for an armistice on October 27.

In other words, further fighting could have been halted by that date, but the carnage continued until the morning of November 11, adding fifteen days to the bloody conflict that took untold lives.

The converging feature of this plan had the British armies, supported by the French on the left, continuing their assault toward Cambrai. The center of the French armies west of Reims would carry on with the actions already under way to drive the Germans past Amiens. The American Army, flanked on the right by the French, would direct its attack on Sedan and attempt to capture a vital railroad system that ran between Sedan and Mézières.

After the Saint-Mihiel salient had been nipped off, Marshal Foch decided that the converging plan, originated by General Haig, should be attempted, and when Pershing accepted the responsibility for the Meuse-Argonne front, the marshal could withdraw a quarter of a million French soldiers from the area taken over by the Americans.

The cutting of the Carignan-Sedan-Mézières railroad that was connected to a transport junction at Lille, might prove to be the most important strategic blow of the campaign; if this line could be severed before the German armies facing the French and British could withdraw to the east of it, their problems of supply would be so difficult, an orderly withdrawal might be turned into a rout. The railroad was about thirty miles from where the Americans would make their jump-off.

The area to be taken lay between the unfordable Meuse and the rough wooded hills of the elaborately fortified Argonne Forest. A defile, some fifteen miles in width at one point, stretched out to twenty-five at the village of Buzancy. The high points of the Meuse looked down on a valley to the west and across the broad plain of Woëvre to the east, thus providing observation and positions from which the Germans could deliver heavy oblique fire all along the west bank of the Meuse River. The River Aire also skirted the Argonne, and was fordable in only a few places. The eastern edge of the forest dominated its valley and any batteries located there could cover the German right flank and cross their fire with that of the batteries dug in along the west bank of the Meuse.

The watershed between the Meuse and the Argonne Forest is a massive, sharply crested mound that runs from the southeast to the northwest, and the heights of Montfaucon, Romagne, Cunel, and the wood at Barricourt are natural strong points along or near this axis. Not only could the entire open country south from the enemy positions be seen from their elevations, but the watershed crest divided the twenty-mile front into two parts, offering cross fire both ways. In other words, the Americans had assumed the problem of forcing two defiles.

To all these difficulties was added the lack of roads. The one good highway from the north to the south passed down the valley of the Aire that was wide open and exposed to direct observation and fire of the enemy. The only other passable road was one that followed the Meuse Valley from the American front northward, and this was dominated even more completely by German artillery. Between these two roads a single country lane crawled in and out among the hills from the American front through Montfaucon to the ultimate German position. This track was unsuitable for motorized traffic, and was promptly put out of use by shellfire.

There also was the problem of communications. This American Army, well in excess of 250,000 men, required enormous amounts of munitions and supplies, to say nothing of the strength of artillery needed to support it. Medical stations, and ambulances to evacuate the wounded were necessary, as well as thousands of replacements to keep the various divisions up to strength. Many first-class roads could have been used, but those available did not begin to handle this tremendous traffic.

Once the jump-off was made on September 26, the American soldiers had to move through the tangle and debris of previous battles. The Battle of Verdun had been fought here, and Dead Man's Hill and Hill 304 that marked the limit of the German advance, were the points of departure. It is almost impossible to describe the devastation and destruction that faced the doughboys.

The Germans had ten divisions in the line at the opening of the battle, and an equal number in reserve on the front between Fresnes-en-Woëvre and the forest. They had been expecting a continuation of the American Saint-Mihiel push toward Metz, but a number of ruses had been staged, and French troops were retained as a screen along the new American front until the night before the jump-off, all of which conspired to set up a tactical surprise. The operations in the Meuse-Argonne actually formed a continuous whole, but they extended over such a long period of fighting, they have to be considered in three phases, the first running from September 26 to October 3, the second from October 4 to October 31, and the last from November 1 to November 11.

Nine divisions went over the top with the opening of the first phase, and headed out over country lying between the Meuse and the western edge of the Argonne Forest. The idea was to attack and make a deep penetration in the center that, with the French Fourth Army advancing west of the Argonne, would force the enemy to evacuate the forest without its being necessary to deliver an all-out attack in that difficult sector.

After a heavy opening bombardment, and with the support of a number of light tanks, the Americans made some headway over the first two days, or until the enemy brought up trained reserves. Montfaucon was taken after a hard fight by noon of September 28, and a continued frontal attack also captured a few small villages, but the enemy hung on tenaciously in the

Argonne. He produced heavy artillery fire and deadly machine-gun enfilade, and by nightfall of September 29 several
American divisions had to be relieved due to heavy casualties.
Again, the lack of communications for supplies, and the evacuation of the wounded hampered all forward movement. Reserves
were brought in over the next few days and more divisions
were relieved as the engineers and pioneers effected some
substitute for roads.

The attack was renewed on October 4 when it was learned
that the Germans now had sixteen divisions in their defense line.
Bitter fighting continued but only small advances were made.
The American troops worked to drive the enemy out of the
forest and at the same time make him fight to hold his positions
along the heights east of the Meuse. Many kinds of diversionary
thrusts were staged while trying to outflank the enemy in the
forest. The French XVII Corps opened an attack east of the
Meuse against the point on which the Germans would have to
pivot in order to withdraw from northern France. These troops
encountered elaborate fortifications and stubborn resistance, but
by nightfall had advanced six kilometers to a line well within
the Bois de Consenvoye that included the villages of Beaumont
and Haumont.

### Sergeant Alvin C. York

One of the many heroes of the Argonne attack was thirty-one-
year-old Alvin Cullum York of Pall Mall, Tennessee. An elder in
a little mountain church, this man of simple faith, who was inspired with the idea of serving only God, was deeply disturbed
when his country declared war on Germany, but he kept an
open mind, studied the situation, absorbed the history of Germany's treachery, and finally went into the Army with no
qualms. By October 8, 1918, he had advanced to the rank of
sergeant, and on that day, according to an official citation, his
section went into action against the entrenched enemy. He was
told to reach a certain objective, which he did after killing 25

Germans, capturing 135 more, cleaning out 35 enemy machine-gun nests, and in a counterattack wiping out an entire battalion. Sergeant York was awarded the Congressional Medal of Honor and the Distinguished Service Cross for this exploit, and the French bestowed the Croix de Guerre on this Tennessee elder.

Today, Sergeant York is somewhat of a legendary character, and his exploits have been chronicled in many publications and depicted on the motion-picture screen. Each new presentation adds to or revises his glorious day, and it is now difficult to decide what he actually accomplished, or how much of Sergeant York's fame is fact, and how much legend.

When these honors were bestowed on him his chief concern was whether his church would allow him to continue as an elder, and whether his sweetheart in Tennessee would wait for him to come home. America probably never had such a modest hero.

Sergeant York's daring occurred near Hill 223 in the Argonne. The objective was a railroad two kilometers away that required the crossing of a river and a stream, and the enemy reception was so wicked much of York's small force was knocked out before it reached the halfway point.

"We couldn't worry about them," the sergeant explained afterward. "We had to obey orders and take that railroad."

Using the craft he had learned in the Tennessee hills, York made a detour across the valley until he and his depleted party were behind one of the German strong points, but apparently this was not by intent since the sergeant was within a few yards of the gun before he knew it was there. One of his men excitedly fired at the gun crew and aroused the whole defense area, as other machine guns poured burst after burst into the brush cover, and soon friend and foe were scattering in all directions. Sergeant York sat where he was, however, and with his rifle picked off everyone who acted "hostile," and from all accounts Alvin was "shootin' pretty good."

At this tense moment one of his men wanted to crawl back to his own lines, but the sergeant pointed out that one American was worth at least ten Germans, and induced him to stay. Then

turning from that little dialogue, York saw a German officer leading six or seven men who were charging up a hill with fixed
bayonets. He drew his automatic and knocked them down one
at a time.

When he was interviewed after he reached home at war's end,
Sergeant York added to his report: "Then there was a major
who was lying on his stomach to avoid the machine-gun fire. He
yelled at me in English, saying that if I would stop shooting he
would order all his troops to surrender. So I did."

In this version Sergeant York called in all his men, and they
herded the Germans in front of them and started back to the
American lines. He walked so that he was boxed in by four
German officers, and had the wounded men bring up the rear.
When the enemy major asked the sergeant how many men he
had, he grinned and said, "Plenty!"

As they walked back to the lines, they encountered several
German machine-gun nests, and again the major promised that
if York did not shoot, he would order everyone to surrender. "I
didn't shoot," York explained, "and he made the Jerry gunners
give up. In no time we had 132 of the Germans when we got
back to our own people."

During the whole incident Sergeant York lost six of his men,
and three others were seriously wounded.

Not all action in the Battle of the Argonne was so jocular or
profitable. The Americans fought all along the whole front and
had some real success on their extreme left where they captured
the greater part of the Argonne Forest, but the Germans fought
like tigers, chiefly to set up an orderly retirement farther west to
withdraw their forces from northern France before Pershing's
troops could cut the railroad communications through Sedan.

As this heavy action continued it was seen that there were not
enough replacements to build up divisions that were holding the
advance line. Two American divisions were still with the British
and two more with the French, and General Pershing knew that
if his First Army were to maintain this Argonne attack, he would

need to recall the two divisions operating with the French, and possibly take replacements from United States divisions newly arrived in France.

General Pétain agreed that Pershing sorely needed the two divisions attached to the French, but by this time Foch's forces were fighting hard to keep their attack going, and two other American divisions had to be sent to assist the French who were fighting in Flanders.

The U. S. First Army, with more than a million men, was holding a front of 120 kilometers, and to ease the burden of staff work, a portion of this line was transferred to the newly activated Second Army, under Lieutenant General Robert L. Bullard. On October 16 the command of the First Army was given to Lieutenant General Hunter Liggett, and the Commander in Chief, General Pershing, moved his advance headquarters from Ligny-en-Barrois to Souilly on the Bar-le-Duc road.

By October 14 new, and even heavier, attacks were made along the whole front. Resistance was very strong, but a complex of pillboxes on Côte Dame Marie was captured, and this section of the Hindenburg line was broken. Two other important towns, Cunel and Romagne-sous-Montfaucon were taken, and the line was pushed two kilometers north of Sommerance. Sixteen kilometers had been gained since September 26, and the enemy had had to throw in a total of fifteen reserve divisions.

The Americans had met the best of what remained of Germany's elite troops, and captured much of the enemy's complex defense systems, including that portion of the Hindenburg line. The Argonne was in our hands, and 18,600 prisoners, 370 cannon, over 1000 machine guns, and a great amount of valuable matériel had been taken. The railroad artery through Carignan and Sedan was seriously threatened. But this had taken a high toll. Divisions had had to stay in action and fight to the limit of their strength. Combat troops were retained in the line until they were completely exhausted. Artillery batteries could never be relieved, and when they had fired until there was no rifling left in their barrels, they had to be towed out by trucks. All the horses had been killed or severely injured.

Above all, however, the American soldier had once more shown unbelievable fortitude in this continuous action during inclement weather and in an almost untenable position. This heroic accomplishment was highly newsworthy, but whether it need have been fought will long be debated. Before it was over the U. S. First Army suffered 117,000 casualties, killed and wounded, but on the credit side they captured 26,000 prisoners, 847 cannon, and 3000 machine guns.

## The Lost Battalion

Another epic of the Argonne, the story of the U.S. 77th Division's Lost Battalion, will always remain a highlight of that campaign. This small force was never lost, but it might have been—to the enemy—had it not been for the magnificent stand made by Major Charles W. Whittlesey's 308th Regiment to save itself.

A score of writers have told this story, and one will find a dozen variations of the gallant defense. "The Pocket" provides a colorful background for the male-magazine treatment in which earthy "dese-dems-an-dose" characters are created for the leading roles. On the contrary, such was not the case, as a study of the records, dispatches, and personal letters written by the heroes of this dramatic adventure will prove. They were representative of the best of the American forces, highly intelligent men who understood clearly the situation in which they found themselves, and their behavior was a classic of valor and heroism.

On September 30 the 154th Brigade, with artillery support, had driven the enemy from the crests north of a motor-vehicle depot to a ridge south of the Binarville-la-Viergette road where the Germans moved back into previously prepared positions, opposite the front of the 153rd Brigade, and from these earthworks small groups of machine gunners and snipers made a bold de-

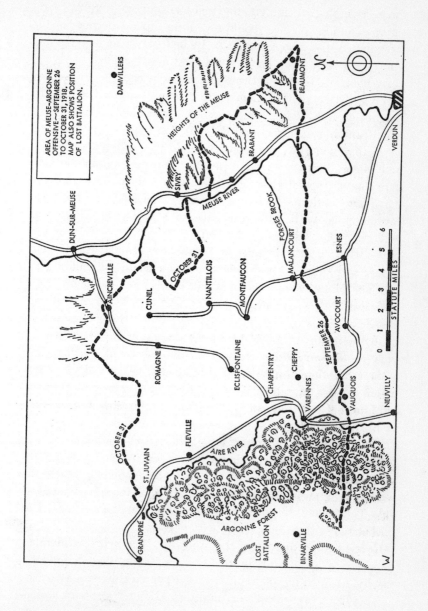

AREA OF MEUSE-ARGONNE
OFFENSIVE—SEPTEMBER 26
TO OCTOBER 31, 1918.
MAP ALSO SHOWS POSITION
OF LOST BATTALION.

DAMVILLERS

HEIGHTS OF THE MEUSE

BEAUMONT

BRABANT

SIVRY

VERDUN

MEUSE RIVER

DUN-SUR-MEUSE

FORGES BROOK

MALANCOURT

OCTOBER 31

NANTILLOIS

MONTFAUCON

ESNES

AINCREVILLE

CUNEL

AVOCOURT

SEPTEMBER 26

ROMAGNE

ECLISFONTAINE

CHARPENTRY

CHEPPY

VARENNES

VAUQUOIS

NEUVILLY

OCTOBER 31

FLEVILLE

AIRE RIVER

ST. JUVAIN

ARGONNE FOREST

GRANDPRÉ

LOST
BATTALION

BINARVILLE

0  1  2  3  4  5  6
STATUTE MILES

fense. Swinging to the left, the 153rd encountered stubborn resistance, and the artillery could give little support because of the crowding of the troops involved. In fact, when any of the big guns were used, they hampered friend and foe alike.

By noon of October 2 the 153rd Brigade had fought its way to an area where the enemy was strongly entrenched on the heights of Bois-de-la Naza, and the opposition was such the Americans were stopped and the situation became most critical.

On that same day the 154th Brigade was ordered to attack, and Major Whittlesey's force penetrated a gap left in the German line, an opening that led them into a deep draw that ran north and south on the left of the brigade sector, and the force continued on with little resistance to a ravine at Charlevaux Mill where it was finally checked.

Whittlesey's six companies had made an advance, carrying out orders to plunge through wherever they could without regard for their flanks. On one side of Whittlesey's force the 307th Regiment was halted by enemy gunfire, and on the other a strong trench system was held by the enemy. When this situation was finally understood, Major Whittlesey was ordered to hold his ravine position until other elements of the line could join him, but a short time later he reported that he was nearly cut off, upon which the 3rd Battalion of the 307th Regiment was sent out to aid him, but only one company of this reinforcement succeeded in breaking through.

Therefore, from October 2–7, Whittlesey's battalion of the 308th Regiment was considered lost, when it actually was only surrounded by Germans and forced to fight against great odds while cut off from supplies of ammunition, food, and medical aid. They were trapped in what later was known as "The Pocket."

Careless reporting after the campaign led many readers to believe that Whittlesey, burdened by a feeling of guilt for having led his men into a trap, was driven to suicide, when on November 29, 1921, the major disappeared from an ocean liner— a tragic conclusion to a heroic career. The fact of the matter is

that the 77th Division's commanding general, Major General
Robert Alexander, had, through a Colonel Stacey, ordered him
"to advance behind the barrage, regardless of the losses," which
he did, and his trouble began with the inability of units on his
right and left to make advances equal to his. Having reached
his objective, there were two good reasons why he could not
retire to safer ground, although he may have wished to. He had
received orders to hold his position until other elements came
abreast of him, but the Germans had filtered through on either
flank, taken positions in his rear and even strung a system of
barbed wire that linked two enemy trench systems to box him
in.

The man in command of these German forces was Lieutenant
Heinrich Prinz of the 76th Infantry Reserve. Prior to the outbreak of the war Prinz had lived in Seattle, Washington, for six
years, and it was he who sent a note to Whittlesey demanding
surrender on humanitarian grounds, to which, according to the
reporters of the day, Whittlesey replied, "Go to hell!"

But the gentle, heroic major made no such remark, and though
he tried for many months to have this phrase stricken from his
record, he discovered, as did so many others of that war, that the
citizenry resented having such myths exploded, preferring to believe the foolish and improbable catch phrases of the campaign.

With the enemy surrounding his position, the major, aided by
Captain George G. McMurty, his second in command, and Captain Nelson M. Holderman who assumed responsibility for the
defense of the critical right flank, took measures to dig in for
the expected siege. There was some water in the ravine, but it
took guile and raw heroism to reach it. In a short time the Americans were on a starvation ration as the enemy harassed them
with machine-gun fire, grenades tossed from the tops of trees,
and taunting yells to surrender. There was, perhaps, justification
for submission, but Whittlesey was determined to fight and hold
on. He deployed his force skillfully, devised new plans, and had
efficient defense systems dug while he himself displayed rare
personal fortitude.

In the tree-shrouded gloom of the evening of October 3 they heard German voices on their left, and later enemy voices were heard in front. Scouts crept out and reported back that a number of enemy soldiers were deployed along a cliff some eighteen feet high, an elevation that overlooked their front line. By the time the scouts returned, a heavy grenade attack had started that lasted for ten minutes. The Americans opened fire with rifles and machine guns, taking the grenadiers by surprise. This deadly action continued for a quarter of an hour, and then the area quieted down for the night.

The next day the enemy tried new tricks, as soldiers who spoke English crept up and gave orders to the Americans to leave their funk holes, but the doughboys sprayed the cover with heavy fire. That night the guns of U.S. troops were heard a short distance to the south, but no one came to relieve them. The next day, however, American artillery was able to zero-in on a large enemy force that was massing to make another grenade attack from the cliff.

By October 6 hunger was taking a toll, as only 275 men were left who could put up a defense, and the ammunition for their machine guns was nearly exhausted. The United States Aviation Service tried to help by dropping supplies from a two-seater, and after this mission First Lieutenant Harold E. Goettler and Second Lieutenant Erwin R. Bleckley, members of Number 50 Aero Squadron, were posthumously awarded the Congressional Medal of Honor for heroic action for trying to relieve the trapped battalion. These two airmen did get some supplies into the ravine, but were themselves shot down and killed.

Next, American artillery started to drop shells into their area. Although Major Whittlesey had had a crate of homing pigeons, there were only two left by October 6. The other winged couriers had not brought relief, but the major decided to make one more appeal, which resulted in a moment or two of frustrated comedy. In reaching into the basket to take out one of the birds, an anxious soldier fumbled, and the pigeon fluttered away before a message could be attached to its legs. Despite his annoyance,

Whittlesey took time to write a new message, that read: *"We are along the road parallel 276.4. Our own artillery is dropping a barrage directly on us. Please stop it!"*

The contrite soldier carefully withdrew the last pigeon, a bird called Cher Ami, and attached the message tube to its leg. Cher Ami rose in a determined spiral, circled the area several times to gain operating height and then glided back and perched in a nearby tree where he—or she—calmly preened his wing feathers. Available histories do not agree whether the pigeon was male or female.

Major Whittlesey glared and muttered, "Well, I'll be . . ."

"Get going!" a soldier roared.

Cher Ami ignored the orders, and the doughboys threw sticks and stones at the pigeon as more American shells burst all around them.

"I told you we should have eaten that one," someone said.

A bristly chinned corporal bellowed, "Back to the barnyard," and then, according to legend, climbed the tree, shook the branch and sent Cher Ami on its way.

This part of the story has a heartwarming ending. The homing pigeon arrived at the 77th Division's loft at four that afternoon, having flown like an arrow through heavy shellfire, and landed minus one eye, his breastbone broken, and one leg shot away, but the message was delivered, and the shelling halted fifteen minutes later.

The brave bird was awarded the French Croix de Guerre, and six months later left for home on the transport *Ohioan*, and became the mascot of the U. S. Army Signal Corps. When it died it was mounted and placed in an honored niche in the Smithsonian Institution.

On the morning of October 7, Private Lowell R. Hollingshead, an eighteen-year-old soldier of Whittlesey's regiment, volunteered, along with six others, to try to get through to their support lines to report their general conditions, and if possible, return with some rations.

This small party, under an unnamed sergeant, moved out through light fog and mist, crept down a hillside, crossed a narrow valley and waded the shallow stream of Charlevaux Creek. When they reached the edge of a wooded area, they huddled down for a brief rest, for they all were exhausted from lack of food and water. When they moved on, they attempted only short crawls forward until a barrage of machine-gun fire halted them. The opposition seemed to come from all sides, and although they hugged the ground, several of them were killed. Hollingshead lay still until he saw that he was being covered by a German soldier who held a large Luger. Realizing he was on the short end, the young soldier muttered, "Kamerad," and the German, a massive six-footer, smiled, walked over, and spoke in English. He pointed to Hollingshead's leg, and for the first time the American saw that he had been hit just below the knee where blood was spurting.

Several Germans now arrived and Hollingshead learned that four of his small party had been killed outright, and the rest wounded. They were taken back to one of the enemy's machine-gun posts where their wounds were cared for, and they were questioned rather extensively.

One of the Germans, evidently a runner, was sent off, and later returned with orders for Hollingshead to accompany him back to regimental headquarters. The others who were wounded more seriously were taken out on stretchers and Hollingshead did not see them again. He was blindfolded and guided some distance to a well-furnished dugout where he was interrogated by Lieutenant Prinz, as a doctor cared for his leg wound, and an orderly provided a full meal of meat and hot vegetables.

While Private Hollingshead refreshed himself, Prinz and two other officers continued the questioning, but the young American gave no more than the required information. During this interview his wound started to bleed again, and the doctor was called back to redress it and stop the flow of blood. Lieutenant Prinz continued to question the doughboy, and explained that he had spent some time in America, having lived in Seattle. The

German officer was especially interested in learning how much
amunition Whittlesey's men still had, and how many men were
left alive. Hollingshead courageously refused to satisfy any of
these queries.

"You'd better lie down and take it easy," Prinz suggested when
he saw he was getting nowhere, then he added thoughtfully,
"Would you like to take a message back to your commanding
officer?"

"That all depends. I would want to see the letter first," the
young private replied.

Prinz went to a typewriter set on a table, and wrote what
proved to be a "Demand for Surrender." Hollingshead read it
and agreed to take it back, if he could have a short rest before
starting out. It was then about 2:30 in the afternoon, so in an
hour or so Lieutenant Prinz aroused the private and said, "If
you hope to get this message back before dark, you must start
now."

"I'm ready," the wounded doughboy replied.

Prinz tucked the letter in Hollingshead's blouse pocket, and
taking a stout cane from a corner, handed it to him, saying,
"This will help you in walking." Then he procured a portion of a
white sheet from the doctor's office and tied it to another stick
which Hollingshead was to carry while crossing no man's land.

Hollingshead's trip back was a classic one. He was blind-folded
again and put in charge of a German soldier who guided him
carefully back to the critical area. He was provided with two
packs of German cigarettes and a chunk of black bread. Once,
he was left alone, while the guide made final arrangements for
his mercy-mission release, and he dropped to the ground to rest.
Someone threw a heavy overcoat over him, and then he was
helped to his feet again and moved on as machine guns could
be heard snarling from a post nearby. Finally, the guide halted
him, the blindfold was removed and the American was surprised
to find he was on a road that he had not encountered before.

The German guide smiled, shook hands with him, and pointed
down the road. Limping, using his cane, and holding his flag

of truce high, Hollingshead started his fearful journey back. He fully expected to be cut down by one side or the other, but he eventually reached one of his own outposts where he was halted and given a thorough questioning. Once he had satisfied his own countrymen that he was an American, he was passed on to a lieutenant who in turn took him to Major Whittlesey.

He was interrogated again as Whittlesey read the letter which was as follows:

To the Commanding Officer—Infantry 77th Division

Sir: The bearer of this present, Private Lowell R. Hollingshead, has been taken prisoner by us. He refused to give the German Intelligence any answer to his questions, and is quite an honorable fellow, doing honor to his Fatherland in the strictest sense of the word.

He has been charged against his will, believing he is doing wrong to his country to carry forward and present this letter to the officer in charge of the battalion of the 77th Division, with the purpose to recommend this commander to surrender with his forces, as it would be useless to resist any more in view of the present conditions.

The suffering of your wounded men can be heard over here in the German lines, and we are appealing to your humane sentiments to stop. A white flag shown by one of your men will tell us that you agree with these conditions.

Please treat Private Lowell R. Hollingshead as an honorable man. He is quite a soldier. We envy you.

The German Commanding Officer.

As soon as Private Hollingshead had delivered his message he staggered to a funk hole where he fell unconscious.

Although Major Whittlesey denied afterward that he had used the "Go to hell!" reply credited to him, he did employ a restrained gesture that proved him to be a real hero. Instead of sending back a man with a white flag marking surrender, he ordered that the white ground panels, laid out as markers for

17.   Admiral William S. Sims, who commanded American naval operations in European waters during World War I. Born in Canada, Sims came to the U.S. as a child, graduated from Annapolis in 1880 and after the war presented a lengthy report in which he charged that serious errors had been made by the U.S. Navy Department in the management of naval operations. His postwar book, *The Victory at Sea*, written in collaboration with Burton Jesse Hendrick, was in 1921 awarded the Pulitzer prize for history. U.S. NAVY PHOTO

18.   The famous Liverpool ferryboats, *Daffodil* and *Iris* which played such an important role in the successful blocking of Zeebrugge. Without *Daffodil's* assistance, the cruiser *Vindictive* would have been unable to move up to the sea wall to support the action. *Daffodil* has since become a legendary vessel, and many British soldiers who escaped from Dunkirk more than thirty years later, still swear they were rescued by an old ferryboat named—*Daffodil*—although that ancient hulk had been dismantled years before.   COLONEL G. B. JARRETT PHOTO

19.  H.M.S. *Vindictive* returns from Zeebrugge. This photograph clearly shows the famous old cruiser and the battering she took when the British attempted to block Zeebrugge harbor. The oblong pads hung from the bridge and superstructure were armored shields carried for the occasion. *Vindictive* was later sent to Ostend where she was sunk in an attempt to block off that U-boat haven.     COLONEL G. B. JARRETT PHOTO

20.  Brigadier General William Mitchell, stormy petrel of the Aviation Service, who commanded America's combat squadrons on the western front. Mitchell, inspired by General Hugh Trenchard's original ideas of strategic aviation, conceived an early form of airborne infantry with which he hoped to capture Metz. Unfortunately, aircraft capable of such loads and range were not available before the war ended.     U.S. AIR FORCE PHOTO

21. Britain's first air V.C., 2nd Lieutenant William B. Rhodes-Moorhouse, who won the coveted decoration after giving his life to turn in a reconnaissance report. After bombing Courtrai station, he was seriously wounded, but instead of landing immediately to get medical attention, he determinedly flew back to British GHQ to explain the critical situation, a flight that saved the British Army which had fallen back after Germany's first gas attack.

22. Britain's first two-seater fighter, the F.E.2b pusher which held the line until the Bristol Fighter appeared. The author began his front-line flying aboard one of these aircraft, serving as an NCO aerial gunner for several months. It carried two flexible machine guns, one of which could be raised to fire over the top plane at an enemy attacker. To use this weapon, however, the gunner had to stand with his feet on the edges of the nacelle. It is amazing what young men will do for flight pay.

23.　Royal Flying Corps' famous D. H. 2 single-seater pusher biplane, Britain's answer to the early Fokker fixed-gun fighter. Here is shown the front-firing Lewis gun and the outboard racks for carrying extra drums of ammunition. Since the engine and propeller were behind the pilot's seat, the D. H. 2 did not require an interrupter gear to enable the gun to fire forward. The variations of uniforms worn by British pilots in 1916 are particularly interesting.
IMPERIAL WAR MUSEUM PHOTO

24.　Captain Albert Ball, Britain's outstanding airman who scored forty-four victories during 1916–17. Ball, a poet and musician, was the most aggressive airman on the front. Never a skilled pilot, he was a daring antagonist and would attack no matter what the odds. Strangely enough, he was eventually shot down by a German infantryman hiding in a church tower. Ball usually flew low past this building to check on the time and this habit betrayed him and ended a brilliant career.

25. Victor Chapman, the first American to die in air battle on the western front. A short time previously he had been wounded in the head, but had refused to take convalescent leave, and continued to fly. On June 17, 1916, he was fighting five Fokker pilots and apparently fainted in mid-air and crashed inside the enemy lines. PAUL A. ROCKWELL PHOTO

26. The original Mad Major of legendary fame. While there were many airmen on both sides of the line who because of their antics above the trenches were dubbed Mad Majors, it was Major Christopher Draper who won the title with his daring and violent attacks against enemy ground troops. After the war, Draper continued his antics by flying under the fifteen bridges that cross the river Thames, and only recently renewed his flying license, although he is well over seventy years of age.

27. Major Raoul Lufbery in the uniform of the U.S. Aviation Service after being transferred from the Lafayette Escadrille. Lufbery, who was born in France and who had lived in Wallingford, Connecticut, served in the U.S. Army in peacetime and had teamed up with Marc Pourpe, a French exhibition flyer. When Pourpe joined the French Aviation at the outbreak of the war, Lufbery went into the Foreign Legion but eventually transferred to flying and became a 17-plane ace before he was killed. U.S. AIR FORCE PHOTO

28. Dudley Hill, famed Lafayette Escadrille pilot, aboard his Nieuport scout. This shows the mounting of both the Vickers and Lewis guns. The belt-fed weapon above the engine cowling was synchronized to fire through the propeller, using the British Constantinesco gear. The drum-fed gun above was set to fire over the tips of the propeller blades, but could be tilted back to fire upward at an enemy plane; thus it was semi-flexible and often proved most valuable. CHARLES H. DOLAN PHOTO

29.   Major Raymond Collishaw, leader of the Black Triplane flight which
destroyed eighty-seven enemy aircraft, for a loss of but one plane and pilot.
Here Collishaw is shown aboard a Sopwith Camel when he commanded No. 13
(Naval) Squadron. He ended the war with 68 victories, and after the Armistice
led the British air arm against the Red Russian revolutionaries, and downed
twenty more. He remained with the Royal Air Force serving all over the world
and during World War II commanded a fighter group operating from British
aircraft carriers. A short time ago he retired to his home in Nanaimo, British
Columbia.   BRITISH INFORMATION OFFICE PHOTO

30.   The birth of the flight deck. It was from a lighter towed by a destroyer
that Sub-Lieutenant Stuart D. Culley of the Royal Naval Air Service took off
aboard a Sopwith Camel to intercept and shoot down German Zeppelin L.53.
Culley, of course, had to land in the water and hope to be picked up by the
destroyer which had helped launch him. It was a series of experiments of this
kind which led to the development of today's aircraft carrier.   ROYAL NAVY
PHOTO

31.   Pilots and observers of "A" Flight, No. 22 Squadron RFC shown before
a Bristol Fighter of early 1918. The famous Major McKelvie, wearing a field
cap, stands behind the officer holding the squadron mascot. The Nissen huts
beyond accommodated the NCO gunners. This picture was taken at Vert
Galland Farm aerodrome.   BRITISH INFORMATION SERVICES PHOTO

32.   Bringing truth to the legend. As early as 1918 the Royal Flying Corps
was experimenting with a "secret weapon." This guided missile was to be
loaded with an explosive warhead and homed to its target by radio. The prototype was built by a garage hand, a design-engineer and a department store
radio-parts salesman. It was not too successful, but became the forerunner
of a number of guided drone planes.   IMPERIAL WAR MUSEUM PHOTO

American airmen trying to get supplies to them, be taken up, thus cutting his last link with the United States Army knowing that his action might delay or even prevent their rescue.

Another interesting feature of Hollingshead's part in this drama is that some versions of his story relate that none of the men of his patrol had been given orders to break out, and writing in his report of four o'clock that afternoon Whittlesey states that a private from H Company reported that Hollingshead and eight others had left without permission in the morning, and encountered a German outpost. Five of the nine were killed, the rest captured. However, in a signed article that appeared in a booklet titled *History and Rhymes of the Lost Battalion,* published in 1919, Hollingshead said that the unnamed sergeant told them Major Whittlesey had asked for eight men to volunteer to make the dangerous journey. It is noted that Private Hollingshead was never rewarded with any decoration for his part in the event.

Private Abraham Krotoshinsky, Major Whittlesey's runner, was honored with the Distinguished Service Cross for another risky adventure. After five days and nights of their entrapment, during which time several volunteers who had tried to get to the headquarters of the 77th Division were killed or captured, Major Whittlesey once more asked for volunteers, and Krotoshinsky stepped forward. At dawn of the sixth day, weary, hungry, and in a devil-may-care state of mind, he made his way to some bushes just behind the German lines, and while lying prone a German officer walked by and stepped on Krotoshinsky's fingers. He stifled his cries, and because of the enemy traffic was pinned down there for several hours.

All that time he was under the heavy fire being exchanged by both sides, but he took the fatalist viewpoint, and thought of nothing but getting the message through. When he dared leave his hiding place, he wandered back and forth, retracing his route and making detours designed to deceive his enemies. By nightfall he stumbled into an abandoned German trench, and lay there exhausted trying to regain some strength.

Finally he heard American voices, but suddenly realized he

did not have the password of the day, so he risked everything by crying, "Hello! Hello!" He was lucky, as a small scouting party found him and led him to their headquarters where his message was read and acted on. After some rest, food, and medical attention, he was ordered to lead a number of relief troops back to The Pocket. On the way in he was wounded and gassed, but his little force got through and received a tremendous welcome from his despairing comrades. The relief troops were the first of the 307th Regiment infantrymen to reach them, and half an hour later patrols from the 308th were reported to be coming in from the south, and the next morning 252 survivors of the 679 men who had entered The Pocket, marched out with their sick and wounded to a well-earned rest. Major Whittlesey, Captain McMurty, and Captain Holderman were awarded the Congressional Medal of Honor.

*Foulup at Sedan*

Early in November all the Allied armies were pushing on, and the enemy was retreating in wild confusion, with little opportunity to make a stand anywhere—his artillery was more of a hindrance than an asset. Needless to state, all Allied commanders made the most of this favorable situation to press the pursuit.

Sedan was the main objective on the American front, and the German divisions, broken and exhausted, offered little resistance. It was at this time that one of the prize foulups of the war was written into the records. Some generous staff officer, with a spirit of poetic justice rising from the flush of victory, suggested that the French be given the honor of retaking Sedan where they had lost a decisive and historic battle to the Germans in 1871. General Pershing was in one of his less benevolent moments and ignored, or missed the importance of such a gesture. Instead, he was determined that his First Army should be the first to march into the old city, particularly when he saw that the French would not be able to overtake the Americans.

He first communicated with Major General Joseph T. Dickman,

I Corps Commander, stating that he would like to see his troops have the honor of taking Sedan. Then Pershing found himself in a tactless debate with the French general, Paul A. M. Maistre, that only contributed to the approaching bitterness. In fact, before cooler heads could govern, the race for Sedan turned into a military nightmare that completely tangled two important divisions, and left a sector of the American front wide open for a possible counterattack, but fortunately the Germans were not strong enough or sufficiently alert to take advantage of the ridiculous situation.

It should be added that General Pershing explained in his postwar memoirs that he had suggested to General Maistre that the prescribed boundary line between the U. S. First Army and the French Fourth Army might be ignored in case the Yanks should outrun the poilus, and that instead of objecting General Maistre "warmly approved."

This competitive tangle began with an order directed to the commanding generals of the United States I and V Corps that read: "General Pershing desires that the honor of entering Sedan should fall to the First Army. He has every confidence that the troops of I Corps, assisted on their right by V Corps, will enable him to realize this desire."

Unfortunately, Brigadier General Hugh A. Drum, First Army Chief of Staff, added a sentence to this message that read: "In transmitting the foregoing message, your attention is invited to the favorable opportunity now existing for pressing our advance throughout the night. Boundaries will not be considered binding."

General Hunter Liggett, commander of the First Army, was away from his headquarters and did not learn of this order until two days later—November 7—and by that time the big foulup was at its zenith.

This is what happened. On receipt of the order, Generals Joseph T. Dickman and Charles P. Summerall, commanders of I and V Corps respectively, moved to carry it out—to the letter. Summerall ordered Brigadier General Frank Parker's 1st Infantry Division to head for Sedan in five columns *by the most direct route.* This meant that his division would have to cut to the left, directly across the path of the advancing I Corps and elements of the French Fourth Army. Summerall had taken General Drum's added sentence to Pershing's message as an order, one that eliminated the boundaries between I and V Corps, whereas it was intended only that V Corps commander would assist Dickman if called on during I Corps' advance toward Sedan.

The 1st Division set out on its forced march in the mud and rain on the night of November 6, and proceeded over deep-rutted, shell-pocked roads, through thick forests, and supplied by trucks that moved without headlights. It eventually blundered into the path of I Corps' 42nd and 77th Divisions and blocked them off, although I Corps had been closer to Sedan when the frantic march began.

Unbelievable confusion reigned. Lead elements of the 1st Division fired on two companies of an Iowa infantry regiment, and received return fire before the situation was clarified. Brigadier General Douglas MacArthur, while moving about his 42nd Division command post near Beaumiel Farm, was "captured" having been mistaken for a German officer as he was not wearing a complete military uniform. Hours passed before he was identified and released. That same night Lieutenant Colonel Theodore Roosevelt, Jr., marched his regiment into the French Fourth Army where he was challenged immediately. The French commander told him in no uncertain words that his troops would come under heavy barrage-fire, unless they were moved out within an hour. Colonel Roosevelt quickly retired.

With the coming of dawn a local war threatened between the French and American commands. The 42nd Division by now had started toward Sedan, proceeding through French Territory which brought on another threat of French artillery opening up unless the American troops stopped obstructing the French advance.

Meanwhile the 1st and 42nd Divisions had reached heights south and west of Sedan, but just as they were about to move on to victory and glory, orders were received by radio from GHQ that held them where they were. When the boundaries were finally confirmed, the French gained the honor of first marching into Sedan, although some perverse newspapermen claimed later that a few American patrols had entered the city a short time before.

For a day or two, top-level furor seethed from division to division; many charges and countercharges were made. An inquiry was ordered, but with so many high-ranking officers involved it came to nothing. Those of the 1st Division who had been responsible for the movement across the zones of action might have been demoted under normal conditions, but the splendid record of the unit, and the approach of the end of hostilities placed the matter in a more lenient light.

## Final Drive to Victory

The end of the war came when least expected. When General von Ludendorff resigned, many other German officers followed him. The German Navy was in mutiny at Kiel, and the Italian Army, in revenge for its defeat at Caporetto the year before, was driving the Austrians across the Piave River. The Hapsburg monarchy selected a new prime minister who took the office with a pledge to make a separate peace.

British mounted troops had occupied Aleppo in Syria, then belonging to Turkey, and Turkey wisely withdrew from the war. By November 11 British cavalry officers who had fought at Mons in 1914 were once more on the scene of their original encounter with the German Army. Most curious of all, the 2nd Battalion of the Royal Irish Regiment that had fought in the loop of the canal northeast of Mons on August 23, 1914, was back with the 63rd Division cutting the same loop when the hostilities ceased.

The armistice was signed in a railroad car that had been sidetracked in a forest near Compiègne. For hours a hush fell across the grim battlefields, then there was a wild celebration, old inter-Allied feuds were forgotten, and the top brass began a round of formal dinners, parties, and decorations parades. Hardly had the final gun been silenced, than newspapers and pressure groups in the United States demanded that the boys be sent home at once. The war was over, and from all accounts America wanted no more of Europe's burdens. There were the inevitable arguments as to who "won the war," with a dozen chauvinistic claims echoing from all sides, depending on one's national ties and prejudices. Those of us who were still serving were sickened by it, until we realized that the most vociferous in these pointless exchanges usually were civilians who never had heard a shot fired.

The battles were over, but the months of service were not. The AEF had to move into Germany and form part of the Army of Occupation, and it stayed there until 1923. The British and French, however, were required to remain in Germany for six more years. A peace was signed that was supposed to contain German militarism for all time, but the free world renounced its responsibilities, and before long another dictator rose and set the wheels of war rolling again.

Through the 1920s the world wanted nothing more than to get back to "normal" living. Civilization had been saved, so why not enjoy the promise of prosperity? We had not learned that we must work as hard for peace as we had to win a war.

ON THE SEA

# CHAPTER IX

*Britain Blockades Germany . . . U-Boats' First Triumph
. . . The Great Armada . . . Battle off the Falklands . . .
Frightfulness at Sea.*

## Britain Blockades Germany

Any cursory reflection on World War I and its history will
arouse memories of trench warfare, bayonet charges through a
maze of barbed wire, flashing combats between darting aircraft,
or thundering artillery battles that pounded towns and villages
to dusty rubble. We all are fairly glib concerning famous campaigns and the generals responsible for the bloody battlefields.
Some of us can recite the names of a few individual heroes who
were awarded the Congressional Medal of Honor or the Victoria
Cross, but landlubbers that we are, we seldom remember or
are willing to grant that possibly the most important blows in
that war were delivered by naval forces.

Except for a very brief meeting with King George VI, I have
never met a man who fought at Jutland, and throughout the
war I had only a vague understanding of the seriousness of the
U-boat, nor did I appreciate the broad program of naval protection required to bring men and supplies across the Atlantic. Understandably, I was more concerned with my own personal
safety, on the ground or in the air, and it was not until some
years after the war that I had a concept of the part the Allied
navies had in the ultimate decision.

This, indeed, was the Silent Service.

Anyone who takes the time today to study the early history of the Great War cannot but be amazed at Great Britain's audacity in accepting the German challenge. Her army was little better than a token force; military aviation was scarcely more than a phrase, as in August 1914 she had only enough airplanes and pilots to organize three eighteen-plane squadrons; only her Royal Navy was prepared for anything resembling a war, and was ready, and standing by at assigned war stations. Why this was so is almost a legendary story, generally forgotten, but it may be read in Winston Churchill's *World Crisis*.

Churchill had been First Lord of the Admiralty for three years when suddenly one week before Britain declared war on Germany, he ordered the Grand Fleet of 200 fighting ships and 70,000 men to slip out of Portland Harbor and head for battle stations in the North Sea, a move that was one of the most decisive in that war's history. Any surprise attack was forestalled, and the safe transport of the British Expeditionary Force to France assured.

What had triggered Churchill's timely decision? Why, after a routine test mobilization had been completed, and when most of the reservists were being paid off before returning to their homes, did the First Lord of the Admiralty decide to send the world's greatest navy into the North Sea?

On Friday, July 24, 1914, Churchill had attended a banquet in London. One of the guests was Albert Ballin, director general of the Hamburg-American Steamship Line and a close friend of Kaiser Wilhelm. He had just arrived in England from Berlin, and when Ballin was placed beside Churchill, the First Lord of the Admiralty questioned the German shipping man on the international situation.

Ballin indicated that the situation was grave, and added reflectively: "I remember old Bismarck telling me the year before he died, that one day the great European War would come out of some damned foolish thing in the Balkans." Churchill sat deep in thought as Ballin continued to outline various possibilities, and then closed with some earnestness: "Suppose we had to go to war with Russia and France, and suppose we defeated

France and yet took nothing from her in Europe, not one inch
of her territory—only some colonies to indemnify us. Would that
make a difference in England's attitude? Suppose we gave such a
guarantee beforehand?"

A short while later when a proposal, based on Ballin's supposi-
tion, was telegraphed from Berlin to London, it was rejected immediately. Churchill knew that war was uppermost in Germany's
mind. And with that the Grand Fleet moved into the North Sea,
stood off all important German harbors, and the Imperial German Navy, second only to Great Britain's in size, was bottled up.
Without this precaution the enemy's High Seas Fleet could
have steamed from its shelter and wreaked great havoc on ports
and shipping of Britain and France, spreading a destruction that
might have evened the scales of sea power.

Whether the Admiralty would have demobilized the fleet after
Austria's ultimatum, in which Germany fully supported her, is,
of course, debatable, but the fact remains that Britain's immediate blockade of German ports had a great part in winning the
war. The U-boat phase was dramatic and menacing, and had it
not been for the British Navy's early determination to eradicate
this threat, the war might have been won by Germany long before the United States could have joined the Allies. The British
blockade, by clearing the oceans of practically all German ships,
naval and merchant alike, held the Kaiser's empire in a relent-
less grip from beginning to end. If the German people did not
actually starve, a considerable number suffered from hunger, and
their military machine was handicapped by the absence of necessary materials available from the outside world. Great as was
the physical and material hindrance imposed by the British fleet,
the moral blockade was more deadly. Germany was isolated from
the world, while the products of America's farms, mines, and
factories flowed into Allied ports. Hamburg and Bremen were
literally deserted.

As Frank H. Simonds pointed out in his *History of the World
War*, the war on the sea was as unromantic, as hard, as painful
as war in the trenches; yet it had a more shining reward. On the

day a German admiral brought the German High Seas Fleet into Scapa Flow under its own steam, and, on Admiral David Beatty's order, hauled down the German ensign, Great Britain had achieved a greater triumph over a naval rival than had been seen since the days when Rome conquered Carthage. The Kaiser had challenged British supremacy of the seas, and the end of the conflict was the scene at Scapa Flow, a victory that not only destroyed the enemy's power to resist, but shattered a tradition without which no navy can exist.

Without the British Navy there could have been no victory on land, and if Beatty had no triumph comparable to the Second Battle of the Marne or the Hindenburg line to reward his labors, Foch was no more successful in reviving the tradition of Napoleon for the French Army than Beatty was in preserving the prestige of Nelson for the British. That the United States Navy served usefully and gallantly under Beatty must be a cause for national pride, no less than the Meuse-Argonne achievement of the Army.

## U-Boats' First Triumph

Admiral Beatty, in command of Britain's battle cruiser squadron, made a memorable initiative decision by planning a daring ambush of Germany's light cruisers. These warships had adopted the practice of moving out to bring in the British destroyer guard that presumed to take command of the North Sea. His was a daring plan, for with inclement weather, enemy submarines, and the possibility that the German High Seas Fleet might dart out suddenly, the admiral risked his valuable squadron time after time.

Admiral Beatty also believed that the German Navy was not yet ready for modern surface tactics—the handling of ships at high speed, the coping with the increased range of guns, and the possibility of accidents while maneuvering through smoke screens. Unfortunately, what he hoped would happen to his adversaries became the bane of the British fleet. For one thing, the new submarine flotilla that had joined his battle cruisers was most troublesome and seemed unable to conform to planned sailing courses.

On his first contact with the Germans, his light cruisers were outnumbered and outgunned when his light flotilla moved daringly into the Heligoland Bight, but luckily, Beatty brought his heavy cruisers over the horizon just in time, and the Germans were soon outnumbered. Three enemy light cruisers, *Coln*, *Mainz*, and *Ariadne*, and one destroyer were sunk. The British cruiser *Arethusa* was hit, but all returned safely to their stations.

This success raised the morale of all Britain and for a few weeks everyone was convinced that Britannia still ruled the waves, but a new setback was suffered on September 22, one that cast a deep pall of gloom over the world of naval designers, particularly those of the mighty dreadnought school.

There had been much discussion before the war concerning the value of the submarine. Few "big navy" men would admit that this ungainly little vessel, even when armed with Whitehead torpedoes would ever have an important role in naval operations. They were afraid of them, so dismissed them from their calculations. During the first few weeks of the war submarines on either side caused little damage, but suddenly, on September 22, Lieutenant Otto Weddigen, in command of U-9 on a patrol off the Hook of Holland, sank three British cruisers in less than an hour. It was an outstanding feat, achieved under ideal circumstances, and one that was never repeated. But for a few weeks the threat of this underwater vessel was awesome beyond words.

Lieutenant Weddigen, a thirty-two-year-old officer who had been associated with the submarine flotilla for about five years, had been married to his sweetheart on August 16, and the following day was ordered on a duty patrol. Setting out from the Kiel Canal he took U-9 on a southwesterly course and cruised off the coast of Holland where he settled down to await developments.

Early in the morning of September 22 he caught sight of a British cruiser at a point eighteen miles off the Hook of Holland. The sea was rough and whitecaps shielded his periscope that had been out of the water a distance of five feet. A short time later two more cruisers appeared in his periscope. He then submerged and moved into position, well within range of his torpedoes. Bringing his periscope to the surface once more he found his targets again, and accurately determined their course.

He fired one torpedo at the nearest cruiser, the *Aboukir*. This shot exploded near the magazine which also went up and finished the British ship in minutes. Lieutenant Weddigen then had some unearned luck when both the *Cressy* and the *Hogue*, instead of turning away, wheeled hard to pick up survivors from the *Aboukir*. This gave the German U-boat commander another sitting shot, and his next torpedo was aimed at the *Hogue* which had steamed directly into his gunnery path. The torpedo ran true, scoring a clean hit, but in this case was not aided by any magazine explosion. However, the *Hogue* was brought to a halt and lay wallowing helplessly until at last she took in enough water, rolled over and sank.

Perhaps realizing by now what was taking place, *Cressy* tried vainly to fire her guns and torpedoes, but slowed to lower liferafts and boats to aid the men already floundering in the rough water. She next moved into a zigzag course until Weddigen had to come in dangerously close to get a shot at her. He even surfaced completely, risking the cruiser's gunfire in order to determine where the British cruiser was moving. Then he submerged once more to periscope depth and sent off his third torpedo. A fourth soon followed, and both struck cleanly, severely damaging *Cressy*. She was soon going down by the head, but even in this position her gun crews continued to fire on anything that looked like a periscope. Then *Cressy's* boilers burst, she turned turtle and went to the bottom.

Knowing that calls for help had been sent out, Lieutenant Weddigen wisely moved for home. He was chased for a time by destroyers and torpedo boats, but he reached Kiel safely, and was awarded the Iron Cross First Class. In March 1915 he was lost at sea when his new command, *U-90*, was sunk by British antisubmarine forces.

The loss of the three light cruisers caused a greater respect for the submarine, and tactics had to be devised to counter this new weapon. It also was soon apparent that such mercy attempts as *Cressy* and *Hogue* had made were foolhardy.

## The Great Armada

The loyalty and devotion of the British colonies to the Motherland was a mystery to the German High Command, who did not believe that Canada, Australia, New Zealand, South Africa, and even India and Egypt, would rally to Britain's cause. The Prussians had the impression that these overseas people had been under a type of oppression that they themselves would have employed in their governing, and expected the British colonies to take advantage of the war in Europe to break their fetters with the homeland. Little did they realize that the loyalty of the colonies would be a major factor in Britain's eventual victory, and the High Command discovered too late that the colonials, as they were known, were bound to Britain in the Great Cause by fair and generous dealing, not by force.

In North America, the Dominion of Canada in particular displayed how wholeheartedly aid was given and rushed to the Old Country; in four years of warfare she contributed 600,000 men, a remarkable amount considering that the Canadian population at the time was less than 10,000,000. The highlight of this help was the first shipment of 33,000 men, the greatest number to be sent across the Atlantic as a body. Later on, the United States topped this mark, but by then the convoy system was a successful venture, and America, of course, had a larger population from which to draw.

This Canadian effort deserves more than passing mention. Here was a peace-loving, non-military people who, prior to the war, had ignored German aggression in Europe, having been too involved in their frontier-type of life while struggling to carve a new country out of an inhospitable continent. Yet, in seven short weeks, Canada created a volunteer army that a few months later was to save Calais on the battlefield of Langemarck. This effort was a sterling example to Australia and New Zealand who responded immediately, and matched Canada's great effort.

At first, the Canadian Parliament had asked for 20,000 men but 33,000 volunteered within two months. They formed cavalry squadrons, artillery batteries, infantry regiments, engineers, signalers, and staffs required for ammunition columns, ambulances, and hospitals. They also furnished their own rifles, machine guns, field guns, some heavy artillery, and a store of ammunition.

The manhood of Canada hurried to arms from the wheatfields of the west, from the farms of the east, from the slopes of the Rockies, and the shores of Hudson Bay. Also, a large number of idealistic Americans crossed the border and begged to join them. To finance all this effort, the Canadian government raised an initial fifty million dollars for war purposes.

A military camp was soon erected at Valcartier, sixteen miles west of Quebec, a short day's march from important ports. A line of rifle targets 3½ miles long was constructed and three miles of railroad siding was run in. Within four days some six thousand men had arrived and were under training. A transatlantic fleet gathered at the Gaspé Basin off Quebec on September 23, and over the next three days the complete Canadian 1st Division, with its reserves, horses, guns, and weapons was abroad and on its way down the St. Lawrence River. They arrived in Plymouth, England, on October 14. Censorship and secrecy had been so strict, this Canadian armada arrived unexpectedly, but once their uniforms were spotted the people of Devon gave them a welcome that none of them ever forgot. How could an Empire lose a war when backed by such a loyal and unflinching spirit?

### Battle off the Falklands

Germany had a number of warships and auxiliary merchantmen scattered over the various oceans at the start of the war, and some of them carried out prearranged programs of piracy and destruction until they were tracked down and sunk.

The famous *Emden* had a profitable cruise until she was caught and destroyed by the Australian cruiser *Sydney*. There was also the *Prinz Eitel Friedrich*, a luxury passenger steamer that had been converted into a raider. She finally sought shelter in a United States port where she was interned.

The most dangerous fleet was Germany's Asiatic Squadron that sailed under Admiral Maximilian von Spee. It cruised through the southern Pacific and off the west coast of South America where, on November 1, 1914, the German admiral trapped a lighter British flotilla under Admiral Sir Christopher G. F. M. Cradock. Admiral Cradock daringly gave battle, and had his force practically destroyed.

Admiral Spee had as the bulk of his fleet the famous *Scharnhorst* and *Gneisenau*, which should not be confused with two other vessels of the same names that made history in World War II. He had gathered in innocent-looking German traders that he used most efficiently as colliers and supply ships, and, eventually, his fleet was comprised of five cruisers with their attendant supply ships concentrated at Valparaiso.

The British knew that this enemy force would have to be vanquished quickly, but at the time only Admiral Cradock's small squadron, with *Good Hope* as his flagship and the large cruiser *Monmouth* that was armed with nothing heavier than six-inch guns, was available. Another ancient, *Glasgow*, was some distance away, but was steaming to join the squadron. Admiral Cradock's flagship was capable of twenty-five knots and carried two 9.2-inch guns, but they were of an old pattern. *Otranto*, an armed liner, served best as a supply ship. *Canopus* with four 12-inch guns was also on her way to join this puny force.

Had Admiral Cradock met only German light cruisers, he might have had a good chance of taking the day, but the *Scharnhorst* and *Gneisenau* were comparatively new, heavily armored ships bearing 8.2-inch guns, and the scales were tilted against him. The 6-inch guns aboard the *Monmouth* and *Good Hope* were turreted on the lower deck and were of small value in a heavy sea. Whether *Canopus* could have been of any help had she arrived in time is questionable since she could do little better than fifteen knots, a deficiency that possibly saved her.

Cradock was sailing north from Cape Horn on November 1, 1914, when he ran into Admiral Spee off Coronel on the coast of Chile. The weather was what was to be expected in those latitudes as an angry gale whipped the sea into a violent battleground. While running parallel to the five-cruiser German squadron about twelve miles away, Cradock sent a message to *Canopus* still far to the south: "I am going to engage the enemy now." That was at five o'clock in the afternoon, and when the German commander spotted the British vessels he turned quickly and drew in toward the land. The weather worsened with winds of almost hurricane force and nightfall was approaching. Spee's move was masterful since he not only found some shelter, but his ships were scarcely visible against the vague outline of the coast, while his enemies' were suddenly silhouetted in the last level rays of a betraying sunset.

Success and defeat were swift: after a third broadside, *Monmouth* staggered around completely in flames; *Good Hope* was totally aflame and out of control. Signals were heard from *Monmouth* for half an hour, as *Glasgow,* an unarmored vessel exchanged broadsides of 760 pounds with *Gneisenau* whose gunnery was 3300 pounds. The hopelessness of the task forced *Glasgow* to withdraw, and she was lucky to escape and head south where she hoped to join *Canopus.*

Not one man of the 1600 aboard *Good Hope* and *Monmouth* was ever found, and no attempt at rescue seems to have been made. Once the sun set, the weather made it impossible to lower boats or take time to rescue any men who had scrambled onto rafts or other debris.

This was Germany's last victory on the sea against her hated enemy, but Admiral Spee was thankful to steam out of the vicinity, head for his colliers, and then plan to set up a fixed supply base in the Falklands, a move that brought on his end when he unwittingly sailed straight into the lion's paws.

On receiving the dreadful news of Cradock's defeat, the Admiralty made a swift, and most fortunate, decision. An avenger squadron, under Admiral Sir Doveton Sturdee, arrived off the Falklands by December 7, where it was to coal, and then search for Admiral Spee. Admiral Sturdee had the battle cruisers *Invincible* and *Inflexible*, backed by five other worthy warships.

Here the fortunes of war took a decided turn on the morning of Sturdee's arrival, when the German Asiatic Fleet arrived almost on cue. This time it was the British who were hidden behind the land, coaling quietly while the unsuspecting Spee drew closer. By nine o'clock that morning *Canopus* fired a shot or two over the projecting heights of the harbor, as *Gneisenau* and *Nürnberg* moved well within range. After this unexpected welcome, the two German cruisers moved off and waited for the rest of their squadron to join them.

Possibly believing that some small force of British ships was skulking in the harbor, the German admiral then risked all. Having no aircraft to spot for him, it was not until he reached the opening of the harbor that he saw how he had been tricked by the strength sheltered there. Instead of running for it, he waited and pondered the situation until *Glasgow*, now repaired after her battering off Coronel, charged out of the Falklands' shelter. She was followed by *Kent*, and behind them, making use of the carefully laid smoke screen, came the British battle cruisers. By that time Admiral Spee saw that only speed and retirement could save him.

In contrast to the Coronel engagement, this battle was fought in bright sunshine on a glassy sea with just a mere breeze to stir the smoke of action. The chase began, and the British made no great haste to open the ball. All hands were piped to dinner as usual and some time was allowed for smoking before Admiral Sturdee decided to close with the enemy.

As soon as the noonday meal was cleared away, the bugles rang out with "Action Stations!" and everyone took his post. *Scharnhorst* was leading the enemy pack when the British opened fire. The three German light cruisers broke away from the line and appeared to be dropping mines. As they scattered to the south they were followed by *Glasgow, Kent,* and *Cornwall. Bristol* had already been ordered to destroy the enemy colliers and so the main battle was fought by four big vessels of both flotillas.

*Gneisenau* and *Scharnhorst* changed course to the southeast, and by three in the afternoon *Inflexible* and *Invincible* engaged them. This time it was the Germans who were outranged, and both their cruisers took a severe beating, while unable to reply in turn. Shell after shell pierced the armor of *Scharnhorst,* fire leaped out, and by four o'clock she was rolling helplessly, and sank with her entire crew.

*Gneisenau* held out a little longer, but the concentrated fire of both British battle cruisers soon finished her, and she rolled over slowly as a number of men were seen to be climbing over the greasy hull. The British picked up nearly two hundred of *Gneisenau's* crew.

*Glasgow* pursued *Leipsig* until she too disappeared by nine that evening. *Kent* and *Nürnberg* had a fierce engagement that lasted until 7:26 P.M. The British ship had been hit thirty-five times, but eventually sank her adversary. *Prinz Eitel Friedrich,* the armed liner, and *Dresden,* a light cruiser, escaped, but the latter was finally trapped and captured by *Kent* and *Glasgow* early in 1915 off the Juan Fernández Islands in the South Pacific Ocean four hundred miles west of Chile. As explained before, the armed liner reached an American port where she was interned.

The Battle of the Falklands reversed the decision at Coronel. Only the *Emden* had great success in her raids across the endless seas and before she was forced aground by the guns of the cruiser *Sydney* on November 9, 1914, she had sunk an aggregate of 80,000 tons of shipping.

## Frightfulness at Sea

Early in 1915 Germany took a drastic step, one that challenged the whole world to war. When her High Seas Fleet had been driven to cover and eliminated as a naval threat, she turned to the submarine, especially after Lieutenant Weddigen's success against the three British light cruisers, *Aboukir, Cressy,* and *Hogue.* She declared, on February 4, 1915, that her U-boats would sink on sight any merchant ship that they suspected of being an enemy.

This decision struck at the base of all international law, as for generations sailors the world over had been guaranteed safety at sea. This was not breaking some individual treaty, as in the case of the invasion of Belgium, but all treaties. It claimed the right for Germany to be the sole arbiter of all her acts, including the killing of foreigners who had committed no crime, and with whom she was not at war.

Amazingly enough, the neutrals raised no serious objections, but made every possible allowance for the pressing factors. Even the United States did no more than present formal appeals against this threat of killing her people. But Germany was far more skilled with words than any of her antagonists, being most adept with obscure discussions and replies while her top officials arranged bewildering delays in answering any charges. In the meantime her U-boats were showing her real intent.

Actually, this was done in the hope of blocking the bulk of neutral trade from the Allies by terrorizing neutral seamen. She had little intent of dragging other foes into war, but did hope to put quaking fear into the hearts of all by her pattern of "frightfulness" at sea, just as she had done on the land. As far as France and Great Britain were concerned, Germany was bent on breaking every pledge, every restraint of morality or humanity, if by so doing she could increase her chance of victory.

The British losses from the torpedoes of the U-boats alone were tremendous. In the next four years 5622 British merchant ships were sunk, about half of all Great Britain possessed. Norway also suffered greatly, and during more than two years of neutrality the United States lost 19 merchant vessels, and 126 more in the months of her active participation. More than

15,000 British merchant sailors were lost, and 775 Americans aboard vessels that flew their own flag.

But while this frightfulness blackened the pages of German history, submarine warfare had its epic moments, and not a few legends. One in particular that reads like a tale concocted by a "thriller" magazine hack endowed with a keen plot mind, is actually on record with the British Admiralty. It is said to have happened early in 1916, but can be presented here to draw a balance between the horrors of submarine warfare, and the ingenuity of one man who found himself involved in an unusual pigboat circumstance.

A mine-laying U-boat had crept into a British harbor to plant a pattern of underwater explosives, and on this occasion, intent on doing a complete job, the German commander submerged to the bottom of the harbor for safety as considerable surface traffic was passing overhead at the time. During this rest period members of the crew reported that they heard *tap-tap-taps* that seemed to come from the outer surface of the hull. The officer of the watch listened and then called the commander, for it was obvious that the taps were suspiciously like Morse code signals.

Every crewman aboard stood stock-still, listening intently. Unwilling to accept the idea that they were on the outside, the commander decided they were sounds from a machinist's hammer, possibly from some repair work going on in their engine room. A thorough investigation convinced everyone that the sounds *were* coming from the outside. Someone was tapping a message on the outer shell, and the intent was clear.

The German crew stared at one another in dread and disbelief. It was fantastic, unbelievable, but someone was tapping what sounded like a message. The commander who understood English jotted down each letter as his junior officers peered over his shoulder. He exchanged glances with them, and took down the message a second time. The sheet of paper was passed around and their blackest suspicions confirmed: *Surface and surrender, or depth charges will be exploded against your hull.*

For a minute there was a faint expression of revolt, but the signal taps began again, and this time the message was delivered with more emphasis, as if to insist on immediate action, and then a postscript was added: *Depth charge has been lowered and wired.*

There was no argument. The commander blew his tanks and rose to the surface. When he reached his conning tower he saw an armed trawler about one hundred yards away. The crew aboard the trawler appeared surprised, but in seconds her decks bustled with activity, and before the sub captain could take advantage of the situation, a shell screamed out and pierced the conning tower. There was no chance to submerge and escape. Surrender was the only way out. The trawler's boats took off the crew, and then passed a line to the U-boat.

As the bewildered German commander demanded some explanation for this unfair trick, the dripping helmet of a diver rose from the depths of the harbor. He was hoisted aboard the trawler by the men who had been tending his pump and air line. As they unscrewed his headgear, he sat on a capstan and grinned.

"Good! I hoped you chaps would be alert and nail the blighter when I sent him up. I didn't try to tell you, because I knew you wouldn't believe me."

The German commander was still confused.

"It was like this," the diver continued. "There I was down there working on the hulk of a drifter and as I was putting a patch on, your bloomin' submarine slides past and settles on the bottom. I had an idea you were up to some mine-laying game."

"But I don't understand how you made him pop up alongside of us," the trawler captain broke in.

"Well, you see, I had been a signalman before I took up diving, so I just walked over to this Hun bloke and began talking to him—with my hammer."

The trawler captain wiped his brow. "I wish you'd make yourself clearer."

"Simple! I used Morse code. Clank . . . clank . . . clank. I just hoped one of them would understand English. Of course, I could have sent up word to you, but this seemed easier and not so messy. I rather liked the idea of capturing a submarine singlehanded, so to speak."

"But where did you get the depth charge?" the German commander demanded.

"Depth charge? I made that one up. You mustn't believe everything you hear in the British Navy, chum."

## Britain's Subs Strike Back

As the ground war in France and Flanders rumbled on to its
stalemate and the massive armies dug in until the issue was
brought out into the open by the tanks, the British Navy, said
to be worth 500,000 bayonets to the land war, searched its hoary
head for an answer to that insolent weapon of ill-repute, the submarine. It had few friends in the Royal Navy, since by tradition naval action was to be fought by recognized surface fleets
in the accepted manner. The thought of a four-hundred- to
seven-hundred-ton upstart darting about unseen and delivering
lethal torpedoes at proud capital ships was unimaginable. Mahan
had predicted none of this; naval wars were to be fought as
Nelson, Jones, Farragut, and Dewey had prescribed.

Once the German High Seas Fleet was bottled up, the Royal
Navy felt impotent, and the planning staff searched its collective
mind for something to do. When *Goeben* and *Breslau* evaded
the British Mediterranean Fleet and escaped into the Dardanelles, it was imperative that they be contained there, and a
force of two battle cruisers and other large naval craft were
assigned to watch this rathole.

Among this mixed force based at the island of Tenedos—now
Bozcaada—off the west coast of Turkey in Asia, were three
antiquated British submarines. *B-19* was commanded by Lieu-

tenant Geoffrey Warburton, *B-10* by a Lieutenant Gravener, and *B-11* by Lieutenant Norman D. Holbrook. The French had three more, but, like the British boats, they were old and in need of repair because of heavy prewar service. The battery power on *B-9* and *B-10* was almost exhausted, but Lieutenant Holbrook's craft had just been fitted with a new storage battery and generator system.

Western Turkey is separated from the main portion of Asia Minor by the Dardanelles, the Sea of Marmara, and a narrow channel known as the Bosporus that connects the Marmara with the Black Sea. Istanbul, then called Constantinople, is situated at the southern end of the Bosporus. British Naval Intelligence had learned that somewhere inside and below the slimmest portion of the Dardanelles, an area known as the Narrows, were five lines of Turkish mines that prevented surface ships from moving into the Sea of Marmara. The Narrows are about twelve miles from the entrance to the strait, and the Turkish capital and its important shipping appeared to be fairly safe.

A few French submarine commanders had enlivened their dull patrol work in the Aegean Sea by penetrating the Dardanelles and running wild against the Turkish fleet. These exploits were noted by Lieutenant Commander P. H. Pownall who was in charge of the British submarine base, and he suggested that his boat commanders might play the same game.

Lieutenant Holbrook, who was keen to give it a try, pointed out, "My boat, *B-11*, is the only one that could do it. I have a new battery, and if I restricted my speed to two knots, I might be able to run submerged for almost twenty-four hours."

Only by comparing distances, space, and other features of the Dardanelles against the performance of those early 1914 submarines, can one have any conception of what Lieutenant Holbrook was taking on. When submerged, the speed of these vessels was between five and six knots, but this could be maintained for only about two hours; by the end of that time they would have to surface and recharge the batteries by running the Diesel engines. To forestall this, Holbrook planned to move at his slowest speed and thereby have electric power for a full day's submerged sailing.

One of the difficulties in penetrating the Turkish strait is a strong flow of fresh water about ten fanthoms deep that runs from the Narrows all the way to the entrance. At the Narrows the natural current is increased to twice its force, so to make any progress, Holbrook knew he would have to move at fairly high speed, thus drawing heavily on his battery power.

These submarines had no anti-mine gear, no metal blades that could sheer off mine-mooring cables or nets; on the contrary they bore all sorts of jagged projections that invited entanglement with mine-mooring ropes or cables. With this in mind, Holbrook rigged some temporary mine guards, and his *B-11* was ready for one of the first great submarine exploits of modern warfare by Saturday, December 12, 1914.

At 4:15 the next morning she was on the surface three miles from the entrance to the Dardanelles. The Turks had mounted searchlights that swept the strait continuously during the night, and in order to use his battery as economically as possible, Holbrook waited until dawn when these lights were extinguished. Then he moved on the surface as far as he dared. About a mile from Cape Helles on the southern tip of the Gallipoli Peninsula he trimmed and began to dive. In these old subs the conning tower was not shut off from the main boat hull during submerged sailing, for the inner end of the periscope was located there, and the commander had to stand inside to observe and control his vessel when the hull was under water. While hazardous, this arrangement had one advantage, for the commander, without changing his position, had a view through the conning tower ports when the submarine was forced suddenly to surface, and this factor was an important feature in *B-11's* exploit.

Commander Holbrook moved along the northern shore, which was fairly straight, at a depth of between sixty and eighty feet. Any enemy mines would be moored between sixteen to thirty feet where they would entangle surface craft, and if all suppositions were correct, if Holbrook's mine guards worked, there was a fair chance of his getting through.

*B-11* had proceeded about a mile when telltale vibrations told the crew that their mine guard had fouled in some manner. Coming to the surface, Holbrook discovered that the guard on the port forward hydroplane had twisted around, forming a hook that would collect mines rather than evade them. The young commander had to unbolt this mine trap quickly and proceed without it.

Progress was slow over the next few hours, but by 9:40 A.M. Holbrook decided that he was somewhere near the Narrows, and on making an observation through the periscope saw that he was right. Off his starboard beam was a large, two-funneled, gray ship, flying the Turkish ensign and bristling with naval guns.

Knowing that a good torpedo shot would be difficult in the strong current, Holbrook decided to move up as close as possible before attacking. He dipped his periscope, altered course, and after a short run came up to periscope depth again and found he had been swept down by the current, so, closing in gradually, he moved to get into a position for a shot from his starboard torpedo tube.

The current held him fast and he had to increase his battery output to get his nose around to draw a bead on the Turkish man-of-war. Then, risking being seen, he gave his orders: "Stand by! . . . Fire!"

Holbrook watched the torpedo through his periscope as it churned a white streak and sped for its mark. At that instant his boat was caught in a swirl and his periscope went under. The coxswain gradually brought her up again, but before the commander could get another look there was the thud of a great explosion. Everyone aboard *B-11* knew that their torpedo had scored. A cloud of black smoke enveloped the ship, and as Holbrook watched, the guns aboard the man-of-war, and others on shore, snarled in revenge. The water about *B-11* was churned with the eruptions of the bursting shells; the Turks has spotted him at last.

Holbrook swung away and lowered his periscope after noting the enemy vessel settling by its stern. This was his first victory but it was immediately tempered with consternation. The man at the helm reported that he could not read the compass as the lens was fogged, but Holbrook was too busy to waste time on that problem. He took one last look around to choose a safe course of escape, but the land had few distinguishing features. The only definite mark was the Turkish warship, now on fire as she wallowed. As it turned out, however, he had guessed correctly that he was in Sari Siglar Bay, a gouge in the southern coastline just below the Narrows. But he had been swept in by the current much farther than he had intended, and the course he selected to take him clear was more westerly than he realized, and carried him into an area of shoals.

There was a sudden bump indicating that B-11 had struck bottom. Her commander knew that the first effect of striking bottom is for the nose to go up, and on that presumption he ordered full speed ahead, hoping to move into deeper water. There was some satisfactory scraping below and B-11 seemed to be moving into the clear, when she struck another bump and practically came to a standstill. On glancing through the conning tower ports, Holbrook saw that the submarine was well out of the water.

Guns that were mounted in nearby forts lost no time in opening fire until columns of spray blotted out everything. Had a chunk of shrapnel from any of those shells even nicked the conning tower the crew would have been interned behind barbed wire. The batteries were still providing power and the screws twirling, as old B-11 slogged along on her belly, yard by yard; it was bump, scrape, waddle, flounder as she fought like a hooked pike for deeper water.

While this had been taking place, an American vice consul, G. Van H. Ingert, had been enjoying a row in a small boat. When the Turkish man-of-war, later identified as *Messoudieh*, a cruiser of 10,000 tons, went up, Mr. Ingert played a heroic role. He rescued a few Turkish survivors who had been blown overboard, and then, attracted by the cries of a number of men who seemed to be imprisoned in one of the turrets, he rowed about until he found an open porthole. He peered through and saw that it provided access to the gun deck. With the aid of his oars and some pieces of rope, he extricated about sixty Turkish seamen and helped them into other boats that were joining the rescue work. Then, exhausted, drenched, and half-frozen, Mr. Ingert withdrew from the scene. So far as can be learned, he was never thanked for his assistance, or given any recognition for his timely kindness.

As Lieutenant Holbrook's *B-11* bumped and bounced over the sand and shale, the Turks hammered away with much noise but little accuracy. At last the bumps and scraping ceased, she floundered into the clear and surged forward, diving as she went. Gradually the conning tower went under and she was fully submerged.

The crew breathed a thankful sigh, relieved to learn that the conning tower had not been hit.

"How's her head?" Holbrook called down to the men at the control platform.

"We can't see, sir. The compass is still blurred."

"Tell Lieutenant Winn to have a look."

Holbrook's first lieutenant could not determine anything from the instrument, and the skipper decided that the shock of shells bursting on the water so close to them had shaken the compass box, but he said nothing and raised his periscope again and searched the horizon for other Turks to conquer.

He spotted a Turkish wreck, apparently standing on one end, and he figured that she was on his starboard beam, and if he kept *B-11* so, he would be steering toward the northern shore. After about ten minutes of submerged sailing a break in the land appeared on the port side. This was the entrance to the Dardanelles showing up to the southwest, so, putting his helm over, Holbrook steered for it.

The passage out was made once more at eighty feet to avoid the minefield, but this time the current was in his favor. It was almost impossible to keep direction without a compass, but Holbrook held her as steady as he could, and by frequent surfacing to periscope depth he made his way to the entrance where he came to the surface. In the excitement the crew had not noticed that the air was becoming foul in their long submergence of nine hours. Their oxygen had been almost used up, as was disclosed when the Diesel would not run until the boat had been completely ventilated.

All Turkey was astonished by this feat. How could a British submarine bash its way through their minefield with four miles of shore batteries on each side, and torpedo a warship right under their noses and escape?

When Lieutenant Holbrook was honored with the Victoria Cross for his submarine exploit, other young bloods soon begged for the same chance. By 1915 the submarine still had to prove itself. Practically everything about it was experimental; its size, shape, speed, and armament, and the manner in which it should be used. How much of this claustrophobic life beneath the sea could a man stand? There also was a psychological block in the minds of men that submarine warfare was a form of barbarism that could only result in the destruction of all of them. How often have peaceful men said the same thing about the atomic warhead? But these early underwater boatmen were in much the same class as the young adventurers of the early flying services; a breed apart from the other military forces, a daring, minority group with a strange esoteric excitement of its own, determined to prove that it was capable of exploits of which no one had dreamed.

Instead of cracking under the strain, these volunteers relished it. They brought a new brand of courage, a controlled recklessness, a kind of joy in the power of the human frame. It was not a question of how much these men could stand, but of how designers could meet their demands for more speed, longer hours in action, and more deadly gadgets.

During the Gallipoli campaign a few British submarines were sent against the Turkish peninsular defenses. Their commanders also hoped to get through to the Sea of Marmara and create destruction in shipping that was supplying Turkish forces. Up to the time of the Gallipoli landing on April 25, 1915, every attempt at forcing the Narrows had failed. One Australian Navy submarine, *AE-2*, made a brave try but was caught on the surface and sunk. The French submarine *Joule* was destroyed before she even reached Chanak. But despite these disasters the possibility seethed in the minds of several youthful commanders who had been sent out from the North Sea command, and, because of their weeks of undersea experience were brimming with high morale. Most of them believed that if new tactics could be tried, they would get through.

On the other side of the ledger, the German U-boats engaged in the Gallipoli defense presumably had a simpler problem. They had a complete set of sitting-duck targets—the whole British Mediterranean Fleet that was cruising in the open Aegean, but they were deprived of this easy objective, not by the Narrows, but by the wide expanse of the Atlantic and the length of the Mediterranean. In April there were no U-boats at Constantinople or in the Mediterranean, and the only way for the Germans to reach the scene of this action was to sail around western Europe and slip through the Strait of Gibraltar, which meant running their Diesels until the last ounce of oil fuel was gone. At one time there was a scheme for sending small U-boats in sections by rail to Pola on the Adriatic, but nothing had come of this as yet.

Both sides were balked in their undersea offensive at Gallipoli. The prize for the British and French was the massed Turkish shipping in the Marmara; for the Germans the unprotected Allied battleships in the Aegean. So far, with the exception of Commander Holbrook's plucky, but lucky, exploit against *Messoudieh*, neither antagonist had been able to strike.

Toward the end of April a series of events began that were to alter the whole character of the campaign. On the very day of the Gallipoli landing, Lieutenant Commander Otto Hersing, aboard *U-21*, set out from the mouth of the Ems River in northwest Germany for the long journey around the north of Scotland to the Mediterranean. Two days later Lieutenant Commander E. Courtney Boyle, skipper of *E-14*, slipped silently into the Dardanelles and headed for the Narrows.

Commander Boyle, who became an admiral, planned to work his way through the Dardanelles on the surface under the cover of darkness. He set off at 2:00 A.M., but had not proceeded very far when enemy searchlights spotted him, and the Turkish guns drove him down to ninety feet. He continued at this level until he judged he had passed under the Kephez minefield. He then came up to twenty-two feet intending to make the actual passage of the Narrows with his periscope raised, but the sighting tube carved a distinct feather on the sea, and there was a frantic half hour when the enemy guns around Chanak got his range. At one time the crew of a Turkish patrol boat snatched at the periscope whenever Commander Boyle brought it to the surface. In retrospect this seems amusing, but *E-14* stood a good chance of being damaged seriously. She escaped unscathed, however, and came up in the Sea of Marmara soon after dawn.

For the next three weeks *E-14* cruised about at will. Her greatest success was the sinking of a former White Star liner that was on her way from Constantinople with six thousand troops destined for the battle on the Cape Helles front. There were no survivors, and Boyle's submarine feat was a bigger victory than any the British had on land. There was wild elation when *E-14* came out safely and surfaced in the Aegean Sea on May 18.

On hearing of Boyle's feat, another young lieutenant commander, Martin E. D. Nasmith, decided to take his *E-11* through the Narrows, and within sixteen hours was resting on the bottom of the Sea of Marmara. Unknown to anyone, he had decided on a plan more daring than any essayed heretofore—to attack Constantinople itself.

Nasmith's cruise reads like an anglicized Baron Munchausen tale. On coming to the surface, his first act was to seize a Turkish sailing vessel and lash her to *E-11's* side so that it would act as both a disguise and a decoy. But over the next few days no worthy target appeared, so he discarded this camouflage and moved boldly up the Marmara.

On May 23 he sank a Turkish gunboat and several smaller craft, and then he encountered the transport *Nagara* as it was making its way down to the Dardanelles. The American newspaperman, Raymond Gram Swing, who was on board the transport, said later that he had been talking to one of the passengers about Commander Boyle's feat of the previous week, and had remarked that it was a fine morning for submarines.

It was. One minute later *E-11* bobbed to the surface about one hundred yards away. A slim figure in a white sweater called from the sub's comming tower, "Who are you?"

"I'm Swing, a reporter for the Chicago *Daily News.*"

"Good morning, Mr. Swing," Commander Nasmith replied politely. "What ship is that?"

"The Turkish transport, *Nagara.*"

The crew was in a real panic, running in all directions, but generally to the rail to leap overboard.

"Are those men marines?" Nasmith inquired.

"No, just merchant sailors."

"Sorry, but I'm going to have to sink you."

"Can't we get off?" Swing appealed.

"Yes, but be damned quick about it!"

Everyone on board *Nagara* tried to get into a boat or launch one. There was no deck discipline, so Nasmith ordered Swing to take command of the last available boat, and to pick up as many sailors and passengers as he could. When these routine courtesies were completed, the British submariner put a shot into the troopship and she went up in a pillar of orange flame—she was loaded with ammunition.

In this almost comic-opera cruise *E-11* was then driven away from the coast by a troop of Turkish cavalry, but she continued on to chase and sink another transport and to force a third to beach on the shore. The survivors of these wrecks raised the alarm and from early morning of May 25 Turkish artillerymen stood to their guns on both sides of the Bosporus. In order to allay the fears of the general population, a report was issued to the effect that some practice firing might be made during the day.

The *E-11* next surfaced at 12:40 P.M. and Nasmith spotted the large freighter *Stamboul* that was berthed alongside an arsenal. His first torpedo ran amok and almost sank *E-11*. The second struck home, and Commander Nasmith dived, dashed past the famous Turkish city and darted into the Bosporus as a barrage of artillery churned the water of the narrow strait that joins the Black Sea with the Sea of Marmara.

There was wild panic in Constantinople. The old *Goeben*, now *Sultan Selim*, hurriedly shifted her anchorage and moved into the shelter of her attendant ships. Wild mobs ran in all directions, stores were closed, and soldiers who had been embarked for Gallipoli were rushed back to shore again.

But Nasmith and his crew were having a bad time also. The current in the Bosporus was even stronger than that in the Dardanelles and *E-11* was completely out of control for twenty minutes as she bumped from shoal to shoal along the bottom as far as Leander's Tower. Finally she was righted, and with daring skill Nasmith sailed safely back past Constantinople. Over the next day he wisely rested on the bottom in the middle of the Marmara. One can imagine the relief they all enjoyed after such an experience.

Instead of calling it a patrol and sneaking back to safety, Nasmith resumed his attack on May 27 and sank vessel after vessel in the approaches to the Golden Horn. Stark terror spread across the Sea of Marmara, for it was thought that by now a whole fleet of submarines was operating against the Turks. No ship of any size left port without an escort of gunboats or destroyers, and these tried repeatedly to ram *E-11* whenever she rose to the surface to attack. Commander Nasmith eased up on his crusade only when the air in the hull became so foul he was obliged to surface to permit his crew to go out on deck and draw in fresh air.

There now was a shortage of torpedoes and those that were left were set to run on the surface so that whenever they missed their targets the crew could go overboard and recover them.

By June 5 a serious defect developed in the main port motor; the starboard shaft had cracked. Only two torpedoes were left, so Commander Nasmith decided that he had run out his string, and proceeded home. He entered the Dardanelles and moved down as far as Chanak where he searched for the Turkish battleship *Barbarosa Harradin* on which he had made an unsuccessful attack a few days before. He found nothing, however, but a large transport anchored nearby. *E-11* was in a dangerous part of the Narrows and in her crippled state ran a good chance of being washed ashore, but Nasmith had no intention of wasting a target. After all, he had two torpedoes left. He turned back up the Dardanelles and sent the transport to the bottom, and only then returned for the chancy dive through the Narrows. When he was off Chanak the trim of the boat was affected seriously by the change in the density of the water, so Nasmith dived to seventy feet, and as *E-11* crept slowly forward a scraping sound was detected, indicating that their keel might be running over the bottom. On checking his chart, Nasmith knew this was impossible, so he rose to twenty feet and investigated through his periscope and saw that a large mine had been torn from its moorings and lodged forward in the port hydroplane. He made no mention of this hazard to his crew, but ordered *E-11* to proceed slowly for another hour until he was well outside the entrance to the strait. He then ordered, "Full speed—astern!" and with that the bow of the submarine submerged, and the rush of water from her screws carried away the deadly weapon.

That night there was a formal dinner aboard the British flagship, at which time Commander Nasmith told his story. Later he was recommended for the Victoria Cross, and he finally caught the *Barbarosa Harradin* the following August, sinking her in the Narrows. After that exploit he again returned to Constantinople where he found a collier berthed beside the Haidar Pasha railroad station. Coal literally was black diamonds to Turkey, and a committee of military officials was grouped on the dock to decide how this load was to be apportioned. Nasmith fired one torpedo, and the collier went up in smoke and flames. Leaving that area, *E-11* turned into the Gulf of Ismid (Izmit) where the Constantinople-Baghdad railroad ran over a viaduct close to the sea. Nasmith's first officer, a venturesome youth by the name of D'Oyly-Hughes, swam ashore and blew up the line. He was half-dead when he scrambled back to the submarine, but he had done a perfect job on the viaduct.

Commander Nasmith had bagged 101 enemy vessels in three months, and on occasion had stayed in the Sea of Marmara for forty-seven days. But even with all this, these submarine successes were not completely understood; the raids were considered more as sporting gestures, rather than as part of the main offensive. Had they been enlarged to put commandos ashore, a strong British force might have been landed north of Bulair to cut the Turkish land route to the Gallipoli Peninsula.

## The Riddle of Jutland

The one occasion when the rival battle fleets of Great Britain and Germany met in World War I has been recorded as the Battle of Jutland; Germany prefers to call it the Battle of the Skagerrak, and lists it as a victory for her side. The engagement was fought about seventy-five miles west of the Danish coast, and Admiral Sir John R. Jellicoe commanded the British Grand Fleet, and Admiral Reinhard Scheer the German High Seas Fleet. This enemy fleet that had been built to dispute the British mastery of the sea, came, more by accident than by design, upon the fleet that had held that mastery for centuries. It was on the afternoon of May 31, 1916, but the outcome failed to live up to

the billing. When it was over the battered and bewildered
Grand Fleet was steaming about an empty sea. For those who
are interested in figures, the losses on both sides can be sum-
marized as follows:

| Ships | British | German |
|---|---|---|
| Battleships | None | 1 |
| Battle cruisers | 3 | 1 |
| Cruisers | 3 | None |
| Light cruisers | None | 4 |
| Torpedo craft | 8 | 5 |
| Total | 14 | 11 |

| Personnel | British | German |
|---|---|---|
| Officers, killed | 328 | 160 |
| Men, killed | 5769 | 2385 |
| Officers, prisoners | 10 | None |
| Men, prisoners | 167 | None |
| Total | 6274 | 2545 |

On the face of it these figures would appear to leave much in
favor of Admiral Scheer, but since his fleet was driven back to
its haven and never came out again to fight and was eventually
surrendered to the British at Scapa Flow, it might just as well
have been sent to the bottom. It never struck another blow for
the Fatherland.

Jutland illustrates the fundamental difference between the
higher naval and military leadership in World War I. The generals who commanded from their snug rear-area headquarters
were always keen to take an offensive, no matter how unpropi-
tious the situation. On the other hand, the admirals would not
give battle intentionally unless reasonably sure of an initial advantage.

From the beginning of the war the British Admiralty realized
that maintenance of sea supremacy was more vital than meeting

and defeating the German fleet. The whole war effort of the British was based on the ability of the Royal Navy to keep the sea lanes open; the defeat of the German High Seas Fleet was always subsidiary, but if it could be destroyed, the war might be shortened. The U-boats proved to be a far more potent weapon than Admiral Scheer's surface fleet, and already were threatening to starve Britain out of the war. So, if in trying to overcome the enemy fleet, Admiral Jellicoe lost enough to forfeit his strategic superiority, national defeat would be almost certain. Winston Churchill once said, "Jellicoe was the only man on either side who could lose the war in an afternoon."

Germany's strategy was to avoid any decisive action until the British fleet was so weakened that an all-out encounter could be risked. She employed the weapons of attrition, U-boat torpedoes, and underwater mines, to achieve a preliminary weakening, but Jellicoe realized the intent, and early in the war declared that if a chance of battle came, he would regard the turning away of the German battle fleet as a sign it was setting up a trap where submarines and a pattern of mines lay in wait. It was this over-all situation that prevented an earlier engagement. By early summer of 1916, Admiral Scheer became impatient with the failure of his submarine fleet to do little more than sink unarmed merchantmen, and realized that the British blockade was taking a toll, and his seamen were losing their varied skills and most certainly their morale.

His hopes were slim, for he knew that the British had a larger fleet, and their turrets outgunned him, but what he did not know was that as early as August 1914 when the German light cruiser *Magdeburg* was sunk in the Baltic, some Russian seamen had come across a signal-code case that was clasped in the arms of a drowned officer. The case also contained cipher and signal books of the German Navy as well as their squared charts of the North Sea. These were sent to London, and for many months the Admiralty Intelligence staff had intercepted and deciphered enemy wireless messages, and obtained advance information of movements. At the same time a primitive form of directional wireless had been devised that enabled the British to locate the position of ships using this means of communication.

Admiral Scheer, who had been appointed to command the High Seas Fleet by Admiral Alfred von Tirpitz, was an aggressive man and when he learned that a division of the British Fleet had been assigned to protect the east coast of England from hit-and-run raids, he set up a trap for his first nibble. He planned a bombardment of the city of Sunderland by a few cruisers hoping thereby to draw out a portion of the Grand Fleet to intercept them. He was to hide some fifty miles behind the raiders and be in a position to pounce, and in addition he had a number of submarines out, spreading mines and threatening the British ports of sortie. It was one of these mines that sank H.M.S. *Hampshire* which was carrying Lord Kitchener to Russia.

British Naval Intelligence was well aware of the enemy submarine activity, and that the High Seas Fleet was gathering in the mouth of the Jade River, sometimes referred to as the Jade Roads, or Jade Bay. Admiral Jellicoe, therefore, had the three flotillas of his Grand Fleet at Rosythe, Scapa Flow, and Invergordon on Moray Firth. When Admiral Scheer sent Admiral Franz von Hipper with a scouting force to "demonstrate" off the southwest coast of Norway, Admiral Jellicoe moved, but was uncertain just what was afoot, and a telegram from the Admiralty misled him into believing that the whole German fleet was still off the Jade River and that there was no great need for hurry.

In spite of the possession of German naval codes and signals, Admiral Jellicoe was hampered by the lack of immediate intelligence. He knew that the Germans might use naval Zeppelins to spot for Admiral Scheer, but he had no such reconnaissance, which was one of the chief reasons for his failure to inflict more damage on the German Fleet.

The British had been experimenting for some time with a mother ship for the accommodation of naval aircraft. There were no aircraft carriers with flight decks, of course, but the Royal Naval Air Service had visualized several possibilities, and after a few attempts to devise a seaplane carrier, the old twenty-two-knot Cunarder *Campania* was converted into a fleet aircraft carrier. A flying deck of 120 feet in length was built over the forecastle from which it was hoped light single-seaters might be launched. In addition, derricks, booms, and other equipment for launching and "hoisting-out" a number of two-seater Short seaplanes were included. *Campania* also carried an armament of eight 4.7-inch guns and suitable storage facilities for large quantities of gasoline.

In early trials and exercises with the fleet, *Campania* could put off and recover seaplanes if the seas were not too high. The comparatively low-powered seaplanes of that time were not able to get off rough water, and it was deemed imperative that the aircraft be two-seaters since it was believed that a man charged with the difficulties of piloting an aircraft, was not also capable of spotting enemy movements and relaying the information back to the fleet; that had to be done by a second member, which accounts for the decision to use two-seaters when one-seaters would have filled the bill.

At any rate, early in 1916 *Campania* was a fairly reliable vessel for naval air operations. She carried eight reconnaissance seaplanes and four Sopwith "Baby" seaplanes. A balloon well, sheltered by a canvas screen, was set up at the stern of the vessel to accommodate a kite balloon and its winch and basket. The balloon could be inflated, raised, and used for limited-range observation, just as kite balloons were being used on the Western Front.

Ready for action, and fully equipped in this manner, *Campania* joined the Grand Fleet at Scapa Flow on April 12, 1916, where exercises were carried out, and her flying personnel gained reconnaissance experience. It is recorded that a few Sopwith "Baby" single-seaters were actually flown off the flight deck, using a wheeled trolley as a jettison-undercarriage, while the old liner was hitting twenty knots. But *Campania* was not destined for glory at Jutland; she was the victim of a majestic foulup instead.

On the morning of May 30 this seaplane carrier returned from one of her regular flight exercises in which both the aircraft and the balloon worked on a naval-gunfire shoot with commendable results. She dropped anchor five miles from the main fleet and received a preparatory signal alerting all ships of the Grand Fleet. About 7:00 P.M. she received another order to raise steam for full speed and by 9:30 *Campania* was ready to proceed to sea, but her skipper, Captain Oliver Swann, unfortunately did not receive the executive order that was sent out at 10:45 and it was not until some hours later that he was aware that the fleet had sailed. Once he had learned the reason for the general departure, he weighed anchor and passed the outer boom defenses about an hour after the last ship of the fleet had left.

*Campania's* absence from the action was not detected until about midnight, and Admiral Jellicoe did not know until 2:00 A.M. that she had even left Scapa Flow. Then, respectful of the thirteen enemy submarines known to be in the vicinity and the fact that no destroyer escort could be furnished this untried novelty, he ordered her at 4:37 A.M. to return to harbor which she reached safely at 9:15 A.M. The Grand Fleet went into the Battle of Jutland without aerial reconnaissance.

How much this lack cost can be appreciated when it is explained that at 2:30 on the afternoon of the same day, *Galatea*, one of the British screen ships, sighted a stray merchantman and steamed off to examine her. In the meantime the rest of the battle cruiser flotilla had turned west to join Jellicoe's fleet out of the Orkneys. At the same time a German light cruiser, spotting the same merchantman, also decided to investigate, and in a few minutes both men-of-war had sighted each other and sent out warning signals. It was this trick of fate that opened the Battle of Jutland long before Jellicoe had wished, and unquestionably deprived the British of a complete victory. Had one of the seaplanes from *Campania* been available, Jellicoe or Beatty would have known better than to make the first move against their enemy; they would have waited until the German battle cruiser flotilla was farther north—farther from the shelter of Scheer's High Seas Fleet.

When Admiral Beatty turned southeastward to cut off the retreat of the enemy cruisers, his signal to turn—made by flags—was not received or read because of low-lying smoke, and Rear Admiral Hugh Evan-Thomas, commanding the Fifth Battle Squadron, did not turn until nearly ten minutes later, a delay that left him ten miles behind Admiral Beatty's battle cruisers. Whether this signal should have been given by lamp, or even via wireless, has long been argued. Why Evan-Thomas did not turn immediately on his own initiative as soon as he saw Beatty's *Lion* turning, is also discussed by the armchair strategists, and why Beatty did not wait for the Fifth Battle Squadron to rejoin him has consumed gallons of controversial ink.

All this was typical of the Battle of Jutland, however; very few moves went right, and the most unbelievable hits and misses were recorded. One lone shell hit the midship turret of *Lion*, Beatty's flagship, and had it not been for the heroism of Major F. J. W. Harvey of the Royal Marines the whole vessel might have gone up. With both legs shattered, and the only man left alive in the turret, Harvey managed to crawl to a voice tube and have the magazines flooded, before he died. *Indefatigable* which was hit by three shells from the German battleship *Von der Tann,* dropped out of the line, but was hit again and sank, carrying with her more than one thousand men.

When Evan-Thomas did come up and join the battle, his gunners gave a brilliant display of accuracy, but their shells exploded before piercing the enemy armor. Then *Queen Mary* was hit by a salvo and sank with her crew of 1200. This left Admiral Beatty fighting with four ships against five, but when the battle cruiser *Princess Royal* went down next, the admiral remarked to his flag captain, "Chatfield, there seems to be something wrong with our damned ships today. However, turn two points to port," and with that the gallant Englishman moved closer to his enemy.

Actually, the crisis had passed, Scheer's trap was eluded, and the German admiral had to turn and go to Admiral von Hipper's aid. By 4:40 Beatty took his battle squadron north to join Jellicoe who was coming up with the Grand Fleet. Again Evan-Thomas was misled by a signal that was not received, and found himself sailing south while Beatty was heading north, and only through amazing stands made by British destroyers was Scheer held off. During this new period of indecision, Scheer was heading blindly for the combined Jellicoe-Beatty fleets, but neither British admiral had any knowledge of this unbelievable opportunity. Here again *Campania* might have saved the day and set up the annihilation of Scheer's force. Evan-Thomas was in touch with the enemy, but failed to send out any reports. Beatty's wireless equipment had been shot away, and his messages were going out second- or thirdhand from other British vessels. The climax of all this was that no flotilla was where it was supposed, or assumed, to be when the enemy was sighted. The British fleet was in a compact mass, and could not deliver its maximum fire—only when broadsides are brought into action from in-line formations, can this power of gunnery be used. Jellicoe, appealing for some information on the position of the enemy fleet, next lost Beatty who was some seven miles out of position. It was not until 6:10 P.M. that Jellicoe had any idea where Scheer was or in what direction he was steering.

From this point on, the story of Jutland can be understood only by dedicated naval strategists. It is difficult for the non-expert to explain what happened in terms that will satisfy the blue-water purists. The Battle of Jutland, the last great sea engagement in which the contestants actually saw each other and fired their guns at visible targets—unless we so list that melee of confusion and fury, the tragic-comic World War II naval Battle of Guadalcanal—remains the standard staff college critical study, and is bracketed with Gettysburg, the last great land battle which was won, or lost, by the strategic movement of men and weapons.

For the landlubber the Jutland story becomes a maze of nautical nomenclature, as bewildering as today's Pentagonese, and it is difficult to evaluate the importance of the number of points turned, deployment strategy as depicted on battle maps, or the masked movements leading up to "crossing the T." Non-naval historians are left out of their depth, and all we can say is that the Royal Navy did its best to destroy the German High Seas Fleet, and failing that had to be satisfied with driving it back to Wilhelmshaven where it huddled for the rest of the war.

It is apparent that neither Hipper nor Scheer could be successfully trapped, although many wild risks were taken. Hipper lost his light cruiser *Wiesbaden,* but before he made his getaway he sank *Invincible,* and an armored cruiser, and left a third vessel in a sinking condition. By this time the Royal Navy rounded itself up for some concerted action and made its big-gun contribution to the efforts of the destroyer fleet. *Frauenlob,* a light cruiser, was sunk by a torpedo from the badly battered *Southampton.* The *Elbing* was rammed by the battleship *Posen* which became confused by the antics of the British destroyers, and to keep matters at this ridiculous level, the British destroyer *Spitfire* rammed the enemy battleship *Nassau* and brought back a long sheet of plating to prove this impertinence. For more than an hour a flotilla of British destroyers buzzed about like hornets, sacrificing four, but undoubtedly starting the German fleet back to its harbor shelter. Unfortunately, none bothered to tell their superiors what they were up to, and Jellicoe and Beatty were both in the dark as to the progress of events.

Before Scheer could make his escape, the German battleship *Pommern* went down before a torpedo fired by a destroyer, and the Battle of Jutland ended with the British navy steaming up and down in search of the German High Seas Fleet. Jellicoe and Beatty were so out of touch they had to await word from the Admiralty in London to learn that the enemy fleet was near Horn Reef and obviously steaming for home.

As an aside, it might be added that, on August 19, the German Fleet, covered by an airship patrol, moved out once more from Heligoland Bight, toward England, but a reconnaissance Zeppelin warned that the British Fleet was advancing to meet it, whereupon Admiral Scheer turned and raced back to his base. In November of 1918 Scheer again ordered his High Seas Fleet to break the British blockade, but the German crews refused to weigh anchor; a mutinous outbreak that widened the fissure splitting the whole German cause.

## Death For Captain Fryatt

Another German atrocity that aroused all Great Britain, was the execution of Captain Charles A. Fryatt, master of a British merchantman, who in March 1915 had attempted to ram a U-boat. Almost a year later, his vessel, S.S. *Brussels* was captured by a German surface force and Fryatt was taken prisoner and jailed in Zeebrugge. In carrying out this death penalty, Germany broke every existing form of law, created a new rule of her own, and then condemned Captain Fryatt for not having followed this new law before it had been written.

Shocking as was the death of nurse Edith Cavell, Captain Fryatt's execution aroused the British more than any other event in the war. Being a seafaring people, the act only hardened their purpose, rather than weakened it, as Germany intended.

On the afternoon of March 28, 1915, Captain Fryatt was in command of *Brussels,* sailing from Parkeston Quay in Harwich for Rotterdam. When he was a short distance from the Maas Lightship a submarine identified later as *U-33* appeared on the surface moving at good speed. Warned by experience of the enemy's tactics, Fryatt knew that if he attempted to turn away from his present course, he could be torpedoed. Instead, as was his right under international law, he disregarded a summons from the U-boat commander to stop, and putting his helm over hard, ordered full speed and steered for the conning tower of the enemy vessel. When he was within twenty yards the U-boat submerged, and firemen below in *Brussels* claimed they distinctly heard or felt a bumping sensation. Captain Fryatt did not wait for evidence of damage to the U-boat but continued at full speed until he was safely within territorial waters of Holland.

On his return to England the facts of this adventure were widely reported in many newspapers, and Captain Fryatt and his first officer and chief engineer were awarded gold watches by the Admiralty, and praised in the House of Commons for having saved the ship and crew from certain destruction by the U-boat. Mrs. Fryatt received a letter from King George that read: *"The action of Captain Fryatt in defending his ship against the attack of an enemy submarine was a noble instance of the resource and self-reliance so characteristic of his profession."*

By contrast in Germany, Captain Fryatt was bitterly attacked in all newspapers, and it was claimed that he had actually surrendered and was moving up close to the submarine for examination when he treacherously made an attempt to ram the vessel. In rebuttal, British officials cited the German proclamation of February 4, 1915, that declared any British merchantman flying the British flag in these waters would be attacked without notice. They insisted this was sufficient cause for Fryatt to defend himself and his vessel against such illegal violence by the enemy.

The international clamor died down eventually, but on June 22, 1916, more than a year later, Captain Fryatt sailed from the Hook of Holland bound for Tilbury Docks in London. *Brussels* had a cargo of foodstuffs and a number of Belgian refugees, one of whom spoke German and acted suspiciously throughout the succeeding incident.

*Brussels* was captured by a flotilla of German torpedo boats and taken as a prize into Zeebrugge where Fryatt and his crew behaved with quiet dignity the meanwhile comforting a number of weeping Belgian women frightened by the experience.

By July 1 the British asked the American Ambassador in Amsterdam to check on the whereabouts of Fryatt and his crew, and a response explained that all were safe and well and that "the Master of the vessel had desired that his wife be informed."

No one at the time suspected the terrible import of those few words.

About two weeks later, July 16, an Amsterdam newspaper reported that Captain Fryatt was to be tried by court-martial on a charge of ramming a German submarine. The British Foreign Office requested the American Ambassador to inquire into the matter and take proper steps for the captain's defense.

A court-martial was held at Bruges and no independent witnesses were present, the trial being carried out in great haste and behind locked doors. Only the bald statement was put out that "On Thursday, at Bruges, before the Court-Martial of the Marine Corps, the trial took place of Captain Fryatt of the British steamer *Brussels*, which was brought in as a prize."

A requested postponement of the trial was refused on the thin excuse that submarine personnel could not be detained any longer. Fryatt was defended by a Major Neumann, an attorney in civil life, but no names of the judges, or under what principles of international law he was tried were given out. He was found guilty and condemned to death because—according to the German official announcement—"Although he was not a member of a combatant force, he made an attempt on March 28, 1915, to ram the German submarine, *U-33*, near the Maas Lightship."

But according to the prize laws of all the great states of that day, Fryatt's resistance to being sunk, was legitimate. It was also admitted by German prize regulations, in an appendix, dated June 22, 1914, that stated: "If an enemy armed merchant vessel offers armed resistance to the right of visit, search and capture, the crew are to be treated as prisoners of war."

Germany obviously was determined to discourage any imitation of Captain Fryatt's gallantry, and he was shot in an enclosed part of the harbor grounds at Bruges. One alderman of the town was present to witness the execution, and the news of his death was released by the American Ambassador. A shudder of loathing, horror, and incredulity ran through every neutral country. The New York *Herald* pronounced the death of Captain Fryatt as a "Crowning German Atrocity!" and the New York

*Times* denounced the execution as "a deliberate murder—a trifle to the government that has so many thousands to answer for."

The Geneva *Journal* in little Switzerland had the courage to state: "It is monstrous to maintain that armed forces have a right to murder civilians, but that civilians are guilty of a crime in defending themselves."

## U. S. Destroyers Come Through

A flotilla of United States Navy destroyers made a sudden appearance in British waters on May 4, 1917, or within a month after America declared war. Their arrival was timely and welcome, but seldom has been appreciated for its significance. In comparison to the United States Army, the Navy had an immediate force for the defense of civilization, and the work of these destroyers deserves a high place on the scroll of World War I's history.

Previous to 1916 the concept of building up an expeditionary force of several millions to be shipped overseas was very remote, and no such plans had been considered. The task of providing a transport fleet in itself was a prodigious undertaking, but to build, launch, outfit, and train crews for naval fighting vessels to escort these ships and their cargoes, was, for a time, beyond the scope of available organization.

On May 29, 1917, Rear Admiral Albert Gleaves, then commander of the Destroyer Fleet of the Atlantic Fleet, was designated Commander of the United States Convoy Operations in the Atlantic—in addition to his other duties. While the British Navy bore the brunt of antisubmarine warfare in the North Sea and the English Channel, United States Navy vessels accepted the mission of holding the U-boats in the Atlantic, which they did with efficiency and dispatch.

The first actual war service was undertaken by U. S. Navy destroyers, thereby ignoring the Mahan theory that the place of the destroyers was with the capital ships—the battlewagons. It was generally believed in Washington that every dreadnought should have at least four destroyers to act as her eyes, as scouts, or to screen her with smoke. Both Great Britain and France had advised the United States that small, fast vessels would be of great immediate use, and suggested sending a pack of destroyers. Secretary of the Navy Josephus Daniels, after conferring with Admiral William S. Benson, Chief of Naval Operations, and Admiral Henry Thomas Mayo, Commander-in-Chief of the Atlantic Fleet, ordered the first group of destroyers to go, although he was not wholeheartedly in favor of such an early contribution to the Allied effort.

The U.S. destroyer force was manned by a select group of officers and men, skippered by young lieutenant commanders who gloried in their commands and attracted the best for the noncommissioned ranks. These crews were so keen, they were ready and willing for work when they arrived in England, a spirit that was most welcome at the time when the German submarines were striving to make good their threat to starve England out before aid could be obtained from America.

These escorts afforded a standard of protection seldom attained under such circumstances; not one American soldier was lost to U-boat attack on the trips to Europe. On the homeward-bound trips, however, they were not so fortunate because it was not possible to furnish such a concentration of naval defense east-to-west. The United States Naval transports, *Antilles*, *President Lincoln*, and *Covington* were torpedoed and sunk on their return trips; *Finland* and *Mount Vernon* were torpedoed but made port safely; the United States armored cruiser *San Diego* struck a mine laid by a German submarine and sank.

During the U. S. Transport Fleet's first convoy sailing for France, German submarines made a surprise attack well west of the accepted U-boat zone of operations, and the Navy's first war effort was announced through the U. S. Government Press Bureau, then directed by George Creel, noted journalist and publicity director. The report was somewhat flamboyant, and had to be toned down later to coincide with the more constrained reports issued by the British and French navies. Creel's dispatch, reminiscent of the "Sighted Sub—Sank Same," war reporting, was as follows:

"German submarines attacked the transports in force. They were outfought by the American escorting destroyers, and at least one submarine was destroyed.

"No American ship was hit, and not a life lost. The German submarines attacked twice. On both occasions the U-boats were beaten off with every appearance of loss. One boat was certainly sunk, and there is reason to believe that the accurate fire of our gunners sent others to the bottom.

"The first attack occurred at 10:30 P.M. on June 22. What gives it a particular and disturbing significance is that our ships were set upon at a point well on this side of the rendezvous, in a part of the Atlantic which might have been presumed free from submarines.

"The attack was made in force, and although the night made it impossible to arrive at an exact count, it was clear that the U-boats had gathered for what they deemed would be a slaughter. The heavy gunfire of the American destroyers scattered the submarines. It is not known how many torpedoes were launched, but at least five were counted.

"The second attack was launched a few days later against another contingent, the point of attack being beyond the rendezvous. Not only did the destroyers hold the U-boats at a safe distance, but their speed resulted in the sinking of at least one submarine. Grenades were used, firing a charge of explosives timed to go off at a certain distance under the water. In one instance the wreckage covered the surface of the sea after a shot at a periscope, and reports claim that the boat was sunk.

"Protected by our high-seas convoy, destroyers, and by French war vessels, the contingent proceeded and joined the others at the French port. The whole nation will rejoice that so great a peril was passed by the vanguard of the men who will fight our battles in France."

*Doughty* Daffodil

In early 1918 the Royal Navy was fighting the U-boat tooth and nail in its determination to keep these raiders out of the English Channel and the Straits of Dover. Later on, greatly aided by the United States Navy, the British laid a barrage of mines between the Orkneys and the Bergen leads off the coast of Norway, a venture that in time dulled the fangs of the undersea vessel.

Although more than two-thirds of Germany's U-boats operated out of German ports, a large number used Ostend and Zeebrugge in Belgium. Both of these submarine nests, because of their positions, might be bottled up, if an efficient and diligent attempt were made. A plan had been devised by Rear Admiral Sir Roger Keyes, of Gallipoli fame, whereby both bases could be destroyed, and thus block off the Bruges Canal down which submarines that were built in inland yards were delivered to their bases of operations. The general idea was first to create confusion with a storming party while Royal Navy men moved a number of ancient warships into positions where they could be sunk to block the important channels.

Admiral Keyes was a bold gentleman who was willing to stake his future on any plan he conceived. The story has been told many times, and it may be remembered that at both Zeebrugge and Ostend the efforts were carried out with great gallantry and some tragic losses. The U-boat ports were blocked temporarily, or made useless, and some historians state that this action was the greatest and most daring in modern seamanship. Certainly the enemy submarines were kept out of the Straits of Dover for the rest of the war.

But Zeebrugge, an out-and-out Royal Navy classic that was supported by a number of Royal Marines, must share some of its glory with a Liverpool excursion boat named *Daffodil*.

When ships were being selected for this historic raid, Admiral Keyes knew that the gunnery defenses of the ancient port would have to be eliminated if the block ships were to be moved into their proper positions. At the same time some big guns would have to counter enemy guns, and a number of diversionary moves would have to be made by human raiders while the seamen moved the block ships into position. Keyes therefore selected an outdated light cruiser, the *Vindictive,* and had her modified for this venture. She carried many troops, landing ramps, temporary gun platforms, searchlights, mortar, and machine-gun batteries, and it was from her that most of the raiders were to be disembarked to spread out over the Zeebrugge Mole, or breakwater. All well and good, but provision had to be made to make certain *Vindictive* could move up close to this high concrete and granite seawall. If the seas were rough, or if there were strong ground swells, the light cruiser would have to be nudged in with some auxiliary power.

Naval tugs might have fitted the situation, but Keyes wanted a vessel that could also carry additional men and raiding equipment. Someone suggested that a few, old, expendable, pleasure craft might be available, and with this *everyone* remembered two gaudy, much beloved, excursion boats that in happier times had churned in and out of Liverpool—*Daffodil* and *Iris.*

When tight-lipped representatives of the Royal Navy cryptically requested these two craft for an unnamed naval operation, the members of Liverpool's town council protested.

"*Iris* and *Daffodil?* We can't spare those two. Thousands of people visit Liverpool every year just to ride on those two steamers. Think of our tourist trade." And one of the council suggested, "Why don't you take *Carmania?* She's not doing anything but blocking up one of the wharves."

"Sorry. We've got to have *Iris* and *Daffodil,*" Admiral Keyes's representatives insisted, but what was worse they would not explain for what they were to be used. Had they known, the outraged burghers would have pulled out of the Empire—and taken *Iris* and *Daffodil* with them.

The actual bottling-up operation was to be done with three war-weary cruisers, *Thetis, Intrepid,* and *Iphigenia,* which were stripped for the action, loaded with cement, and explosive charges packed in below their waterlines. The raid was to be supported by eighteen coastal motorboats and thirty-seven motor launches that were to lay the smoke screen and engage in the eventual rescue work. Thirteen destroyers and two heavy-gun monitors were to be drawn up in a semicircle outside to protect the flanks of the operation. Admiral Keyes used the destroyer *Warwick* as his flagship.

After two false starts, the operation was called off until the night of April 22–23. Timing was all-important. Wind and tide had to co-operate perfectly. *Vindictive* headed the invasion, towing *Daffodil* and *Iris* so as to maintain flotilla speed. The motorboats started to lay down the smoke screen, and at 11:40 P.M. were roaring impudently up and down Zeebrugge harbor, spreading their stink, and machine-gunning a number of armored barges.

From this point on, *Daffodil* took over. *Vindictive* reached her assigned position on the seaward side of the Mole. Her mission was to land the Marine storming party. Matters went fairly well up to a point, but owing to a strong tide and an unexpected ground swell, *Vindictive* was stalled about four hundred yards offshore and had trouble getting close enough to the sea wall to off-load her men, and it was at this juncture that pompous little *Daffodil* grabbed the laurel.

Down in her boiler room Artificer-Engineer Sutton called on his men for a heroic effort; "We know this old tub can produce only eighty pounds steam pressure, but if the *Vindictive* is to get alongside the Mole, you've got to double that!"

Stripped to the waist, the stokers of *Daffodil* shoveled coal like machines for more than an hour, and *Vindictive* beat the ground swell and moved in. While this epic struggle was being made, the smoke screen lifted and the German gunners at the land end of the Mole had a field day; *Vindictive's* funnels soon looked like nutmeg graters, but *Daffodil* continued to risk her boilers to keep the old cruiser against the sea wall, which allowed three hundred Marines to get ashore.

Meanwhile the other little excursion boat, *Iris*, was nuzzled against the Mole, but closer to the German shore guns. She was trying to unload her landing party, but the grapnels were not enough to overcome the pull of the ground swell, and *Iris* drifted dead under the German guns and had to take their fire. No one thought to move her back beyond *Vindictive's* bulk where she might have found some shelter. *Iris's* captain, Commander Valentine Gibbs, had both legs blown off, and he spent his last hour crawling about in tourniquets, encouraging his men to greater efforts.

This heroic display at Zeebrugge eventually put the three block ships into position by one o'clock in the morning, but not until the Mole had been cleared of every man who could be moved, did *Vindictive* and *Daffodil* break away and turn in a semicircle, belching flame from every perforation in their funnels. This possibly was their worst moment, for they were fully exposed to every vengeful battery, their decks were a shambles, and many of the men who had lived through the main features of the raid were cut down before the two ships could escape into the smoke screens still being laid by the doughty motor launches.

It had been quite a night for *Daffodil*, and no one seems to remember what happened to her after she was towed home, but there is a legend around Liverpool that a side-wheel excursion boat turned up at Dunkirk twenty-two years later and rescued hundreds of weary-eyed British soldiers who had waded out into the Channel. To this day they swear that her name was *Daffodil!*

## Victory by Blockade

With all the action along the Western Front, in the Mediterranean, and against the U-boat, the importance of Britain's "undeclared" blockade against Germany has been forgotten, or not fully understood. In earlier wars blockade was enforced by surface squadrons standing off enemy ports, but by the time of the Russo-Japanese War, 1904–5, the Japanese blockade fleet off Port Arthur suffered severely from submarine mines. Later on, submarines became such a threat, it was almost impossible to maintain blockade ships in limited areas. Any nation fighting for its existence, and depending on its maritime supremacy, cannot afford to see one of the main objects for which its naval strength has been developed, largely displaced by neutrals, who, taking no risks in the struggle, supply the enemy with food and military supplies.

The ultimate aim of sea power is to protect its own communications while denying oversea supplies to the enemy, and in this can be noted the difference between destroying an enemy fleet, and the act of keeping it bottled up where it cannot engage in the duty for which it was designed. Thus, the true victory of the Battle of Jutland.

At the outbreak of the war much of Germany's seaborne trade was passing through Dutch and Scandinavian ports, while owing to the mining of the approaches to the Baltic, Great Britain could interfere but little with enemy trade in that sea. Light torpedo craft, submarines, mines, and aircraft made a standing, close blockade impossible, and from the beginning Britain and her allies had to find means to make their blockade effective, although their squadrons were held off at a safe distance. In some instances boarding squadrons were substituted in which visit-and-search patrols were carried out, but all this took time and too many vessels and crews.

Eventually, Great Britain's most effective weapon was known as "bunker control," which she could enforce because the world's shipping was almost entirely dependent on British coal. By withholding it from owners who were known to be trying to run the blockade, she could control this problem trade. But trying to determine the real destination of goods from the available documentary evidence was questionable, since it was obvious that supplies were pouring into Germany through Scandinavia, Holland, and, for a time, Italy. It was at this point, however, that Germany herself furnished an answer to the problem.

Germany's own shipping had been driven from the seas, and

the efficient development of her submarines induced her to set up her submarine blockade of Great Britain, and sink all merchant ships of any nation found in Allied waters. The *Lusitania* sinking marked the height of this illegal behavior, and Britain and France replied with their "Reprisals Order," that empowered their naval forces to stop all ships of enemy origin, ownership, or destination.

This new nautical rule brought the United States into sharp conflict with Great Britain, and America claimed that her trade with neutrals was suffering, as compared to that of prewar conditions. British officials in turn, proved the American figures incorrect. For instance, whereas before the war America's sea trade with the neutrals had been diminishing steadily for some years, a circular issued by the Department of Commerce at Washington on January 23, 1915, attempted to show that these trade figures had increased instead. Further British figures showed that trade with Scandinavia and Holland had increased by 300 per cent. It was obvious then that these countries' own requirements could not have risen to that extent, and that they must have been re-exporting these American goods to Germany.

In rebuttal, the United States called attention to the magnitude of Great Britain's own exports to these same countries, and proved with reliable figures that Britain herself was doing exactly what she was trying to prevent America from doing. It might be added that this "Business as Usual" attitude largely governed Britain's shopkeeper policy no matter with whom the business was conducted, and, but for this, Germany might have gone down long before she did. Not until she realized that "Business as Usual" was not compatible with a "Nation in Arms," did Britain gain full benefit from her sea power.

Nevertheless, by the winter of 1916 Germany was reduced to terrible distress, and only the fortunate conquest of Romania and the occupation of the Ukraine prevented a complete breakdown. As an instance, the complete loss of all artificial fertilizers at a very early period was a severe blow, for without these the soil could not produce its normal harvest, much less replace the sea-borne supplies. The loss of fats and oils also caused much distress, for not only did the people suffer, but the lack of lubricants caused many breakdowns in all transportation systems. The meat imported from adjacent neutrals never filled the void widened by the British agreement with the American Meat Packers' Association, and cattle killed in Germany in any year, could not be replaced in the next one because of lack of fodder for the young stock.

All this proved that an industrial country cannot be isolated from the outer world and produce both machinery and food supplies. An agricultural country possibly may feed itself, but it cannot provide arms and materials for its armies. Even after the coalition of the Central Powers covered half of Europe, the lack of sea-borne supplies caused deficits that in turn created others, until in the end the entire population of Germany, Austria, Bulgaria, and Turkey broke down under the strain of these progressive discomforts and sufferings.

By the fall of 1918 the German leaders knew that they had lost the war, but they hoped to have all winter in which to negotiate a peace. Then came the Allied hammer-blow that broke the Hindenburg line, and Generals von Ludendorff and von Hindenburg sent word to Berlin that peace must be made at once. A Major von der Bussche was selected as their official representative and was sent to address the Reichstag on October 2.

Major von der Bussche, a baron and a confirmed Junker, was far from frank and bewildered the Reichstag in his demand for peace while boasting of continued military power, so the government did not take him seriously. The starving people of Germany, however, had heard enough of these falsehoods. They certainly were beaten, and were wearied of their German leaders who placed the blame for their troubles on Bulgaria or Turkey. When Ludendorff, the shrewdest of them all, resigned, the full truth began to reveal itself.

Emperor Wilhelm tried to save himself, and selected a new chancellor, Prince Max of Baden, through whom he proclaimed a new consitutional government. He also liberated Dr. Karl Liebknecht who had been put in jail for antigovernment utterances, and who, immediately on his release, appealed for a socialistic revolt. A dozen other would-be leaders made similiar appeals from every beer garden. Strikes broke out, and soldier and sailor groups mutinied, the most notable of these was that of the Imperial Navy at Kiel when the German High Seas Fleet was ordered out to sea. The sailors refused to sail, saying that they would be heading to a useless death. The cry of the hour became, "Down with the Hohenzollerns!"

General von Ludendorff, possibly regretting his earlier shrewdness, or perhaps attempting to retrieve some of his lost glory, wrote later that the German cause was lost because of the weakness of the German people, and their refusal to fight further. In this, he was unwittingly admitting that the Allied blockade had proved more deadly than all the armies on the Western Front.

To paraphrase Napoleon, "A country fights on its stomach."

# IN THE AIR

# CHAPTER XI

*The New Weapon . . . A Rather Funny War . . . The
Quota of the Quirk . . . Burlington Bertie of the Balloons.*

## The New Weapon

The Wright brothers' twelve-horsepower biplane, first flown
in December 1903, became an important weapon of war less
than eleven years later. Whether these Dayton, Ohio, bicycle
makers intended their invention to be a war bird is difficult to
decide, but on May 28, 1905, Wilbur Wright wrote to Octave
Chanute, civil engineer and aviation pioneer: "We stand ready
to furnish a practical machine for use in war at once, that is,
a machine capable of carrying two men and fuel for a fifty-mile
trip . . . We have made a formal proposition to the British
government and expect to have a conference with one of its representatives at Dayton very soon."

Officially, America had ignored the Wrights despite their
continuing success, and had put her money on Professor Samuel
P. Langley, Secretary of the Smithsonian Institution, who had
been given $50,000 to develop a heavier-than-air flying machine,
but his "aerodrome" never got off its launching ramp. In 1908
the U. S. Army Signal Corps purchased an airship from Captain
Thomas Scott Baldwin "for a practical military means of dirigible aerial navigation." This ancient gasbag was no more a dirigible than any county fair hot-air balloon. Later that same year,
after nearly every nation in Europe had bought and was flying
Wright-type biplanes, the U. S. Army purchased a Wright
model for $25,000, and the American Air Force was born—at

any rate, the United States Air Force celebrated its Fiftieth (Golden) Anniversary in 1957, a milestone that was measured from August 1, 1907, when the Signal Corps established an Aeronautical Division to take "charge of all matters pertaining to military ballooning, air machines, and all kindred subjects."

This air arm was placed in charge of Captain Charles de F. Chandler, and Corporal Edward Ward and Private First Class Joseph E. Barrett were assigned to the division. This new service soon lost one half of its enlisted strength when Private Barrett "went over the hill" shortly after he realized to what he was to be exposed.

In one of the early Wright flights, staged to prove the plane was capable of the required Army performance, Lieutenant Thomas E. Selfridge, flying as an Army observer, was killed when the plane crashed. The pilot, Orville Wright, was severely injured but recovered in a few months.

The United States Army did not own an airplane until August 2, 1909, and there were no military pilots capable of flying one until Wilbur Wright trained Lieutenants Frank P. Lahm and Frederick E. Humphreys at a field near College Park, Maryland.

By November 5 the Army lost its only aircraft and both pilots, when Lahm and Humphreys crashed "Aeroplane Number 1," as the Wright machine was listed in official files and the U. S. Patent Office. Some time in the nineteen thirties a plague of simplified spelling swept through the Army, Navy, and the Bureau of Standards and the word "airplane" was substituted, although the services clung to "matériel," "caissons," "guidon," and "musette bag." At the time of the loss of the first Army aircraft neither pilot was hurt, but the Signal Corps lost them when they were returned to their regular assignments shortly after; Lahm to the Cavalry and Humphreys to the Engineers. Legend had it for a time that Lahm had been banished back to the oat-burners because he had taken a woman aloft for a joyride.

In the meantime Lieutenant Benjamin D. Foulois, who had

taken the same pilot course under the Wrights but had never
soloed, was the only officer on flying duty. He had the plane
repaired and shipped to Fort Sam Houston, in San Antonio,
Texas, where the weather was likely to be more favorable in
winter than it was in Maryland. While the aircraft was being
reassembled, Lieutenant Foulois completed his ground-flight
training by mail from the Wrights, thus becoming the first cor-
respondence school pilot in history. Fortunately, before he tried
to gain his solo ticket by this method, the Wrights sent an instructor who helped him master the tricky art of landing. Between March and September 1910 Foulois made sixty-one
flights, still using the same Number 1 Aeroplane, and it was
not until 1911 that a second was made available through the
generosity of the noted publisher, Robert J. Collier, who loaned
it to the Signal Corps. The Number 1 Aeroplane was restored
to its original condition and sent to the Smithsonian Institution
for permanent exhibition.

By 1911 the United States Congress still had not appropriated
a single dollar for military aeronautics—what had been spent
had been drawn from an experimental fund—and when a formal
request was made for such funds, a member of Congress asked,
"Why all this fuss about aeroplanes for the Army? I thought
we already had one." But in March 1911 Congress finally
appropriated $125,000 for Army aeronautics, $25,000 of which
was to be made available immediately. Five new planes were
ordered and a new flying school established on North Island
in San Diego Bay, California, where both Army and Navy pilots were to be trained. Our air arm finally took shape and
substance.

Surprisingly, the first occasion on record in which the airplane
was employed on a war mission, was during the Mexican revolution of February 1911 when a government pilot is said to
have flown over Ciudad Juárez to observe the positions of the
rebel forces. Italy is alleged to have used six aircraft for scouting
work in September of that same year during her conflict with

Turkey, and also used airships for taking aerial photographs.

On November 1, 1911, the first bomb was dropped from an airplane during the same Italian-Turkish War that ended with the annexation of Libya by Italy. In this instance the pilot was a Lieutenant Gavotti whose historical flight was the result of a personal desire to see the effect of explosive missiles dropped from the air. He flew over the Turkish lines near Tripoli in an Etrich monoplane that was powered by a six-cylinder, 130-horse-power Austro-Daimler engine. He carried four bombs in a leather bag, and the detonators were in his pocket. When he arrived over an enemy encampment at six hundred feet, he took one of the bombs between his knees, fixed the detonator and dropped the missile over the side. Observing what he described as "disastrous results," he circled the camp, and dropped the rest of his load.

All this was done in face of the fact that in 1899 forty-four nations had signed a declaration that outlawed the launching of projectiles or explosives from balloons or other "aerial vessels." Five years later, when this pact came up for renewal at the Hague Convention, only twenty-seven of the original signatories ratified it.

It is also interesting to note that Giulio Douhet, famous Italian aerial strategist, pointed out, shortly after World War I, that these early aeronautics opened a new field of action, and in so doing created a new battlefield, and since these aircraft had many limitations they were, of necessity, considered only as military equipment. He argued that they in no way could fill the bill for civil transportation since they were limited in power, range, payload, and certainly in human comfort. The airplane did have an element of speed, a freedom of movement through three dimensions, and as such a vehicle it gave great promise for military reconnaissance. As it proved itself in this phase, the idea of using it as a range finder for the artillery was conceived, but beyond some vague method of attacking the enemy behind his own lines by bombing or the distribution of free missiles, an offensive program was never seriously considered. It was not until the necessity of countering enemy aerial operations was evident that the airplane was armed for fighting in the air.

These demands were not apparent immediately, for once the aircraft was built with sufficient power to make city-to-city flights, over-water hops, and was structurally sound enough to perform varied maneuvers, it was utilized chiefly as an exhibition vehicle and flown by daredevil pilots for the patrons of municipal fairs and expositions. Others joined in thrilling point-to-point air races or attempted long-distance flights for prizes offered by leading newspapers. Between 1903 and 1913 the airplane became the playboy's toy, and hundreds of thrill-seeking sportsmen took up the science for their own pleasure or vanity.

When the Great War broke out, the United States had nothing resembling an air arm, and eventually had to beg or borrow equipment from the French or British. In the beginning America's most outstanding contribution to the air-war history was the Lafayette Escadrille, that valiant band of volunteers who served and fought with the French from early 1916.

But France, Great Britain, or Germany did not start out as air powers, by any stretch of the imagination, for the old diehard, elite cavalry groups still controlled the destinies of the military services, while the navies refused to consider the noisy contraption—just as they had shunned the submarine and torpedo. For instance, in Great Britain, although a number of civilians had built and flown acceptable machines, it was not until 1912 that the War Office grudgingly granted £320,000—at that time $1,600,000—for the development of an air arm. Thirty-six aircraft were purchased, only half of which were British-built, and a white paper issued that same year contained these words:

In consideration of the difficult and hazardous nature of the flying service, H.M. King George V has granted the title "Royal Flying Corps" . . . etc. etc.

Britain's military air service not only gained the coveted "Royal" to its name, but broke away from the ties of the Royal

Engineers who had wielded control over this heterogeneous organization that had begun simply as a balloon company. The first Royal Flying Corps was expected to assume both Army and Navy duties, and indeed, when the Central Flying School was established at Uphaven, provision was made to train 91 military, 40 naval, and 15 civilian pilots. The staff had but 25 aircraft for this bold project.

By 1913 some experiments were made toward equipping certain aircraft with machine guns, and in September a Maxim gun was mounted in the front seat of a Maurice Farman, but the weapon was too heavy and its recoil dangerous to the flimsy nacelle structure and was abandoned.

In February 1914 the British Military Wing had 161 aircraft on its books, most of them early B.E. (British Experimental) types from the Royal Aircraft Factory. The Naval Wing had acquired 62 planes of various shapes and sizes; they were naval only in that they could take off from or alight on water, if the weather and sea conditions were most favorable. On July 1, 1914, the Naval Wing broke away from the Royal Flying Corps and became the Royal Naval Air Service, and so settled many Admiralty-War Office arguments.

This outline is also the general story of the air arms raised by France and Germany, although most of the latter's interest was vested in Count Ferdinand von Zeppelin's famous dirigibles that were establishing amazing passenger-carrying records all over Europe. Everyone seemed willing to invest in Count von Zeppelin's miracle dirigibles, but few civilians saw a financial future in the limited range or payload of the airplane.

By early 1913 the German High Command had placed orders for a fleet of aircraft, half of which were to be biplanes, the rest monoplanes. The latter were almost all Taube types, and the biplanes were manufactured by Rumpler, Euhler, Allgemeine Elektricitäts Gesellschaft, Luft Verkehrs Gesellschaft, Ago Flugzeuwerke, and Deutsche Flugzeugwerke. Twelve months later, when Germany was actively preparing for war, an Army bill was passed that granted $2,000,000 and what was left of an earlier

design prize of $20,000,000, to the Imperial Air Service. More
aircraft were ordered, and all old types replaced, and an additional clause in all contracts specified that all new machines were
to be of German manufacture, and to have seats for a pilot and a
passenger. They were also to be furnished with bomb racks and
fittings for an aerial camera. No engines of less than 100-hp
would be accepted, and a minimum top speed of 65-mph, a ceiling of 8000 feet, and a flight duration of at least four hours were
mandatory.

When the August drums rolled, Germany's air force was well
ahead of any other belligerent power. They had 38 Zeppelins, or
Schütte-Lanz dirigibles and more than 80 pilots to handle these
giants. In their heavier-than-air hangars they had the production
of more than three years that totaled 1954 aircraft built for military purposes. Allowing a certain percentage for crashes, wear
and tear, and unserviceability, Germany must have had a thousand aircraft at the outbreak of the war. Thirty-six of these were
excellent seaplanes for use over coastal waters. Nearly a thousand pilots had finished their training, and there were 487
skilled observers and additional personnel of 2600 men.

These figures may appear puny alongside the numbers of later
aerial armadas, but all situations and conditions are relative. We
are prone to consider all World War I aircraft as "crates," to use
a pointless term, but they were the best at the time and were
competing against aircraft of contemporary design and construction; not against Spitfires, Me. 109s, or Thunderbolts of another
period.

What drawbacks were disclosed in early military airplanes,
may be found in man's concept of their employment. All military
powers of that day looked on the airplane as an adjunct to the
cavalry; to be used on scouting and reconnaissance. As such,
these fairly slow vehicles were ideal for such missions, as was
proved during the First Battle of the Marne. Is it any wonder,
then, that officials of the ground forces with full say in the employment of aviation, were determined to limit their airmen to
these early tactical duties? When the plan to bomb was

broached, the artillerymen said their Long Toms and Jack Johnsons could do a much better job and deliver more explosive in a very short space of time. They argued that it would be better for the airmen to concentrate on accurate spotting for the gunners.

But the men who were doing the flying, coursing over the enemy lines day after day, saw that there were many situations where they could perform more spectacular work. If they could spot the grouping of enemy troops, why couldn't they interfere with their movement by dropping bombs along their line of march? If they could uncover enemy supply dumps, or concentrations of forces, what was wrong with bombing the dumps or concentrations then and there? Also, they were able to find many important targets well beyond the range of the artillery.

This point was clearly outlined on August 13, 1914, less than two weeks after the opening of hostilities, when Lieutenant Franz von Hiddeson of the Imperial German Air Force flew to within a few miles of the outskirts of Paris and dropped two four-pound hand bombs, and then turned his Taube toward home. No damage was done, but an idea was conceived and another seed of aerial bombing planted. A short time later, Jacob Werner, another German flier, risked a flight to Paris and dropped a taunting message that read:

People of Paris! Surrender! The Germans are at your gates. Tomorrow you will be ours.

This note, which is still on view at the Paris Museum, was for years credited to Max Immelmann, but since the Eagle of Lille did not join the German Air Force until November 12, 1914, he could not have made this memorable flight. This note also was the forerunner of a number of air-war legends. Immelmann has always been credited with devising the Immelmann turn, but this maneuver had been performed by prewar pilots in many countries.

German pilots registered some unfortunate "firsts" in the war. A Sergeant Kausen, who was scouting in an Aviatik, was downed by British ground guns near Le Quesnoy on August 24, and on September 2 the aforementioned Hiddeson was shot down and killed by a battery of antiaircraft guns near the Bois de Vincennes. Probably the first airman to be shot down by another in the air was an unknown German who was forced to land a Rumpler inside the British lines by Lieutenant H. D. Harvey-Kelley and his "gunner," Sergeant Major Street, who was armed with only a light automatic rifle that was mounted on a metal peg fitted to the front cockpit of the B.E. biplane. How he managed to fire such a weapon through the tangle of struts and bracing wires has not been explained. Unquestionably, the Rumpler went down, and was captured, but the crew escaped.

Whether Hiddeson's one-man attack on Paris provided the stimulus, or not, the first raid on an enemy airdrome was made on August 29 by a German Aviatik from which three bombs were dropped, hitting a Royal Flying Corps field at Compiègne. The bomber, however, eluded a flight of British machines that was sent up to intercept it.

French military aeronautics can be traced back to 1870 when free balloons were used during the Prussian siege of Paris to fly out important personages, dispatches, and as carriers for an ammunition airlift. In an attempt to block these escape routes, the Krupp factory designed and produced the first high-angle gun that became the basic weapon for all ground antiaircraft batteries.

Early in 1910 the Aero Club of France advised the War Cabinet that the airplane had great possibilities, a suggestion that resulted in the organization of the French Air Service. Four aircraft were purchased, including one Wright biplane, and from that point on events moved with creditable speed.

A Military Aircraft Competition was arranged in which machines would have to fulfill the following requirements. They would have to be two-seaters capable of flying 186 miles, carrying a payload of 660 pounds *besides* the crew, and be able to maintain a speed of at least 37 miles per hour. This, and other competitions, weeded out the culls of the industry and by August 1914 the French Air Service, composed of 21 escadrilles of 6 two-seaters and 4 escadrilles of 3 single-seaters (reserved for the use of the cavalry), was ready, willing, and able. The aircraft adopted included the Blériot, Farman, Deperdussin, Voisin, Caudron, R.E.P. (Robert Esanautl-Pelterie), and Nieuport.

Although the French devoted much time and study to the development of definite types, we find little reliable information as to what steps were taken to furnish weapons for these aircraft, or to produce a so-called fighter plane.

How Roland Garros solved the problem of mounting a machine gun to fire bursts along the line of flight through the whirling blades of the propeller, and thus produced the first true fighter plane, will be related later on. Some historians have published photographs of Morane-Saulnier single-seaters that show both Vickers and Hotchkiss guns mounted *behind* the propeller, which they insist were assembled as early as 1913, but, again, no reliable records are at hand to prove that these guns were ever fired in the air. Certainly no such weapon appeared on the Western Front until Garros went out with his fixed-gun Morane-Saulnier monoplane on April 1, 1915. It should be pointed out, however, that a number of pusher types, such as the Farmans and the British F.B.5 (Vickers Gun-bus) which had their engines mounted aft of the cockpit, could fire a gun forward, either fixed or flexible, but the idea of using the airplane as a winged weapon, as Garros was to employ it, was not considered seriously until the war had been going on for many months.

Russia, Italy, and Belgium contributed men and machines, but it was the aircraft, squadrons, and airmen of Great Britain, France, and Germany that bore the bulk of the war in the air. A new era was upon us, as nothing that was to take place, had been envisioned before, not even by such imaginative writers as H. G. Wells or Jules Verne. Those who took part went into the early war skies with no precedent or instructors to guide them. There were no previous airmen to emulate. This was a new battleground. At first there were no fighter or bomber schools, there were no guns or bombs to speak of; aerial gunsights and bombsights had yet to be invented. Those of us who went into that early fray were completely on our own, and did the best we could with what we had against whatever the enemy could send up against us. But out of that bewildering, glorious, deadly profession we created a new tradition.

## A Rather Funny War

Habitués of the motion picture theater or readers of popular aviation fiction may be forgiven if they visualize the air action in World War I as dogfights between small flights of Spads and vast Flying Circus packs of Fokker D-7s. This is the standard setting and plot for any presentation of that early conflict in the air. It is useless to point out that the Fokker D-7 did not appear on the Western Front until late spring of 1918, and the Spad was not acceptable as a front-line performer until well into 1917. But to all intents this was a Fokker-Spad war, or so the legend goes.

What really happened immediately after the opening of war that summer of 1914 is seldom related, or appreciated fully. But the men of that era flew and fought just as valiantly, and as often as the widely publicized "aces" of the 1917–18 period. But war in the air was not a profitable publication commodity until an American war correspondent in Paris came upon the term "ace" and mistakenly applied it to all airmen who had destroyed five or more enemy aircraft. He had no idea that in this appellative he was to shackle official thinking in the application of aviation to the conduct of war. Obeying the appeal of the so-called dogfight, the air arms went all out for the one-by-one destruction of enemy aircraft, when they should have concentrated on the requirements of tactical aviation, and then built it up to carry out a program of strategic missions that would complement the British blockade, and possibly have pounded Germany out of the war a year sooner.

From the outset, military aviation was not considered to be particularly important, and its history in the opening days is either vague or confused, since no reliable reports seem to have been kept. We do know, though, that the Royal Flying Corps was mobilized immediately for action, but could not be assembled to go overseas until August 13. Only a few of Britain's four available squadrons could be flown across the twenty-three-mile strip of the Channel, although there are some reports that practically all made the over-water hop, and that one plane crashed on take-off, killing Lieutenant R. R. Skene and Air Mechanic R. K. Barlow, the first RFC men to die in the war.

This mobilization and movement to the front had some lively and humorous sidelights. No one had any notion where the war would be staged, or what uniforms the enemy would wear. Michelin & Cie, the famous French tire manufacturers, furnished a few automobile road guides to be used as military maps. These profusely illustrated sheets, interesting to vacation tourists, were of little value to aviators, but they had to do until a London newspaper publisher obliged with a few copies of gaily colored "war maps" that were offered as premiums to subscribers.

A comic-opera collection of aircraft took off at two-minute intervals, and most of them arrived eventually in France. One plane even got as far as its destination, Amiens, the first night, but its pilot, H. D. Harvey-Kelley, received a severe reprimand for taking a shortcut and arriving on French soil before his commander. Lieutenant R. N. Vaughn was forced down with engine trouble near Boulogne, arrested by French authorities and kept in confinement for a week; it seems they had not been advised officially of the arrangements.

Transport was composed mainly of borrowed furniture vans, commercial delivery vehicles, and one bright red truck that had been commandeered from a noted provision firm. This was used by Number 2 Squadron as its mobile service unit, and during the retreat from Mons this gaudy vehicle was superior to any electronic guidance system—for both sides. It could be seen easily, and could travel almost as fast as the military aircraft it was serving.

Aerial operations in those opening days were more hazardous than the action experienced a year or so later. The early aircraft bore no international markings, and since to the unpracticed eye all types looked much alike, they were fired on by both friend and foe. Forced landings in friendly areas were often hairraising experiences, for the civilians asked no questions, but attacked with pitchforks, hatchets, or shotguns. Airplanes that landed near groups of infantry generally were fired on until the unfortunate crew could explain that they were indeed "on their side."

To counter this the British daubed streaks of red, white, and blue on the wings or rudders. Since the French national colors were the same it was soon obvious that more distinct markings would have to be devised, so a few "battleplanes" had Union Jacks painted wherever there was space. This insignia was simplified later to a blue, white, and red roundel which proved to be most satisfactory. The French adopted a like *cocarde,* but reversed the sequence of colors, painting the outer circle red and the inner spot blue. Out of this original precautionary measure came the first military air insignia, and before the end of 1914 the Germans adopted their Iron Cross design.

Basically, most of the flying personnel were sportsmen fliers. This was especially true of the British, whose airmen were often playboy types who had been deprived of their motorcar licenses because of frequent brushes with the law, and had taken up flying to avoid the jurisdiction of the highway bobbies. Lieutenant W. B. Rhodes-Moorhouse, the first British pilot to be honored with the Victoria Cross, was such a culprit.

Observers and gunners were picked (or plucked) haphazardly at first from the ranks of mechanics or orderly room officers who were not otherwise engaged that day. None had had any air experience or gunnery training, their qualifications being the ability to load and fire a cavalry carbine, to be immune to airsickness, have large jacket pockets to hold half bricks for dropping on enemy aircraft, and a general disregard for their own safety.

This "winged" cavalry soon went to work in earnest, and, as has been noted, their scouting had an important role in saving the combined Franco-British forces in the first few weeks of the war. There was no real air fighting, as none of the planes was armed. A few boisterous characters conceived the idea of "having a go" at the enemy with small-arms fire, but nothing really deliberate was attempted. On one occasion a Maurice Farman of Number 3 Squadron reportedly had taken to the war skies with a Hotchkiss machine gun—but not for shooting purposes— it was simply an experiment in weight carrying.

By mid-September both sides were using many aircraft, the skies were comparatively crowded, and naturally with so many available targets, a few imaginative types began taking along duck guns, pistols, and short lengths of rusty chain. Captain G. W. Mapplebeck of the Royal Flying Corps returned from a reconnaissance patrol with a German pistol bullet in his shoulder. But generally speaking, everyone went about his business, checking the movement of troops, photographing the farm country, and wondering what all those people were doing down there. Whenever enemy machines passed by, the ill-mannered clods thumbed noses or shook belligerent fists. Nothing more.

But of course these entrancing conditions could not last, since some uncouth oaf was determined to disrupt the sanctity of harmless patrols and interrupt the industry of others. A few half bricks *were* tossed, lengths of rusty chain *were* flung at opposition airscrews, large lead weights *were* dangled from lengths of wire with the notion of fouling some Rumpler's propeller, and another unruly wretch amused himself by firing a Webley pistol at passing Aviatiks. But it was the Parker shotgun that finally shattered the Entente Cordiale.

The Germans retaliated with rifle fire, and during this early belligerency Lieutenant V. Waterfell and C. G. G. Bayley, who were flying in an Avro of Number 5 Squadron, were shot down over Ath, Belgium, and killed, being the first of the 7589 to die in the British flying services in the next four years of air action.

This situation could be ignored no longer, and measures were considered for mounting regulation rifles to the cockpits of all aircraft. Engagements were being reported from many sectors, and in most cases the observers, who at that time sat in the front seats of the biplane types, were handicapped in having to aim and fire through the network of struts, stays, flying wires, a whirling propeller, and the fluttering wingtips. Also, holding a rifle in the slipstream, made accurate sighting somewhat difficult.

Rifles, shotguns, and carbines gave some small measure of satisfaction, but the German aircraft were so superior in gaining and maintaining height that it was almost impossible for British or French planes to get at them. German Rumplers would buzz over Allied areas while their observers calmly drew maps, took photographs, or wrote out detailed reports. Frustrated British airmen floundered around three thousand feet below, vainly shooting carbines at the nosy Huns, and when they were denied the satisfaction of venting their wrath on the enemy above, they took it out on the ground troops below, thus setting the groundwork for attack aviation.

Bombing from airplanes began late in October when a squadron, popularly known as the Ostend Carrier Pigeons, was formed by the Germans at Ghistelles, Belgium, and shortly after made what was considered to be a mass raid on Dunkirk.

There were several variations of those early aerial bombs. The first took the form of a streamlined canister of gasoline that was designed to ignite on impact with the ground. Another incendiary bomb was a can of explosive wrapped with coils of sticky, tarred rope—burning hemp was supposed to fly off in all directions and complete the conflagration. A treacherous melinite-shrapnel bomb was a converted French shell that had an unpredictable nose striker. These bombs would explode sometimes while being hung in the racks, or on being carried to the aircraft. At one time parachute-braked bombs were tried so as to give the raiding airman a chance to escape from the explosion

and flying debris. Some shell bombs were tied to the upper
*longerons* of the aircraft with common wrapping cord, and when
the airman was ready to release them over the target, he used
his pocketknife to sever the string.

A colorful character, Wing Commander Charles Rumney, took
his Royal Naval Air Service command to Ostend to assist in the
defense of Antwerp, and while that city was being evacuated
Flight Lieutenant Reginald L. G. Marix and Squadron Commander Spenser Grey, flying Sopwith Tabloids, set out to bomb
the Zeppelin sheds at Düsseldorf. Grey ran into bad weather
and had to settle for the railroad station at Cologne, but Marix
reached Düsseldorf, and from an altitude of six hundred feet
dropped his contribution of twenty-pounders on a shed, scored
a direct hit, set the hangars on fire; and a brand new Zeppelin
went up at the same time.

The defense fire was heavy and Marix's Tabloid was so shot
up he had to force-land twenty miles from his base, but he
knew the local geography well, and being a persuasive fellow,
swapped his damaged Tabloid for a Belgian peasant's bicycle
and pedaled to safety.

Twenty-seven years later, almost to the day, Air Vice-Marshal
Marix bombed and sank a German vessel in the harbor of Aale-
sund, Norway.

As was to be expected, Allied and German air forces were
developing the rivalry and competition that were to mark their
activities during the next four years. On October 5, the observer
of a French machine shot the pilot of an Aviatik stone dead
from a range of one hundred yards. The next day a German
claimed to have destroyed a Caudron by throwing a brick into
its propeller. Another among these casualties was a Sergeant
Major Jillings of the British RFC who was flying with Lieutenant M. W. Noel. Jillings was credited with downing an Albatros
two-seater with a single rifle bullet, but while on the way home
from this success someone on the ground peppered the sergeant
major "where he sat down," and he had to be assisted from his

cockpit on arrival at his field. Jillings was made of stern stuff, however; he lived down this indignity, became a squadron leader, and was eventually awarded the Military Cross.

## The Quota of the Quirk

The outbreak of aerial activity was highlighted by the introduction of the world's worst military airplane—the Quirk. This artful appellation was the title bestowed on the infamous B.E.2c biplane, the aerial clown of the Western Front. This notorious interloper was ungainly, grotesque, treacherous, and totally unfit to occupy hangar space on any airfield, but oddly enough, three of the nineteen Victoria Crosses given to British airmen, were awarded to pilots of this farcical contraption.

It was powered with a government-built engine that, according to legend, blew off its cylinders in the order of firing, but the plane was among the first to be sent into action, and surprisingly, when that four-year-long war rumbled to a close, there still were 1308 Quirks in service with the RAF. She was flown against the enemy in France, Belgium, Palestine, Salonika, and East Africa. As a military craft she carried no regular armament during the early months, and her built-in lack of maneuverability deprived her of any evasive action.

However, it is men who win wars, not machines, as the history of this dreadful product of the Royal Aircraft Factory proves.

Aeronautical engineers long sought the secret of the Quirk's tendency to fly backward in a mild wind, and her ability to perform the most unbelievable evolutions for no apparent reason. Nonetheless, and despite her antics, this Bairnsfather biplane continued to swagger in the glory spotlight. If you left her to her own devices, and decided to take a snooze on the way back home, more than likely she would seek out her own strip of turf and make a perfect landing unassisted. An enemy gunner might shoot her to shreds and splinters, but if the B.E.2c took it into her head she would home like a Spitfire. If there were two or three enemy planes at least six miles away deliberately ignoring her, like as not she would shed her wings, and—without a shot being fired—auger into the nearest shellhole.

There is one juicy legend that a Quirk that had been set afire by antiaircraft shells allowed her crew to take bleacher seats on the leading edges of the wings, and then under her own guidance actually flew into an enemy balloon, setting it on fire, crossed into her own lines, and made a perfect landing on top of an empty artillery truck that was heading for the back area. Everyone concerned arrived home safely.

But despite this unpredictable buzzard, pilots and observers of the RFC were doing extremely well on reconnaissance patrols. For instance, on August 22, 1914, Sir John French held a conference at Le Cateau with the Fifth French Army Commander, General Lanrezac. The Germans were thundering toward Paris, and the Allied generals decided to fight a defensive action, hoping to hold on for at least twenty-four hours. Royal Flying Corps reports had given reliable hints that General Bülow was massing across the Sambre River and that an enveloping movement was expected from Grammont, Belgium. The next day the famous Battle of Mons was fought along a twenty-five-mile front. Allied artillery was on hand, beautifully aligned, but there was no ammunition available, so all serviceable planes of the RFC patrolled unceasingly, checking the enemy's movements and pinpointing enemy batteries.

On the night of August 23 the retreat began, and RFC pilots and observers were in the air almost constantly for the next nine days. Their reports made a gallant chapter in the movement that was to save Paris and the Allied armies.

The outstanding hero of this "Eyes of the Army" service was Lieutenant William B. Rhodes-Moorhouse of Number 2 Squadron, the first British airman to be awarded the Victoria Cross. Prior to the outbreak of hostilities Rhodes-Moorhouse, a fellow countyman of mine from Spratton Grange, had been a playboy type of the early motoring age, a charming, devil-may-care lad whose driver's license bore many red-ink citations, proclaiming disregard for his neck on the public highways. Since blue-coated officialdom frowned on such antics, this slim rascal with the toothbrush mustache gravitated to civilian flying at Brooklands where he amazed his instructors with his pranks and violent acrobatics.

Rhodes-Moorhouse had been flying for about two years before he applied for an official certificate, his theory being that if you exposed yourself to officialdom you were likely to come under its ridiculous jurisdiction. He simply wanted to fly, not unravel red tape. He was induced, eventually, to accept a pilot's ticket in October 1911, since by then he was first-class airman. In 1912 he finished third in Britain's Aerial Derby, and established a record later by carrying two passengers across the English Channel in a moth-eaten Breguet. When war was declared he enlisted in the RFC and was posted to Farnborough where, since he was a trained pilot, he fretted and stewed with inactivity until March 1915.

This gentleman was sent overseas finally and posted to Number 2 Squadron at Merville and began his active-service career aboard B.E.2c Quirks. During the Second Battle of Ypres of April 26—a few days after the first German poison-gas attack— a message was received from Air Headquarters that the Courtrai railroad junction and station were to be bombed at all costs. German reinforcements were believed to be pouring through the town. With a hole two miles wide in front of Ypres, where the Allies had been driven back by chlorine gas, the situation was most precarious.

Four aircraft were assigned to the mission, but only Rhodes-Moorhouse reached the target. In place of an observer he carried a one-hundred-pound bomb slung between the wheels of his plane on some prehistoric bomb rack. Before take-off he had been advised to use his own discretion as to how low he would fly to deliver his load. He went in at three hundred feet, released his bomb and scored a direct hit on the signal box attached to the main building. He could have zoomed into the low clouds and smoke to escape and fly back, but he circled the area instead to gather all the information he could, and what he saw convinced him that the Allied troops around Ypres were in for a rough time. (As previously related, Germany's failure to get reserves into the gassed sector in time, nullified what initial surprise the poison-gas attack had created.)

During the several minutes that Rhodes-Moorhouse was over Courtrai he was subjected to heavy rifle and machine-gun fire, but he remained in the area to study all ground movement. Then a bullet shattered the fingers of his left hand so he headed for home, flying low over the city and past the tower of a church where the Germans had a machine gun in the belfry. As the old Quirk buzzed past a long burst caught the pilot; one slug smashed his thigh and another tore through his stomach.

His base was thirty miles away, but there were a number of places below where he could have landed and received medical attention, though well inside enemy territory. However, he thought only of the hordes of Germans moving toward the Courtrai station that might make the difference between hanging on or losing the war at Ypres; the General Staff should know of this concentration—and the fact that he had destroyed the signal box.

No one knows what Rhodes-Moorhouse suffered while flying those thirty miles. Once he was inside his own lines, he could have landed immediately, but he hung on and flew to a rear area and dropped down near the British headquarters. There, huddling in his blood-soaked cockpit, he dictated his report to an infantry officer, and added just before he fainted, "I didn't want them to get my old B.E. It's not too badly bashed about, is it?" Twenty-four hours later Rhodes-Moorhouse died in a hospital without knowing he had been recommended for the Victoria Cross.

The first German Zeppelin destroyed by an Allied airman was LZ.37 that was set on fire by Flight Lieutenant Reginald A. J. Warneford who caught the big dirigible over Ghent on the night of June 6–7, 1915—a victory scored during the pilot's first attempt to fly at night. He, too, was awarded the Victoria Cross.

The first raiding Zeppelin shot down over England was a Schütte-Lanz type, the SL.11. This success was accomplished from the cockpit of a B.E.—Quirk—within sight of a million pairs of British eyes. The wreckage piled up near the little village of Cuffley in Middlesex. The S.L.11 had a top speed of 60-mph, and by jettisoning her war load in an emergency could rise quickly to an altitude of 15,000 feet. The service ceiling of the Quirk with her military load was 11,000 feet, and this could be obtained only after an hour's clambering effort.

The pilot of the Quirk was William Leefe-Robinson, another slim handsome young man who had joined the new service early. He was born in India in 1895 where his father was employed in government work, and when the family returned to England, young William was sent to St. Bee's School in Cumberland, a small academy that was founded in 1583. Although it accommodated only 117 boys, it gave three Victoria Cross winners to the services. After much schoolboy travel in France and Russia, Leefe-Robinson finally settled down at Sandhurst Military College in August 1914. The following December he was commissioned and posted to the Worcester Regiment, but transferred to the Royal Flying Corps as an observer in March 1915. On May 9 he was wounded in the right arm while carrying out a patrol near Lille. As soon as he recovered he was sent to a flight training school at Farnborough and obtained his pilot's ticket the following September. He was eventually posted to Number 39 Squadron, a Home Defense unit located at Sutton's Farm, a convenient clearing a few miles outside London, where for a few weeks he enjoyed himself searching for raiding Zeppelins—aboard a B.E.2c Quirk.

At this juncture the dirigibles were giving Britain a rough time, and although the public had become fairly well adjusted to these raids, it looked with some contempt at the antiaircraft defenses the politicians and War Office martinets bragged about. Week after week passed without anyone emulating Warneford's feat; in truth the gasbags were enjoying some immunity by avoiding the more important military targets, and as a result, though spectacular and damaging from the view of the general population, they were not seriously hindering the over-all war effort.

Then on the night of September 2–3, 1916, in full view of the great metropolis, a giant raider fell in a roaring mass of flames, the entire crew of sixteen died, and millions of Londoners cheered the unknown hero who had sent it down. Within an hour all the roads leading to Cuffley were thronged with the curious who had rushed to see the remains of the first air raider shot down on English soil.

It was shortly after eleven o' clock that night when the heavy Maybach engines were first heard over the sleeping countryside. It was a beautiful clear night with few clouds, and the stars looked down with their habitual aloofness; altogether a wonderful night for a raid.

When the alarm was sounded several Quirks screeched across the sky in search of the raiders, and just before one o'clock a searchlight picked out a low glowing pencil that was aimed for the Woolwich arsenal. There could be no mistaking it, and another searchlight beam slashed across the streaked sky and joined the first. At that instant Lieutenant Leefe-Robinson spotted the dirigible, seemingly held aloft on a bipod of blinding silver, and, although in some danger of being hit by antiaircraft shells, he raced in to attack.

He stalked the gasbag for ten minutes, trying to gain on it and make some altitude as it started to move eastward. He finally managed to get to about eight hundred feet above, but at that point this particular Zeppelin darted into clouds, and he spent the next fifteen minutes searching for the raider. The effort was fruitless, and after resuming his routine patrol, he spotted a new set of indicator flares, and at 1:50 A.M. saw a red glow marking the northeast sector of London. Presuming it to be an outbreak of fire from an enemy bomb, he nosed around toward that direction and at 2:05 A.M. picked up a dirigible in that area.

This time Leefe-Robinson took no chances and headed directly after his quarry, and since he had some height he could nose down for speed to catch up with it. Antiaircraft shells exploded all around him, and pencil-streaks of tracer bullets scored freakish designs across the blue-black sky.

This Quirk had a Lewis gun loosely mounted on a metal peg outside the pilot's cockpit, an arrangement that permitted bursts of bullets to be fired just beyond the arc of the propeller; in other words, to shoot at anything, Leefe-Robinson had to fly crabwise with reference to a target, but luckily, his gun drums were loaded with a mixture of armor-piercing, tracer, and an incendiary slug known as a Pomeroy bullet.

His first attack was made from below, as he fired a full drum of ammunition while holding the Quirk in a mild zoom. This had no effect, so he replaced the drum and climbed to the level of the SL.11 and flew beside it, triggering long bursts of ammunition, but the old gasbag devoured the lot, as the enemy gunners returned the fire with some effect.

Leefe-Robinson then dropped back to the rear of the big airship and wriggled into a position from where he could fire another drum up and under the tail surfaces. He was now at 11,500 feet, and when the third drum was almost exhausted, he got a lively reaction. The big gasbag started to glow, in a few seconds its whole rear end was blazing, then with a monstrous belch she exploded in midair, and the gaunt, black wreckage started its twirl earthward.

Leefe-Robinson returned to Sutton's Farm at 2:45 A.M., where he discovered that his B.E. had been badly shot up; the rear half of his center section had been peppered, and the main spar of his right lower wing had been hacked in two. The old bus should have folded up before she got home, but she was living up to the traditions of the Quirk.

For that night's work, Leefe-Robinson was awarded the Victoria Cross.

Another B.E.2c hero, seldom mentioned in any air history of World War I, was Lieutenant Frank H. McNamara, an Australian who was honored with the Victoria Cross for one of the most audacious feats performed by any airman in any war.

The old-time thriller writers of the yammering-gun pulp school always devised plots wherein the hero gallantly dropped down behind the enemy lines to rescue his bosom pal, or a squadron sparring partner. These tales were popular with the editors of that day who would not believe that this trick had rarely been accomplished in true-life encounters. In the first place the risk is too great because one seldom finds a suitable stretch of ground for a pick-up landing and subsequent take-off. There also are too many factors to consider. Will the rescue plane evade enemy fire to make a safe landing? Will it get off again with this extra load? Will the one to be rescued be physically able to get to the plane and climb aboard in the split-second timing so necessary for his deliverance? It would be futile for anyone, but the possessor of icy nerves and rare flying skill, to attempt the project.

Such a rescue is far different from that in which a pilot delivers and then picks up an intelligence agent over the enemy lines. In that case the area of operations is carefully selected beforehand, the men involved have worked out all details of the plan, and neither makes his move until certain signals are exchanged that prove that every feature of the plan will interlock.

But it was for an act of rescue that Lieutenant McNamara was awarded the first Victoria Cross to be bestowed on an Australian airman. This adventure occurred in Palestine in March 1917, but the announcement of the award was not made until June 8 of the same year; possibly the Honors and Awards Committee wanted to be certain that this unbelievable incident really took place, so spent considerable time authenticating the story.

The beginning of March 1917 saw preparations for the Second Battle of Gaza well under way, and air operations had to be conducted on a large scale. Every available machine was sent into the air on photographic, bombing, or reconnaissance missions, and many important efforts were recorded. McNamara's name is to be found in many of these records, particularly for a strip of photographs he made of the enemy's position near Sheik Nuran. This little remembered front produced many astonishing singlehanded achievements during World War I. It was here that a Lieutenant Felmy, a Turkish airman, landed his Rumpler inside the British lines and blew up a pipeline that ran from Kantara, on the eastern side of the Suez Canal, to the Front to supply water to the British Army in Palestine.

All the available British aircraft—mostly B.E.s—took off on March 7 and bombed the new Turkish railroad that ran from Tell el Sheria to Irak el Menshiye, and during this action received heavy fire from enemy batteries. A B.E. flown by Lieutenant J. V. Tunbridge was hit and the pilot had to force-land near Rafa. He afterward made his way on foot across the desert in an effort to reach the British lines. He was seen in an exhausted condition by Lieutenants Snell and Morgan who were aboard another B.E. With a certain amount of risk, they landed on the desert, picked up Tunbridge, and brought him in safely. How all three men fitted in that flying grape arbor is a mystery.

By March 13 all was ready for the big show, and despite a violent sandstorm, air operations were made according to schedule. Every plane that could carry a bomb was sent out over the enemy positions. In one of these raids a plane of Number 14 Squadron was seriously damaged by antiaircraft fire and compelled to land within sight of the enemy. Lieutenants Vailliou, the pilot, and Ross Smith, the observer, who later achieved fame by making the first flight from Britain to Australia, landed beside the helpless pilot and picked him up after setting fire to his machine. The following day, March 20, McNamara surpassed this audacious feat.

Flying a very ancient Quirk of Number 67 Squadron, McNamara was one of several pilots engaged in bombing a Turkish construction train, and during the excitement of this mission he saw another plane, piloted by Captain D. W. Rutherford, slithering to the ground apparently out of action. Rutherford had to land his bus smack in the middle of the Turkish positions, and enemy troops ran out to take him prisoner.

Meanwhile, McNamara, who carried six 4.5-inch howitzer shells that were fused to give a delay of forty seconds after being released, had been trying to hit a moving railroad train. Three shells were sent out safely, but the fourth or fifth exploded prematurely, damaged one of his main planes and wounded McNamara in the right buttock. The engine escaped damage, however, and the aircraft continued to fly. Bleeding profusely, McNamara decided to break off the action and return to Kilo 143, his airstrip, but as he banked away from the railroad targets he spotted Rutherford's B.E. and saw the downed pilot firing red Very signal lights. He could see also a troop of Turkish cavalry galloping toward the downed aircraft.

So ignoring his own injury, McNamara turned his aircraft once more, and landed as near as he could to the downed Quirk. He shouted to Rutherford, urging him on to avoid capture, and the downed airman sprinted for it with the enemy cavalry in hot pursuit. Mac tried to turn his biplane into the wind for a take-off, but his one leg was quite stiff from the effect of his wound, and added to this difficulty was an uneven take-off strip. Just as the rescue bus was gaining some speed, it swung violently, the undercarriage was sheared off, and the aircraft ground to a halt with its nose to the earth.

McNamara ignored the approaching cavalry, eased himself out of the cockpit, fired his revolver into the fuel tank, and even took time to fire a Very pistol flare into the escaping fuel. As the Quirk blazed, the Turks dismounted, and fired from prone positions at the two officers who by now had decided to go back to Rutherford's Quirk to retrieve a Lewis gun and make a stand of some sort to avoid capture.

This gun was on a flexible mounting in the pilot's seat, and using this cockpit, McNamara was all set to start firing when at this psychological moment a remaining howitzer shell aboard the blazing Quirk went off with a roar. This apparently frightened the enemy cavalrymen who now decided to dig in instead of advancing on the two pilots, and during this lull a quick examination was made of Rutherford's bus. One tire had been ripped off, the center-section wires had been broken, and one *longeron* cracked. McNamara suggested that Rutherford try swinging the prop. To their amazement the engine started after two swings, and they decided to risk another take-off.

Rutherford jumped into the observer's seat, and in a few seconds the Quirk was making a getaway. The Turkish cavalrymen, watching McNamara frantically trying to ease the crippled B.E. through a number of sand patches, made a final charge and were only a few yards behind the tail when the Quirk scrambled into the air and headed for Kilo 143 seventy miles away. How McNamara made it with so great a loss of blood is difficult to guess, but make it he did, and brought off a successful landing to complete this daring rescue.

Three Quirks . . . three Victoria Crosses.

## Burlington Bertie of the Balloons

Early in the air war the Tommies, digging in along the Western Front, concocted a legend they told over and over to brighten many a dreary dugout. It seems there was one wag of an observer who had been a student pilot, but because of his antics and ability to live through a full dozen training crashes, was banished to kite balloons.

This noted gentleman immediately staged a program of revolt that had the whole sector in stitches. Whenever he was assigned to a period of observation, he usually appeared wearing a high silk hat and a plum-colored smoking jacket, and strutted from his quarters to the balloon basket twirling a walking stick. The ground crew, winch men, riggers, and other serfs of the organization highlighted this formal approach with lusty choruses from the old music-hall ditty, "Burlington Bertie from Bow." Whether Bertie personally annoyed the enemy with his makeup, or whether he was one of the unfortunates, he usually had to jump from the basket at least once a day, and, to the high glee of all who saw him, always baled out still wearing his top hat and executing a marvelous pantomime of a man walking on thin air while swinging a dandy's cane.

If this character really existed, he no doubt helped many a footslogger through long hours of sentry duty.

Another legend devised by the infantry was that of the Mad Major, a tale bandied about from the days when aircraft first ventured anywhere near the trench systems. At first the Mad Major was a so-called famous German who flew a red Albatros and was especially good at knocking down Allied balloons and shooting up ambulances. Later on, as the Allied airmen took the offensive, the Mad Major was a Britisher who also flew a red biplane. Eventually, it was Major Christopher Draper who earned this sobriquet; a wild, low-flying character who also managed to destroy twelve enemy aircraft that had been sent out to bat him down. After the war Draper continued his theatrical activities, amusing all London by flying under the Thames bridges as the river police roared up and down in motorboats attempting to put an end to these stunts.

However, there always was a Mad Major of some organization who was created by war-weary soldiers, and from all accounts performed most amazing deeds of daring.

The reader perhaps will ask, "But weren't there any legends connected with the American forces over there?"

There were, but they didn't seem to have the same quality as those conceived by the British and French. Alexander Woollcott, who served in the AEF, related several, but the one that comes to mind when old times are discussed by a group of Quiet Birdmen concerns the pilot of the DH.4 who, during a very violent effort to evade the attack of a German Albatros scout, tossed his observer from the rear cockpit.

The instant the man went out, the pilot sensed the loss of weight behind, and, looking around, discovered that his partner was missing. Legend then has it that the pilot looked below and saw the observer tumbling to earth—minus a parachute, of course. Feeling personally responsible, the pilot nosed down in a steep dive and soon caught up with the tumbling observer. Then, by carefully maneuvering the DH.4 into a logical position, he caught the unfortunate by trapping him in the empty cockpit.

This story ran the rounds for weeks during the war, and like so many other legends, it had some basis of fact. A DH.4 observer was actually tossed out of an American observation plane, but he never left the structure of the machine. What happened was that he was flipped out while the pilot was stunting, but he only slid along the top of the fuselage, came up sharply against the fixed stablizer, and clung there until the pilot noticed the change in trim, and looked around to investigate. He was astonished to see his observer astride the fuselage and clinging to the fin. Thinking that his pal had gone mad or was playing some crazy game, he ordered him back to his seat. So by crawling carefully, and making handholds by ripping holes in the fabric, and gripping the structural members of the framework, the observer returned safely to his place in the plane.

It was from this giddy adventure that the legend of the observer who was flipped out at 12,000 feet and flipped back in again a few feet above the trenches was possibly contrived.

# CHAPTER XII

*Jimmy Bach's Bad Break . . . Winners or Losers? . . .
The Weapon Takes Wing . . . How Fokker Became Famous . . . Advent of the Aces.*

## Jimmy Bach's Bad Break

The first American credited with destroying a German plane
was James J. Bach, a volunteer who has long been forgotten.
He was born in France of American parents and spent a great
part of his life in European cities, where he earned his living
as a mechanical engineer. He spoke French fluently, and
although properly registered with the American Consul in Paris
to assure his national status, he had a natural affection for the
land of his birth. At the outbreak of war he enlisted in the
Foreign Legion along with Bill Thaw, Bert Hall, and other
Americans.

On a raw day in November 1914 a group of these American volunteers looked up from their mud-lined trench and
watched a French biplane gunner exchange a few bursts with a
German Rumpler. It was of small importance as an air battle,
but it triggered a mass decision that was to have international
implications and significance. Bill Thaw, Bert Hall, and Jimmy
Bach were in this group.

After discussing this aerial engagement, Bill Thaw, who had
been a sportsman airman while a student at Yale, renewed an
earlier request for an assignment to a French air squadron.
In order to make this request Bill had to hike thirty-two kilometers to interview an old friend, a Lieutenant Brocard, who

commanded a reconnaissance escadrille. In due time Thaw, Bach, and Hall were transferred from the Foreign Legion, and by mid-December had reported to the French Air Service headquarters.

All three men went through the red tape and training routine of that time, but, because of his immediate experience, Bach's history is most pertinent at this point. He was given a short course in map reading, engine mechanics, and some general instruction in aircraft rigging. He did not reach a flying school until March 10 when he was sent to Pau, a primary field where students were allowed to taxi up and down the turf aboard what were known as Penguin aircraft—ancient Blériot monoplanes with clipped wings. These machines would not get off the ground, but they were powered by aircraft propellers that gave pupils the initial touch, the feel of rudder and aileron controls, and the knack of operating a rotary or a radial engine. By July 4, 1915, Jimmy had graduated to the early Caudron, gained his pilot's brevet, had been promoted to rank of corporal and assigned to Escadrille M.S.38 to fly Morane-Saulniers. He reached the front line on August 29.

The Morane-Saulnier was a two-seater monoplane that had its wing mounted high above the cockpit, and early in the war had been dubbed "the Parasol" by British airmen. It was designed originally as a reconnaissance machine to carry a pilot and observer, but in the course of events some models were fitted with two machine guns; one was mounted up on the wing to fire past the arc of the propeller, and the second, intended for the use of the passenger, was set on a primitive mounting, and could, in fact, be fired through a fairly wide arc at enemy machines attacking from the rear or broadside.

Very early in his flying career Bach was sent on a long-distance reconnaissance that took him into the vicinity of Mézières, and on the way back he met a German Aviatik, that was homeward bound from a similar mission. Jimmy's observer was a Lieutenant Giroux. In those days the French did not consider piloting the premier duty; it was more important to gather intelligent, accurate information, and such data could be entrusted only to a commissioned officer. The pilot was simply an aerial chauffeur.

The observer aboard the German plane fired a long-range burst at the dainty Parasol, an impudence that enraged Jimmy. A second burst was more accurate as slugs ripped through the linen fabric, battered at the engine cowling, and one sizzled through the cockpit, and nipped at Bach's coveralls, making him lunge against his safety belt.

"What are you waiting for?" Jimmy yelled at the lieutenant.

The monoplane peeled off into a tight bank and the eighty-horsepower Le Rhone engine screamed under full throttle.

The Aviatik nosed down to get away but the Parasol was somewhat faster, and as they continued the dive Jimmy's Lewis gun chattered in short bursts. The chase continued until Lieutenant Giroux was concerned that his pilot would follow the enemy plane all the way back to Berlin if necessary, but Jimmy ignored his superior's entreaties and poured burst after burst at the fleeing Aviatik.

When he had come to within seventy-five yards of his target, Bach's gun jammed, so he struggled to reach up to clear the stoppage and change the drum while flying with the stick between his knees. He then noticed that the German plane was acting erratically. He took another look and was positive that the observer had been hit because he was draped over his gun.

Giroux tapped Bach on the shoulder and pointed at his own weapon. "You got him, but I'll finish him for you!" he yelled in the pilot's ear.

Jimmy nodded and nosed down to gain more speed. He went under the Aviatik, zoomed, and curled around to give Giroux a broadside shot. The Le Rhone engine clanked, and every wire and strut was strained to the limit. Two short, but very accurate, bursts slammed into the enemy plane. The propeller on the Mercedes splintered, then broke up, and the hub ran wild.

"Don't let him get away!" Jimmy pleaded.

Giroux took another careful shot, and the Aviatik staggered

under the fusillade; pieces of wood, strips of linen, and spatters of dried paint flew off. Another burst and the wings collapsed as if battered by a massive hammer. She rolled and the body ripped itself clear of the tangle and tore through like a dart. Once free, the fuselage began to spin, and the runaway engine wailed its mournful story, dragging a long, greasy plume of smoke behind it.

Now Jimmy was praying that his own fuselage would stay with his one wing, as he worked to ease down the engine and bring the Morane to a safe pullout. The Parasol had not been designed for this sort of activity, but the pilot fortunately kept her together and turned back for his own lines.

When he opened the throttle again, the rotary engine sniffed, choked, and coughed. Jimmy had probably fouled the plugs while easing out of the wild dive, as had happened so many times to other fliers. The chase had taken them deep into the German lines, and as matters stood, with the prevailing wind against them, Jimmy knew that he had a dead-stick glide ahead of him if he hoped to reach friendly territory.

"You chased him too far," Lieutenant Giroux complained.

"I had to to get him."

"I admit you got him, but now they'll get us. Prisoner-of-war compound."

"Don't give up so easily. We're still flying," Bach taunted.

The jagged pattern of trenches and sapheads that made up the front line seemed miles away, and the wind blew telltale ground smoke toward the enemy back areas. Risking everything, even a deadly spin that could follow a stall, Jimmy stretched his glide mile after mile. The French lines were now clearly visible, and he knew that hundreds of infantrymen would be watching this little airplane as it dipped and fluttered in its effort to reach safety.

With their share of luck, they made it as the wheels crossed the friendly line with only feet to spare. There was no flat, cleared space, and the plane stumbled through tangles of barbed wire, thudding and bouncing, and floundered into water-filled shellholes that finished the undercarriage; what was left slithered along on its belly and finally came to a halt.

Lieutenant Giroux who had been standing up advising Jimmy how to handle the situation was tossed out and suffered a broken arm, but Jimmy, who was well belted in, didn't have a scratch. On their return to their squadron, and after all details of the fight had been written out, the credit for the victory was given to Corporal Bach, the pilot, who had first given chase, delivered the first blow, and had "courageouly stayed in action until his observer could finish off the enemy."

This was a good beginning, and it was unfortunate that Jimmy could not continue in this vein, but he was taken out of the play while trying to save a comrade in dire distress. He, and a Sergeant Pilot Mangeot, were given the assignment to deliver two Intelligence agents into the enemy lines. Mangeot wrecked his Morane on landing, and Bach, who had carried out his part of the mission, went back to pick him up, but in the second take-off his wingtip brushed against the branch of a tree and the plane piled up. The two men made a bold bid for freedom, but were finally caught and spent the rest of the war in German prison camps. In fact, Bach had a rough time evading a *franc-tireur* court-martial charge, which could have put him before a firing squad. But he was cleared, and so paved the way for other American volunteers who were taken prisoner while serving with Allied forces before America entered the war.

### Winners or Losers?

Bach's experiences point up several problems that all Allied airmen had to face in fighting the Imperial German Air Service. The enemy quickly went on the defensive in this war-in-the-air, for which no one could blame him, but the French and British were continually on the short end of the deal. In other words, if you want to fight an enemy on the defensive, you must go into his territory and make him fight. Only on rare occasions did German airmen bring the battle to the Allies, and they therefore had nearly every facet of the action in their favor. For one thing, any Allied aircraft a German pilot shot down, fell in his territory where he could clearly establish his claim. Any aircraft shot down by an Allied pilot usually had to be fully confirmed by members of his squadron—who often were too busy to note another pilot's success—or by kite-balloon observers, if the action had taken place close enough to the line for them to determine what had actually happened.

Allied airplanes took a double risk in these ventures, for if they had engine trouble, there was little choice but to force-land in enemy territory. Also, under these circumstances they could be noted by German pilots who had but to follow them down and claim a victory.

A variation of this situation was seen during World War II. When the German Air Force attacked in strength during the Battle of Britain, it lost large numbers of fighters and bombers, to both British fighters and antiaircraft fire. When the circumstances were reversed and British and American aircraft attacked German key cities, it was Allied airmen who suffered the great losses that are the lot of the attacker.

A group of air historians have, for years, presented the air-war of 1914–18 as proof that German airmen and aircraft were far superior to that produced by the Allies. This is far from true, because the final statistics show that the British, in particular, had by far the better of the fight. Although, prior to July 1915, no records were kept of enemy aircraft downed, official statistics disclose that between that date and November 11, 1918 enemy aircraft destroyed on all British fronts numbered 7908, whereas only 2810 RFC-RNAS planes were lost or considered "missing." This does not include aircraft and crews, that, although damaged or badly hit, returned to their own side of the line, after which the airmen were lost from squadron strength temporarily, or died of their wounds. Since in so many instances, enemy airmen who were also wounded in contests with British airmen, but got back to their home fields and landed in hospitals or died of their wounds, the score balances, and the above figures represent fairly well the actual ratio of victory against defeat.

From the dramatic point of view, it is always well to intimate, if not prove, that the enemy has all the advantages. How else can the gallantry of the hero be presented? This theory is especially true in the popular action story, whether set in the prize ring, on the baseball diamond, or in a battle with the redskins; the enemy must be presented so superior that the reader wonders by what stretch of the imagination the underdog is sent against such overwhelming opposition.

On the basis of many widely distributed magazines, books, motion-pictures, and the more recent TV presentations, it is understandable that so many people believe in the over-all superiority of the German airman and his mounts. The output of a handful of conservative writers, most of whom had an active part in the aerial campaign, attempts to correct these impressions, but the quest is hopeless.

Getting back to the winners or losers of this chapter, we must point out that even American airmen who participated but a few months and have always claimed that they were mounted aboard castoff aircraft provided by the French and British, did exceedingly well. At the close of the war Billy Mitchell's Air Service was composed of 740 planes assigned to active-service squadrons at the front, or about ten per cent of the total aircraft strength of the Allies. American fighters officially destroyed 781 enemy planes and 73 kite balloons, while losing only 298 planes in these combats. Seventy-one fighter pilots qualified as aces, and this select group downed 450 planes and 50 balloons.

As to their equipment, it is only fair to state that they had mounts equal to any used by the French or British. Most of them started off with the Nieuport scout, the same aircraft used by such gallants as Georges Guynemer, Billy Bishop, Albert Ball, and many others. Later, when they were available, the much-publicized Spads were used. Although not in the same class as the Sopwith Camel or S.E.5, it was exactly the same plane as that flown by a host of French airmen of renown. Several Americans who were attached to or were members of British squadrons did very well aboard S.E.5s or Camels, and it was only in the two-seater or light-bomber categories that the Americans were shortchanged. The most efficient Bristol Fighter, so popular with the British, was not available outside of the Royal Flying Corps, which was unfortunate, for I am certain American airmen would have recorded some startling performances with this aircraft.

It is regrettable that this famed two-seater fighter could not have been mass-produced in America, but at the time the Munitions Board was entranced with the new Liberty engine, and an attempt was made to reproduce the Bristol Fighter airframe and power it with this monstrous engine. The result was mortifying because the scoutlike B-F could scarcely haul this heap of cast iron off the ground.

## The Weapon Takes Wing

The man who turned the airplane from an aerial eye to a winged weapon was an ex-concert pianist, Roland Garros. When the early air pioneers began circling the Eiffel Tower for prize money, Garros induced Alberto Santos-Dumont to teach him to fly. By October 1910 Garros was a member of the French aviation team that competed in the memorable Statue of Liberty race. It was won by Count Jacques de Lesseps who flew a Blériot monoplane. Garros was aboard an early Paulhan that was not maneuverable enough to make the required tight turn around the harbor goddess and he had to be content with third place. In 1911 he won the $100,000 Paris-to-Rome race, was also first in the Paris-to-Madrid feature, and led the pack in the Grand Prix d'Anjou event that same year.

When war was declared Garros was in Germany giving exhibitions with an early Morane monoplane. He was most popular, for, after holding crowds spellbound with his acrobatic displays, he would later delight music-salon groups with his skill at the piano. One can imagine his amazement and despair when he saw the newspaper headlines late one afternoon that said the Kaiser's troops had invaded Belgium and declared war on France. According to international rules of war he could be interned for the duration of hostilities, but even worse, the Germans might confiscate his exhibition machine—and might fly it against his own people!

Determined not to be trapped by such legalities, Garros crept back to his hotel, packed his bags and left by a rear door. He scurried through the busy streets and made his way to the exhibition grounds, where luckily, most of the guards had gathered at the nearest *Gasthaus* to toast the Kaiser and drink to Germany's coming victory. Garros had little trouble dragging his monoplane from its shed and starting the Le Rhone engine. He stowed his bags in the fuselage, and climbed aboard.

At that time few men had flown at night, but Garros took off boldly and flew to the nearest border, landing safely in Switzerland. After several days he continued on to Paris where he volunteered for military service. Along with Armand Pinsard, another prewar airman, he was sent to Saint-Cyr-l'École where he donned a uniform, was taught parade-ground drill and what went for aviation tactics at that time.

Morane-Saulnier Escadrille Number 23 was being formed at Buc, near Paris, and Garros and Pinsard were ordered there, and to their great delight were soon joined by other exhibition pilots, including Adolphe Pégoud, Jules Vedrines, Eugene Gilbert, and Marc Pourpe. With Pourpe was Raoul Lufbery from Wallingford, Connecticut. Lufbery had worked as a mechanic for Pourpe for nearly four years of exhibition flights that had taken them all over the world. Pourpe and Lufbery were in Paris to buy a new machine when the war broke out, and exhibition flying was, of course, out of the question; there were more important adventures to be had with the French Air Service.

During the next few weeks these exhibition headliners were actively engaged in attempting to stem Germany's rush for Paris, and did their share in turning the enemy advance along the Marne into a crushing defeat.

Reconnaissance was important, but Garros and several of the

other pilots thought that much of their efforts were wasted. Pinsard was all for dropping bombs on the enemy, and when Armand was forced down later and captured, Garros conceived a harebrained scheme to organize a rescue flight to spirit him from the prison compound. But this made him realize that the airplane was a talonless war bird, and he wondered how a gun or guns could be adapted to its framework. Eugene Gilbert was also pondering on this problem. He believed that to make the airplane earn its fuel, it would have to be flown fast, handled with maneuverability and skill, and be able to strike—or thrust —exactly as a swordsman. Thus, an important seed of military aviation was sown. But all these factors indicated that the gun had to be mounted so that it would fire directly forward; it couldn't be set out on the wings outside the propeller arc or even mounted below on the undercarriage. It would be of limited value there since simple stoppages could not be rectified and the ammunition drums or clips could not be changed. No, the gun had to be available to the pilot at all times. It had to be mounted conveniently somewhere behind the propeller.

Gilbert knew that in any such mounting a percentage of the bullets would hit the whirling blades and pierce them, and it would take but a few to sever the wooden blades, and then . . . *Boom!* . . . no prop!

Legend, hearsay, and rumor now curdle the tale. Some armament men have stated that Gilbert wrapped the butt ends of a propeller with strips of steel tape, others have reported that he fitted a curved block of metal at the point where the bullets might strike the airscrew; but obviously some form of metal protection was used.

Gilbert's first experiment was made at Luxeuil as early as December 1914 when he mounted a Hotchkiss gun on the engine cowling of a Morane Bullet. Some statements indicate that Gilbert actually shot down an Aviatik with this gun arrangement in January 1915. If so, one may naturally wonder why this device, crude as it was, was not used more widely. Why didn't

Garros or some other pilot of M.S.23 know of it and show more interest?

History is imperfect at times, and so is often nothing more than the crystallization of popular beliefs. The real story is probably somewhat as follows: After this legendary success against the Aviatik, Gilbert tried to improve his deflector device and fabricated two identical V-shaped wedges of armorplate that were bolted to the back of each blade on the assumption that the propeller would be better balanced in that manner.

During gun-butt experiments he asked some fellow officers to help him raise the Morane into flying position, steady the wingtips, and hold the plane relatively secure while he ran the engine and fired a test burst at the wall of sandbags. But apparently the deflector blocks were shaped incorrectly, and two officers were killed by richocheting bullets. Eugene was so distressed by the accident he dropped his experiments, and from all accounts never considered them again.

By coincidence Garros had thought of the same plan of protecting the butt end of the propeller blades, and spent long hours in the armorer's shed figuring weights, recoil, loading procedures, and the rate of fire. Once he touched on this last point, he felt that he was on the right track. He checked the 300-rounds-per-minute of the Hotchkiss gun against the varied speeds of the propeller and concluded that less than 7 per cent of the rounds fired would strike the deflector. From that point on it was a simple matter to go into the air, aim his nose at an enemy plane, pull the trigger, and shoot it down.

Learning of Gilbert's tragic experience, Garros decided that Eugene had used a deflector that was curved at an incorrect angle, and he induced a Parisian machinist to turn out a collar of armorplate that could be bolted around the base of the propeller blade. This was designed with a slight angle so that any deflected bullet would continue on in a narrow vee off the line of the undeflected rounds. He sacrificed some propeller efficiency, but he intended to avoid further accidents.

When the collars were finished and delivered, Garros bolted them into place on the propeller of a discarded Morane Bullet, and then had the armorer mount a Hotchkiss gun over the cockpit and engine cowling. They devised a trigger cable that was connected to the joystick to permit the pilot to fire the gun with the same hand that held the control lever. In that convenient position the machine gun could be easily loaded and minor stoppages quickly cleared.

Once more legend and hearsay befuddle the tale. In one yarn an unidentified pilot mounted a Hotchkiss gun outside his cockpit with no protection for the propeller. He is said to have gone into the air to test out the arrangement—and promptly shot himself down. Another version states that some young enthusiast stole Garros's plane and went over the line to engage the enemy, and the pilot hammered the propeller clean off the shaft and spun down out of control.

None of these accounts can be substantiated.

Garros left nothing to chance to assure his device would work perfectly; clip after clip of Hotchkiss ammunition was fired at the buttress as the engine ran at varying speeds—what few bullets did strike the propeller were deflected off harmlessly.

But Garros did not try his device against the enemy until April 1, 1915. On that morning a crew of an Albatros two-seater was flying a reconnaissance patrol near Epernay, and as French antiaircraft guns barked and spattered the sky with telltale blobs of white smoke, Garros turned to inspect the area.

The two Germans watched him with only casual interest, and when the Morane came into position behind their tail, the German pilot assumed that the Frenchman was on an observation mission also, and since the Allied machine carried no observer who might have a rifle, the Albatros pilot took no precautions. So long as the Frenchman didn't crab alongside from where he might trigger a few rounds from a loosely mounted weapon, it could be only another observation mission.

Ten seconds later a burst of fifteen rounds of Hotchkiss machine-gun fire tore through the pilot's shoulder blades; the bullets had come *straight* from the Morane mid-wing monoplane directly behind. Only the observer, Franz Dietrichs, sensed that the slugs were screaming through the sheen of the propeller, and realized, too late, that a gun was mounted on top of the engine cowling, not on an elevated, or cockpit, bracket. This weapon was really firing through the whirling blades of the propeller! But how could that be? Dietrichs never lived to find out; he knew nothing about piloting an Albatros and went down to his death, helpless to aid himself.

A new weapon and a new breed of men had been created. The military force had been given a most lethal piece of armament. It made the airplane as important a war machine as the naval dreadnought. It turned a collection of rickety flying machines into an air service, and overnight the airplane became the platform for sky-high gunnery, not simply an airy-fairy vehicle of observation.

The Dutch airplane designer, Anthony Fokker, had nothing to do with any of this. He had never heard of a front-firing gun, or conceived such an idea; he was too busy trying to sell to the German government a sports-type monoplane that was powered by an engine copied from the French Le Rhone rotary. Roland Garros gave the aviation service the fixed-gun fighter.

The day after his first success against the Albatros, Garros was returning from a visit to another escadrille when he met an L.V.G., also a two-seater, and shot it down near Dunkirk. Once more a German aircrew was deceived by the Morane's nose-on approach. Two days later he spotted one of the newer Aviatiks, armed with a Parabellum mounted in the observer's rear seat, that was flying toward the French lines. The German pilot hurriedly dropped his bombs to gain maneuverability, and the observer's first burst caught the Morane's wing root and punctured the reserve fuel tank. Trailing a cloud of gasoline vapor, Garros disregarded the possibility of fire in the air and closed in. The German observer died with five bullets in his chest; the next five of the same clip tore through the pilot's head, slammed through the instrument panel and ignited the fuel line. The Aviatik went down and burned to a cinder in a marsh.

On April 11 Garros stalked two more unsuspecting Aviatik two-seaters, and using the same strategy, sent one down under a torrent of Hotchkiss fire. The observer of the second German plane stood and fought with a revolver and Garros could not get in a finishing burst.

On the morning of April 16 Garros was attacked by four Albatros two-seaters that were returning from a bombing raid. A number of rifle bullets penetrated his machine, one of them hit the engine cowling and fell back into his lap. The moment the Frenchman's fixed gun began to spark behind the sheen of the propeller, all four two-seater pilots turned back for their airdrome, but one appeared to be slower than the rest and gradually lagged behind. Garros darted in to get within range. Noting their companions' danger, the other Albatros pilots turned about to head off the determined Frenchman. But Garros would not be denied and his bullets tore away the left wing of the laggard Albatros, and the ill-fated crew went down in a fuselage that threw away the other wing before it spun in.

Five victories in sixteen days! This was the initial harvest of Roland Garros's front-firing gun. He was immediately cited for the Legion of Honor and nearly every newspaper in France and Great Britain carried the astounding news of his aerial accomplishment. The boulevardiers cheered and toasted their newest war hero. "Oh that Garros," they cried. "Roland Garros, our aerial savior! Five enemy flying machines he has destroyed. Garros is an ace!"

The word "ace" was a popular catchword of that day, and was applied to anyone, but in particular to athletes who had performed anything unusual. The latest Grand Prix winner was an ace. The newest cycling hero was an ace. Popular jockeys were included in this category of headliners. It was natural then that it should be applied to Roland Garros.

These continued references were noticed by an American newspaperman in Paris at the time who interpreted it to mean any war pilot who had shot down five enemy planes, and in his next dispatch to New York applied the reference to Roland Garros without explaining how the Frenchman had made his score or with what new weapon. So the word soon became the journalistic standard by which a French fighter pilot was rated.

The British ignored all references to individual fighting scores, and still refuse, officially, to accept the ace designation. They did not keep any authentic records of enemy planes shot down until late 1915, and did not publish the names of their stars, or the day-by-day records of their outstanding airmen. Only on the occasion of the publication of awards and decorations were these scores ever mentioned. When I was awarded the Military Medal (an Army decoration since no actual flying decorations had been designed or authorized), the official announcement coincided with what I considered my seventh victory in the air, but the citation just mentioned my "devotion to duty, for courage in action and determination in the face of the enemy." No mention was made of any specific accomplishment. I believe this was typical of most citations for awards.

However, the term ace and its requirements has persisted to this day. Roland Garros became the world's first ace, and the man who to a large extent revolutionized aerial warfare. He was invited to appear before the Directorate of Military Aeronautics to present his views on this new phase of aerial combat. The date for this appearance was set for April 26, but, unfortunately, Garros could not keep the appointment. Dame Fortune suddenly withdrew her patronage.

On the afternoon of April 19, 1915, Garros went aloft to bomb the railroad sidings at Courtrai, an assignment that indicates that the importance of man-to-man air combat was not yet fully appreciated. Once over his target, Garros cut his Le Rhone engine, went into the glide approach, swept over the freight yards, and dropped his contribution. He had no idea whether he had scored or missed; he was too concerned with getting the impact-fuse bombs overboard without blowing himself to bits. Then when he tried to switch on the rotary engine again, nothing happened; the propeller just windmilled in the slipstream. He knew immediately what had occurred and probably swore at his carelessness. In the long approach glide for the railroad yard he had allowed the spark plugs to oil up and had forgotten to burn them off by blipping the ignition switch intermittently. He had no alternative but to stretch his glide until he found a suitable spot to land.

He came down near Ingelmunster, about forty miles from the Dutch frontier, and his first concern was to destroy his plane and the secret of his front-firing gun. He did his best to set fire to the Morane, but all the fabric was damp and refused to burn.

A squad of German soldiers soon appeared and Garros made one last desperate bid for liberty by running across the field and sliding into a ditch for cover. The depression was full of muddy water, weeds, and half-frozen sedge, but he stayed there until darkness and then crawled out and headed for the Dutch border. As luck would have it he wandered straight into a group of enemy soldiers who were foraging for firewood. The game was up.

German aviation men soon examined the undamaged Morane, and were intrigued by the steel wedges that were bolted around the propeller blades. Blued bullet streaks soon disclosed the purpose of the plates, and the secret of the gun that could fire bullets between the blades of the whirling propeller was revealed. The Germans moved fast. The French *cocardes* were daubed out, and the Morane flown to Berlin where Anthony Fokker, a young Dutch engineer, was called in to examine its gun mounting.

## How Fokker Became Famous

Fokker's role in the development of early aircraft armament is well known, although his part has been greatly exaggerated. In short, once he sensed what the deflectors were for, he soon devised a mechanical interrupter gear—one that controlled the fire of the weapon and synchronized it with the position of the propeller blades. He bolted a cam gear to the back of the pro-

peller boss that, through a series of metal rods, actuated the
trigger of the machine gun. Thus, when a blade was opposite the
muzzle of the weapon, the trigger release was taken out of action and no bullets were fired.

Anthony Fokker was not alone in this idea. A Sergeant Mechanic Alkan of the French Air Service was working on a similar
arrangement. In Great Britain three other interrupter gears were
in the process of development, but Fokker's device was put into
production first, and when German airmen started to score with
this weapon, the propagandists in Berlin made the most of it. No
mention was made of the British DH.2, a single-seater pusher on
which a semi-flexible Lewis gun was mounted to fire forward.
Since the DH.2s engine was set behind the pilot's cockpit, no
interrupter gear was necessary. This little gadfly biplane was
equally effective as a front-gun fighter as was Fokker's more publicized Fokker E.1. In fact, most of Britain's early high-scorers,
notably Major Lanoe Hawker, had their successes aboard the
DH.2, but since the RFC did not play up individual perform-
ers, little was known of this early fighter aircraft.

Fokker's interrupter gear, fitted to his early E.1 monoplane,
had an important role in the development of the German Air
Force. Once it was tested and proved workable, the first squad-
ron-service model was given to Lieutenant Oswald Boelcke. After
several days of instruction he took Fokker's device into action on
June 30, 1915, while escorting a number of two-seaters on a
special mission. He was not successful in his first attack on a
French plane, because the little Fokker was more sensitive than
anything he had flown before. After one burst at the foeman,
Boelcke withdrew, as he was still concerned with the gun-
control mechanism.

Boelcke finally scored a week later—but not with the Fokker
gun. He was flying a two-seater Albatros and was attacked by a
French Morane. Neither of these aircraft was equipped with a
front-firing gun, but in the ensuing scramble Boelcke's observer
put a burst into the French pilot, and the Morane crashed in

German territory. This victory was credited to Boelcke, of course, not to his gunner.

Meanwhile a few Fokker gears had been hurriedly assembled and mounted aboard E.1s that were rushed to Boelcke's squadron at Douai. One of these machines was given to Max Immelmann, and it was this ace-to-be who scored first with this novel weapon. This success came on August 11, but he did not score again until September 9. On September 21 Max himself was shot down by the observer in a Farman two-seater, and was lucky to wobble in for a safe landing on his own field.

Immelmann had run his score up to seven by December 15, which hardly justifies the Fokker-fodder appellative. In the meantime Boelcke was making a calm study of the weapon and its potentiality, and although he too began to run up a creditable score, he was more intent on the full tactical use of the combination. It was he who devised the mass formations, the proper tactics in air fighting, and the rule that no German plane equipped with the Fokker gear was ever to cross the line into enemy territory. However, a very impetuous young German pilot who was flying a new Fokker monoplane became lost in the fog, and running out of fuel, landed in French territory; unwillingly handing the Allies an undamaged Fokker-gear monoplane. In this misfortune we can note poetic justice for the undamaged Morane Roland Garros had presented to the Germans.

It was soon evident that fixed-gun fighters, or at least aircraft that could have bursts of bullets fired along their line of flight, were vitally necessary. Although Fokker's device was first fitted to his own Eindekker monoplane, Boelcke soon showed a preference for a new Albatros D.1, and this mount was next selected to be the standard German fighter, and a very fine aircraft it was. In good hands and flown in the Boelcke squadron-strength formations, it became Germany's first real threat in her attempt to gain control of the air.

At the same time the British were flying the F.E.2b, the Vickers F.B.5 and F.B.9, all good two-seater fighters capable of taking care of themselves, and carrying skilled gunners who had been induced to transfer from the ground forces. These pusher machines soon offset the initial success of the Fokker mounts; so much so, in fact, that by the spring of 1916, and certainly through the Battle of the Somme, British air squadrons were making such inroads on German air strength that Boelcke had to devise the Flying Circus system. He joined, not only complete squadrons, but complete fighter groups into great massed forces that flew up and down to beat down smaller flights or squadrons by sheer power of weight and numbers.

Boelcke and Immelmann who gained great renown as fighting airmen did not live long to enjoy the fruits of their victories. Boelcke was killed in an air accident when one of his companions collided with him in midair. Immelmann was shot down by a British aerial gunner, Corporal J. H. Waller.

## Advent of the Aces

War in the air took on a new grim reality with the development of the fighting plane. No longer were "intrepid" airmen staging comic battles with Parker shotguns, half bricks, or potshotting at one another with cavalry carbines. Only the old Quirk was filling the lighter side of the program, or adding to the scores of the German airmen.

The airplane had proved itself in many situations. Engines were more powerful and reliable, gun mountings for observers were improved, and aerial cameras, though still loaded with glass plates, were highly efficient, and men were learning to glean important information from their prints. Bombing progressed as fast as the development of the aircraft for this payload purpose, and because antiaircraft ground crews could not keep up with the pace, both sides had to rely on their fighting airmen to prevent the other from snooping too often. Is it any wonder that the ace and the fighting squadrons enjoyed the fruits of wide publicity and universal acclaim?

The year 1916 saw the beginning of this mad race for victory scores. Thousands of servicemen who were thrilled by the air

fights above them, begged for a chance to climb out of the mud
of the trenches. Everyone wanted to be a pilot, of course, for few
could see any particular glory in serving as an observer or an
aerial gunner. In Great Britain where designers were developing
efficient two-seater fighters, there was some difficulty in obtain-
ing volunteers to fill the secondary posts. Finally, it was decided
that all commissioned officers who had volunteered for the Royal
Flying Corps would first have to put in fifty hours over the
enemy lines as observer-gunners. If they survived that ordeal,
they were sent back to Britain and given the standard pilot-
training course. Noncommissioned aerial gunners, enticed from
cavalry and infantry regiments, were usually promised the same
plan, but seldom, if ever, did any of them close out their gunners' servitude in so short a time: three hundred hours of active-
service flying was more often their lot before they were rewarded
with a rest and the comparative safety of the flying schools.

Once Oswald Boelcke had organized his Flying Circus defense, air fighting as an individual science was necessary, and
British and French designers had to concentrate on single-seater
fighters that were capable of countering these swarms. The
French improved their Nieuport scout that, by now, used the
British Constantinesco gun gear—a far superior hydraulic system
—and a semi-flexible gun mounted high on the top plane that
could be tilted upward to attack an enemy plane from below.
The Spad was well beyond the blueprint stage. The British were
developing the Sopwith Camel, S.E.5—and the Bristol Fighter.
It should be added to their credit that they were still hopeful
of some form of strategic aviation and were planning long-range
bombers, tactical bombers, and aircraft designed especially for
low-level or attack aviation. But all this good intent was delayed
by the frenzy for the development of fighting aircraft and the
training of fighting airmen. Still, the air services that had to
counter the defensive tactics of the Germans had little choice.
We know now that had true tactical and strategic aviation been
pressed earlier—the first to operate more efficiently with the
troops in the trenches, and the second to hit the enemy at his

chief bases of supply—the war might have been brought to a successful conclusion many months earlier. By the time all this was apparent, the aircraft needed were not far enough along in development and production to make these efforts possible. As an example, the four-engined, long-range Handley Page bomber designed for strategic attacks on Berlin and important German munitions centers, was not in full production.

During 1918 the British Air Board had decided that Berlin could be bombed from bases in England. The possibilities of heavy night bombing had been demonstrated by the Handley Page 0/400, and on the basis of this, it was decided to bring the German capital within reach of British bombs by rushing into manufacture a super Handley Page bomber, that had been developed as the V/1500 that was capable of a 1200-mile range, and of carrying thirty 250-pound bombs. When the Armistice brought an end to hostilities, only three of these giants were ready for war, but their performance was a cardinal event in the development of the heavy bomber and a triumph of aeronautical engineering.

The concept of long-range strategic bombing was not abandoned between the two world wars, and descendants of the V/1500 were designed on the assumption that a long-term policy would prove successful in a future war. The wisdom of this can be found in the later types developed by Handley Page and other British manufacturers.

An organization of American volunteers was accepted into the French Air Service on April 20, 1916, and for want of a better name was called the Escadrille Américaine. On French rosters it was known as N.124 Squadron. The volunteers were William Thaw, Elliot Cowdin, Kiffin Rockwell, Norman Prince, Charles C. Johnson, Clyde Balsley, Victor Chapman, Laurence Rumsey, and James R. McConnell.

The airplane they were to fly was the Nieuport 17.C1, one of the first of the Allied single-seaters designed to fire a fixed gun along its line of flight. This was not a weapon controlled to fire between the blades of the propeller. The Lewis gun was mounted on two V-brackets set on the spars of the center section, and its bullets passed just over the tips of the whirling propeller. The first models carried the infantry-type ammunition pan that held only forty-seven rounds, but a larger type that held ninety-seven rounds was provided later. In the early mountings it was impossible to tilt the weapon to replace an empty drum, and with this primary armament the pilot went into action with only forty-seven rounds of ammunition. The bracket was improved by the British, and by means of a curved rail the gun could be drawn back to a tilted position. The weapon was still secure with the fixture, and some Nieuport pilots, notably the famous Captains Albert Ball and Billy Bishop used this device to fire up at enemy planes ahead and above them.

After a few days of preliminary formation flying and visits over the line in the custody of Captain Georges Thénault, a seasoned French airman, Escadrille Américaine gradually assumed routine patrols, but the ace influence was soon noted, and they often went over on lone patrols hoping to encounter enemy aircraft. On May 18 Kiffin Yates Rockwell scored the first American victory when he downed an enemy two-seater over the old town of Thann with the expenditure of only four rounds of ammunition. It was his first combat, the first time he had seen an enemy plane, and the first time he had fired his machine gun.

With time and experience the American squadron was moved to the Verdun front where Bert Hall scored the second victory for this volunteer group. This legendary character is not to be confused with James Norman Hall, the noted writer who joined the escadrille later. Bert Hall was the typical soldier of fortune, a mystery man who could delight and confound his companions hour by hour. He was a careless braggart, and in one mood would swear he had been born in Kentucky around 1880, and an hour later before the same audience would credit Higginsville, Missouri, as his birthplace.

Old Bert was at his best when telling his amazing stories of military prowess. He had fought on one side or the other, as an airman of course, in the Turkish-Bulgarian war of 1912. In the next breath he had been a Gor-bli-me Tommy fighting with Kitchener's Army when it was making its heroic stand during the Battle of Mons. Before his listeners could get a few facts substantiated, Bert had transferred to the French Foreign Legion and was taking credit for active service from August 1914 to December 1914. His tales were so credible, few of his listeners bothered to check his credentials.

But there were times when Bert was a lovable character and no one would have questioned him had he insisted that he had been with Captain Scott on his tragic trip to the South Pole. It was useless to argue with him, for, like as not, he would produce a page or two from Scott's diary, or a medal awarded to him for making the trip.

Hall made his way into the French Air Service by saying that he had fought for the Turks—or the Bulgarians—in a number of air battles, but when asked to show his skill aboard a Blériot, he displayed no evidence of having encountered an airplane before. Nevertheless, he scrambled through the schools and won his wings on August 19, 1915, and through that summer and following autumn was a member of MS.38, a Morane-Saulnier squadron that carried out routine observation missions. Apparently Bert held his own, for he was accepted for the new Escadrille Américaine late in April 1916. Here with his own countrymen he was a happy-go-lucky, garrulous, ne'er-do-well adventurer, and his social behavior left much to be desired. His manner of playing cards or rolling dice soon banned him from most companionable groups, and eventually, although he had downed three enemy airplanes and had been decorated twice, Bert was "invited" to leave the squadron.

He was then posted to another French Nieuport escadrille where he was awarded another citation for his courage and energy. But he stayed with this escadrille for only a short time, and by January 1917 was granted permission to accompany a French Aviation mission to Romania. Following this, he was allowed to

return to the United States, ostensibly to join the United States
Aviation Corps, but he failed to turn up at any American enlist-
ment bureau, and to this day is still listed as a deserter in French
military records.

After the war he roamed the world in various roles, some not
too savory, and died in an automobile accident. Few historians of
the Lafayette Escadrille have given Bert Hall much space in their
journals, which is regrettable for he must have been a fascinating
character.

The outstanding figure in the Lafayette Escadrille was Raoul
Lufbery, who was not a native American. He was born in France
in 1885 and was somewhat older than the average World War I
airman. His mother died one year after his birth and his father
remarried in 1890 and shortly after took his new wife to the
United States, leaving Raoul and two other sons with their grand-
mother.

When he was in his teens Raoul found a job in a chocolate
factory, and for nearly four years sent most of his earnings to
his father; money that helped M. Lufbery to establish a comfortable home and a stamp business in Wallingford, Connecticut.
In 1904, at age nineteen, Raoul set out to see the world and
eventually came to the United States. Unfortunately, Raoul arrived in New York on the very day his father had sailed from
the same port for Europe on business. As events turned out, they
never did meet again.

Raoul stayed in Wallingford for about two years where he
picked up a smattering of English, but he was not geared to
settle down, and next went to Cuba. Then swinging back to the
United States he evaded the panic of 1907 by joining the United
States Army, and was sent to the Philippines for a military hitch
that enabled him to claim American citizenship. After a two-year
service he took his savings and headed for Japan and China.

In 1912 he was in Saigon where he made the acquaintance of
Marc Pourpe, a noted French aviator who was giving exhibition
flights with a Blériot monoplane. Lufbery signed on as a general

handyman and mechanic, and these two men barnstormed around Europe and Africa during the next two years. They returned to France in the early summer of 1914 to buy a Morane Parasol. They fully intended to go back to the Far East for another exhibition tour but war broke out, and Pourpe offered his services to the French Aviation.

Contrary to popular belief, Lufbery did not join up with his companion, but accepted the breaks of fate, bid Marc goodby and was among the first American volunteers to gather at the Hôtel des Invalides in Paris, and on August 24 joined the Foreign Legion as an infantryman. Whether or not Pourpe pulled any wires, or whether Raoul's mechanical skill had anything to do with it, within a week Lufbery was transferred to Pourpe's squadron as an aviation mechanic. Three months later Marc was killed in action.

The aviation mechanic stayed on to service planes, but over the next few weeks perceptive officers had sensed the intense spirit of devotion that had developed between Pourpe and Lufbery, and one of them suggested that Raoul be relieved and given pilot training. This opportunity was gratefully accepted by Raoul with no dramatic gestures or theatrical threats of revenge. He was not capable of such histrionics; he simply picked up his gear and strode out of camp.

He received his primary training at Chartres and won his wings on a Farman. Later he had bombing instruction on a Voisin, and his first active service flying was with VB.106 where he proved to be a workmanlike performer, although he made no outstanding contribution and received few official citations. After a reasonable number of hours on bombardment duty he applied for *chasse* training. Knowing that experienced bomber pilots were at a premium, his commander tried at first to dissuade him and used every recourse to keep this impassive, but reliable airman. But Lufbery was rewarded eventually, and sent to Plessis-Belleville for training on the Nieuport. He displayed no particular skill or brilliance here, for he was clumsy and heavy handed, and for a time his instructors feared he would have to be sent back to the bomber squadron. Raoul persisted, however, until he gained some proficiency and was sent finally to the Escadrille Américaine.

He was a total unknown when he arrived at Luxeuil, and in appearance small, chunky, not much over five feet tall. He had broad shoulders, a perpetual scowl, and apparently no emotions of any kind. He seldom talked of his past and his language was a polyglot of every patois he had picked up. Certainly, he did not speak like a New Englander, but there was no doubt of his daring. Had history been kinder and had he remained with the French after America entered the war, he might have become an outstanding airman with a lengthy record of "kills."

He soon became an ace, however, and gained great popularity on both sides of the Atlantic, but he was not the first American ace. Fred Libby of Colorado who had joined the Royal Flying Corps already had been accepted in that gallant company. But Lufbery was widely publicized, and Libby was not.

Lufbery became the fighting mainstay of the Lafayette Escadrille until America entered the war and reclaimed her flying sons. This move put Raoul Lufbery once more in his former situation of uncertainty and dilemma. When President Wilson signed America's declaration of war, he unknowingly scrawled Raoul Lufbery's death sentence.

After many weeks of waiting for an American squadron to be formed and outfitted, Lufbery was killed while fighting a German airplane not many yards from his own airfield. He jumped to his death when his aircraft was set on fire by the enemy aerial gunner. Like so many others of the ace group, he died in a manner contrary to all expectations.

Jimmy McCudden was killed in a foolish attempt to turn back to his field after his engine had failed on take-off. No one knows how Georges Guynemer died or where he is buried. The great Baron Manfred von Richthofen may have been shot down by Roy Brown, a Canadian pilot, but most wartime airmen believe he was brought down by two Australian machine gunners who were protecting an artillery park. As mentioned before, Boelcke was killed in a midair collision. Mickey Mannock was downed by ground fire while showing a novice pilot how to attack an enemy plane. Albert Ball was shot down by a German gunner hidden in a church tower. George Lanoe Hawker was killed by a "creaser" bullet, one of several hundred fired at him by Richthofen. Werner Voss, a most redoubtable German airman, was trapped well behind the British lines by McCudden's Number 56 Squadron and shot down. He was one of the few Germans who dared to attack Allied planes over their own territory.

Captain G. E. H. McElroy, who downed forty-two enemy aircraft, disappeared one morning in the summer of 1918. Some reports have it that he is buried at Laventie, but no one knows how he died. Reggie Warneford, who downed the first Zeppelin, was killed a few days later when he was thrown from an aircraft that had no seat belts. Alan McLeod, a Canadian V.C. hero, was decorated at Buckingham Palace, went home for a rest and died of influenza during the epidemic that swept North America. Roland Garros who devised the first front-firing gun, finally escaped from the Germans, and on trying to continue his fighting career was shot down and killed one month before the Armistice.

Frank Luke, second only to Eddie Rickenbacker among American aces, was shot down during an attack on three German balloons. He landed safely and could have been taken prisoner, but he elected to shoot it out with an automatic pistol trying to hold off a platoon of enemy infantrymen. Italy's Luigi Olivari, who downed twelve enemy planes, was killed during a take-off when he climbed too sharply and went into a spin. Germany's Max Mulzer was killed while testing a new Albatros plane, as was Heinrich Gontermann while testing a Fokker Triplane.

And so the great aces passed, denied the end fitting the knights of the sky.

# CHAPTER XIII

*The Epic of Captain Ball . . . The Legend of the Lady
Flier . . . Two-Seaters at Cambrai . . . The Black Tri-
planes . . . The Birth of Strategic Aviation . . . Aircraft
Carrier Operations.*

## The Epic of Captain Ball

I am often asked which of the great aces of World War I intrigued or impressed me most. I met many of these war fliers,
both in the field and in later years, when their old exploits could
be discussed quietly and with some objectivity. This first war-in-
the-air produced all sorts on both sides of the line, and although
the service did appear to attract the best of the youth of that day,
it should not be assumed that the Galahadian factor was uppermost in all of them.

There were braggarts and cowards who would have acted the
same no matter in which service they fought. There were professional Hun-haters, and true gentlemen who dueled with
knightly skill, patrol after patrol. There were those who were
shocked when they realized what war flying entailed, but being
true heroes who had to make themselves go out day after day,
they somehow lived through it, and to their amazement discovered they were regarded as gallant men and decorated for their
efforts. There were many such.

Few air heroes went into the flying services determined to be
high-scoring knights of the air. A number of them have intimated
in reminiscences written years after they had grounded themselves for good, that that was their goal, but most of them, and

I include myself in this company, selected military flying rather than trench warfare as the lesser of two evils. After months of aimless training with no hope of engaging the enemy, cavalry-men willingly transferred to the aviation services, and in all honesty it must be said that few of them made this decision in the belief that they might become internationally known heroes. Once they were in and had survived the training courses, they realized at last, and not until then, what they had signed on for.

I am speaking, of course, of the early years of war flying before the ace qualifications and romance of air fighting had been widely published. I made my first move to evade ground war-fare in 1916, but at the time had no preconceived notions of becoming a fighting airman. I had never heard of such a type. Looking back, I see that I did not know what I was volunteering for, except to get out of the trenches, and take on a new and more appealing method of doing my bit. At first, I did not feel qualified for a commission and pilot training, but I was willing to fly in some capacity, or even learn to be a mechanic and service the aircraft. When it was pointed out that I might be employed as a machine gunner aboard a "battleplane," I jumped at the opportunity, but initially, had no idea of becoming a pilot. That was for "officers and gentlemen."

In the United States and Canada, at least by the time America was moving toward a declaration of war, hundreds of youths straight out of prep schools or universities were begging for flight-cadet appointments with the understanding that they would be taught to fly and awarded commissions some time be-fore they crossed the Atlantic. I suppose some of these candi-dates may have had hopes and yearnings for an ace status, but I never met anyone who made such a statement publicly. How in-terested they were in this service must be tempered with the reminder that national conscription was soon to be enforced in the United States, and like many of us already in action, they decided that the air was less hazardous than the trenches.

A study of the German aces reveals much the same pattern. In the early years most of them were volunteers from cavalry regiments who felt that as flying men they could contribute more on a patrol than they could astride a horse. A few of them hoped to aid the Fatherland as bomber pilots, for they, too, had not conceived of fighting in the air. It was the later newspaper buildup of Oswald Boelcke and Max Immelmann that attracted the more belligerent types.

To my mind, the most fabulous character of World War I flying was Captain Albert Ball who dominated British aviation between the summer of 1916 and the spring of 1917. He downed forty-four enemy aircraft during a wild pugnacious career that had no equal on any front. Albert Ball would have made Frank Luke, the Arizona Balloon Buster, seem like a chastened choirboy.

I knew Ball for a few short weeks in 1917 when he was a star performer with Number 56 Squadron, RFC. He was tending a hutch of rabbits with adolescent concern, and because he was a commissioned officer and I a mere first class air mechanic (gunner) our intercourse was limited to this barnyard level. We could not decide whether his mangy brood preferred dandelion leaves or cabbage stalks. Such a scene was the last I remember of him, and I often wondered what became of his pets.

Albert Ball was the world's leading air fighter before he was twenty-one years of age. He had the tenacity of a bulldog, and the expression of a poet. He enjoyed music, books, paintings, and could write, but not spell, with the skill of an essayist. Aflame with boyish patriotism, and driven by what he considered to be his bounden duty, his life reads like that of a contrived character of fiction.

The product of a Victorian family, Albert Ball would not fit the matrix of today's concept of a war hero. His father was at one time Mayor of Nottingham, England, Albert's home town. He went to a middle-class school, served in the Boy Scouts, pursued all the usual hobbies, and had a knack for general engineering. He was devoted to his mother, adored his sister Lois, but his brother Cyril was someone to be endured, a feeling that was mutual.

When he was seventeen Albert Ball organized what he called the Universal Engineering Works, and his business cards stated that the firm was "On Admiralty and War Office Lists," giving the impression that the Nottingham youth was turning out battleships and sixteen-inch guns on order. The war put an end to this project, and Albert enlisted in his county regiment, the 7th Battalion of the Sherwood Foresters, the Nottingham company of which was known as the Robin Hood Rifles.

He gained his sergeant's stripes within a month, a promotion that doomed him to the role of an instructor, which nettled him no end. From what he had gathered from the casualty reports, he thought that he would be of more use in Flanders. Then he read about Rhodes-Moorhouse and realized for the first time that men were actually flying airplanes on military duty, so one morning in May 1915, after he had been commissioned, he threw a leg over his motorcycle and roared over the sixty miles from his base to a private flying field at Hendon. Making a quick, specialized deal, he paid out ten pounds from his own pocket for a few flying lessons, and before he started back, had a few minutes of dual-control experience on an old French Caudron. He whizzed back to Luton, dusty, begrimed, and road-streaked, and his colonel had him on the carpet for appearing in an oil-stained tunic. So Albert simply arose a half hour earlier each day so that he could get back in time to change into a clean uniform.

He finally earned his "ticket," despite two amusing crashes that he deleted from the records, and, by October 1915, had sufficient time in to warrant a transfer to the Royal Flying Corps. Early in the new year he was given an opportunity to go to France—but not as a pilot; the RFC was short of observers and aerial gunners. Albert thought that because he had bought his wings, he was entitled to fly the machine. His luck changed by February 15, however, and he was posted to Number 13 Squadron in France where old Quirks were being flown.

He soon learned that flying Caudrons, Farmans, and Avros in England in no way compared with the activity along the Western Front, and he wisely concentrated on learning the ropes. The old BE.2c was no "battleplane," but for a time it was too much for him, and there was a period when his CO, a Major Marsh, considered sending him back for further training, but Albert put on such a scene, the major permitted him to stay.

This young man, who was considered most inexperienced, volunteered for intelligence missions in which he boldly flew British agents over the line, deposited them in enemy territory, and went back a few days later to pick them up. In addition, there were artillery shoots to carry out, and at that time the weather was dreadful. Machine after machine failed to return, and Albert began to view the "intrepid-airman" activity in a new light. Once in the cockpit, he nonetheless went headlong into every task, accepting extra work and additional patrols with no question or complaint.

Ball became a reasonably good Quirk pilot, but was never spectacular, and what stunting he attempted was not smooth or precise. At best, he was just another journeyman pilot, who found it difficult to work in harmony with other airmen, particularly in Army co-operation work. It was soon evident that he was an individualist, and he saw that if he hoped to be happy in this war, he would have to transfer to a single-seater squadron; an example of the fact that few airmen started their war flying with the intent of becoming aces.

It was the practice in those days to assign to two-seater squadrons one or two single-seaters that could be flown in support of the co-operation machines. There were two Bristol Scouts for such sorties at Number 13, and Ball spent more time on these single-seaters than he did on the Quirk. He became quite adept with them, too.

Major Marsh, possibly hoping to be rid of this young firebrand, sent Ball across the field one day with a note to the CO of Number 11. The note explained that, "this young man can be entrusted with the best single-seater on the front. Please give him something to do."

Major W. H. Hubbard of Number 11 was delighted. He had

a few decrepit Nieuport scouts and assigned one to Ball and ordered him to protect the tails of his Quirks. As a matter of fact, Ball carried out these escort patrols for both squadrons all through the early summer of 1916, but it is not known if he downed any enemy aircraft because few RFC pilots at that time bothered to make official reports on such activity.

Ball performed this double-duty work until he had a mild physical breakdown and was to be sent home on leave, but the Battle of the Somme was about to open, and all leave was canceled. However, Major Marsh realized that Ball was at the end of his tether and sent him home for a much-needed rest. He returned in time to zoom into the worst of the Blood Bath activity.

The Somme battle afforded trench-strafing, kite-balloon attacks, fights with enemy aircraft, and low-altitude co-operation with the advancing troops. Numbers 11 and 13 Squadrons were in the thick of it and Ball put in ungodly hours and registered his first official victory, an enemy kite balloon. This feat brought him the Military Cross. A short time later, fighting along with a number of F.E.2b pushers, he barged into six Roland two-seaters. The Fees destroyed one, and Ball got another.

Ball flew with both squadrons all through that memorable summer, and even made a number of reconnaissance flights aboard the Quirk. He got his second enemy plane in the middle of August, and was promoted to captain and transferred to Number 60 Squadron, which was to produce the famous Billy Bishop. On the day he left Number 13 Ball attacked six Rolands and downed one of them.

Albert Ball was a problem at Number 60 because it was impossible for him to accept restraint and work in standard formations. Major Barry-Smith, then CO, wisely allowed him to fly as a free-lance pilot, a situation seldom met in any British squadron. From this time on, Albert Ball came into his own. Flying the new version of the Nieuport scout, he perfected the trick of getting below and behind his enemy, then tilting the flexible Lewis gun upward, he would drench his opponent

with deadly bursts before that unfortunate knew that a Britisher
was anywhere in the area. He displayed savage enthusiasm in
all his flights and took dangerous chances. On returning from
a show he would hound the mechanics until his bus was serv-
iced again, then he would roar away once more. He attacked
singles, doubles, and complete flights of enemy aircraft, showing
no fear of anyone. When night crept in to end his day, he would
often retire to his cubicle and play dreadful passages on his
violin until he drove everyone else off to Amiens. Either that,
or he bored his flight mates stiff with his concept of poetry.

By October 3, 1916, Captain Ball had scored thirty-one
victories, but these figures were not made available to the
British press, although at this time Germany was flooding the
world with detailed reports of her leading aces, and American
newspapers, in particular, were giving these accounts wide circulation. But Fleet Street argued, "If we expect young men to
volunteer to fly with the RFC, we must offer them the chance to
become heroes, like Captain Ball. [Ball had tried to keep
the details of his record from the press, but the facts leaked
out.] Here in Britain, we are playing down our air heroes and
are having to go into the trenches to beg young infantrymen to
volunteer for flying. What a chance! They see war in the air
every day—and all its grisly action. But over in Canada and
America every kid who can read wants to learn how to fly. Why?
Because all they know of war flying comes from the French and
German reports, and how their aces are winning all the
medals!"

This was true, up to a point, for the people of France knew
more about Captain Ball than did the good folk of Nottingham;
he was simply a young man who for some reason or other had
won the Distinguished Service Order and the Military Cross.
What he had done to earn these honors was offered as "most
conspicuous and consistent bravery," but none of the details
was available.

While on a leave in England, Ball designed a single-seater

which was built by the Austin Company. It was a boxy, chunky
affair that looked something like a Spad, and performed even
worse, and luckily never went into production.

Late in February 1917 Ball returned to France to join the
crack Number 56 Squadron. In this, he was both pleased and
disappointed; he was delighted to leave England again, but was
disturbed to learn that he would be expected to fly the S.E.5.
What he had against this splendid aircraft is a mystery.

It was here at Estrée-Blanche that Ball indulged in animal
husbandry, and learned that the squadron was replete with
high-scoring fighters; men like Jimmy McCudden, A. P. F. Rhys-
Davids, G. J. C. Maxwell, and A. Mayberry. Back at Number
60 Billy Bishop was racking up Huns, and the Lafayette Escadrille was lighting a glory trail across the French front. In other
words, Ball returned to France to learn that he was expected to
act like an ace, and he begged for a Nieuport scout, instead of
the S.E.5. Once more his well-known red-nosed single-seater was
a-wing over the Bapaume-Cambrai road.

In the period from April 22 to May 7, Captain Ball shot
down eleven more enemy aircraft, raising his score to forty-two,
which led the Allied field. Gradually he acquired an air of
maturity and forsook the 1916 Nieuport for the S.E.5., a more
practical warplane.

Captain Albert Ball reached the end of his short, but wild,
flying life, on the evening of May 7, 1917. His passing has been
the subject of more arguments and myths than that of anyone else in the history of the air. Probably no one knows how he
died.

Another Battle of Arras was in progress, and the British were
concentrating on the village of Bullecourt. Officials of the 9th
Wing, RFC, decided to maintain a formation of Spads, Camels,
and S.E.5s in the Douai-Cambrai sector throughout that day.
Ball headed a flight from Number 56 Squadron.

After a number of general attacks on anything available, and

dodging cloud conditions over Bourlon Wood, Ball suddenly
went into a dive, apparently shooting at an Albatros single-
seater below. That was the last anyone saw of him. The most
reliable story that can be made of the available evidence is
that Ball had just shot down his forty-fourth victim, and then
turned for home well below the cloud level. He passed over
the village of Annoeulin, and following an old habit checked on
the time. Although he wore a wrist watch and had a small clock
set into the instrument panel of his machine, Albert, the Sunday-
school boy, trusted implicitly in church clocks. Whenever he was
in that area, and on his way home, he usually sped past the
Annoeulin church and checked with the time-encrusted hands
of the tower clock.

The villagers knew of this, and the Germans occupying the
sector finally learned of his habit. They all recognized the
British scout with the red nose-spinner, and Ball's routine was
an invitation. Early in May the Germans put a machine gun
in the church tower—and waited.

When Captain Ball flew past to glance at the church clock,
a spray of machine-gun bullets caught him and he crashed just
outside the village of Annoeulin. There was no other aircraft in
the vicinity.

At the end of that month, more than three weeks later, the
German newspapers proclaimed the death of Captain Albert
Ball. The reports said that he had been shot down by Lothar
von Richthofen, brother of the Baron. But the villagers of
Annoeulin knew better. The British knew better, since Lothar
von Richthofen stated in his combat report, or in a combat
credited to him, that he was victorious over Captain Ball, and
had shot down Ball's *Sopwith Triplane* near Annoeulin. He
somehow had produced the engine number of Ball's S.E.5, but
could not give the aircraft number!

When this Richthofen was charged later with the mistake of
calling an S.E.5 a triplane, he foolishly stated that in the heat
of an action he *often* mistook biplanes for triplanes. What he

never could explain, however, is that on the day Ball was shot down, May 7, 1917, Lothar von Richthofen was in Berlin—on sick leave!

The years have added bewilderment to the Albert Ball story. Many writers, starry-eyed over the Flying Circus, have credited this victory to one or the other of the Richthofens, ignoring the fact that Manfred was also on leave in Berlin, after scoring his fifty-second victory. He left the front on May 1, 1917, and did not return until June 14. Other reports claim that Lothar, who had been wounded early in May was in a hospital in a state of shock, and facing a long period of convalescence.

More reliable reports state that a peasant woman in Annoeulin told Ball's brother Cyril that it was she who pulled Albert out of the crash. He was still alive at the time, but had a serious head wound and died shortly after as she held him in her arms. Recent information indicates that Ball was buried in a German military cemetery at Annoeulin, the only British grave in this ground. The early wooden cross has been replaced by a more formal monument and is tended by a French pensioner. The British War Graves Commission at one time suggested that Ball's remains be removed to a British cemetery, but his father declined, and added that he wished his son to lie among the German dead. He also bought the field on which Ball fell and had it cemented over to mark the tragic spot.

On June 3, 1917, less than a month after his flight, Captain Ball was honored posthumously with the Victoria Cross, the tenth V.C. to be awarded to a British airman in nearly three years of air-war fighting.

## The Legend of the Lady Flier

Some time after Captain Ball's death, a new air legend ran the length of the front. In this period every German aviator who was shot down and captured within Allied territory—and there were very few—when brought in for interrogation claimed that he had been downed by a girl who was flying a red Sopwith triplane. In some instances the plane was a red-nosed S.E.5, exactly like Captain Ball's.

No one refuted these claims, not even when some of the captives went so far as to request an introduction to this militant female, before being sent to POW compounds. This gay tale trickled along the wire of the front, and was repeated in nearly every mess. The British wisely let the story ride. Dozens of Allied airmen claimed to have seen this blonde siren skipping about at twelve thousand feet, shooting the tails off unsuspecting Fokkers and Halberstadts. It was no optical illusion, brought on by equal parts of mist, sunshine, and Guinness's stout. They had seen her clearly, and she was a beautiful dish. Her Irene Castle-style bobbed hair fluttered in the wind as she zoomed and banked all over the sky. The infantry adopted this fable with wholehearted enthusiasm, and in no time this flossy figure was zipping up and down the enemy wire, shooting Hun gunners out of machine-gun pits, and performing all sorts of fantastic deeds of aerial daring. Nothing in *La Vie Parisienne* could match this charmer.

Some of the time she was Captain Ball's sister Lois, a tomboy who loved him devotedly, and was carrying out a scourge of family revenge. This revenge motif played a large part in several variations that followed. Whenever the war situation became grave for the Allies, the girl in the red-nosed S.E.5 sometimes became a German *fräulein* flying a black-and-white Fokker. This particular damsel had long yellow braids that seemed to streak back all the way to the tail surfaces of her plane, and by mid-1918 American soldiers impressed with the story of the Red Knight of Germany, were certain she was a sister of the Baron, out to take revenge for the death of her famous brother. His only sister, Frieda, had married the British novelist David H. Lawrence, and was interned in Great Britain, thereby spoiling that myth.

The most popular version of this high-flying girl was rife throughout Amiens. Everyone there knew her, for she flew an

S.E.5 and won the collective hearts of a certain RFC squadron, and by some mysterious arrangement had been taught to fly a British single-seater. Now she was the master of Sop triplanes, Camels, S.E.5s, and even Salamanders.

I think I know the actual basis for this flossy legend that began innocently enough on a field near Chipilly on the Somme. We had a squadron of S.E.5s on the same field with us, and these young scout pilots were always up to some healthy devilment. Around Christmas of 1917—long after Ball had gone west—they decided to enliven the dreary days by organizing a squadron party complete with a theatrical performance. They were especially good at this, and one of the ringleaders was a clever female impersonator. He was young, beardless, and probably should have been back at Rugby conjugating Latin verbs. He was hilarious in the show and fooled most of us because he had been listed on the program as a well-known theatrical ingénue who had been brought over from London. After the show he appeared at the bar and flirted so outrageously with the squadron major, the whole outfit was almost granted fourteen days' leave.

The gag proved so genuine the youth was induced to stay in character and liven matters around the field. The mechanics were goggle-eyed as this dainty bit flounced in and out of the hangars, showing a shapely leg, and brazenly climbing into S.E.5 cockpits in such a manner as to acquaint them with the very latest in French lingerie. Then, one bright lad got the idea that "she" should lead them on that afternoon's patrol.

The mechanics, still unaware of the sex of this "lass," were once more lifted to heights of delirium as she was assisted into a plane while the pilots gallantly turned their heads at the flutter of lace and silk. They watched in astonishment as she put on a pair of flying goggles, refreshed her make-up and fluffed out her blond tresses.

The rest of the act produced the basis for the story of the girl in the red-nosed S.E.5. The formation went over the line and made certain that every other formation on the front got a look at their leader who appeared to be a girl with beautiful fair hair.

The mechanics back at the field were still dizzy with what they had seen, and gave the legend full, detailed circulation.

## Two-Seaters at Cambrai

An erroneous impression that has been held for a long time is that almost all air fighting was done by pilots of single-seater squadrons, which is understandable because all ace lists are composed of pilots who flew scouts or monoplace machines of the day—Spads, Fokkers, Camels, S.E.5s, or Nieuports. So it may come as a surprise for many readers to learn that the famed Bristol Fighter may claim the championship for aircraft destroyed, although the Sopwith Camel with its score of 1634 victories is generally considered to be the star of them all.

There are no official records credited to this British two-seater, and the successes scored by the observer-gunners were never credited to the men in the rear seat, so because of this hard and fast rule of the British service, it has been impossible to know exactly how many enemy aircraft fell before Bristol Fighter guns. The gunners aboard D.H.4s and Armstrong-Whitworths also fought valiantly, and downed their share of the opposition, but their conquests could not compare with those of the Bristol Fighter airmen.

There are a number of Bristol Fighter pilots, however, who are listed in some unofficial records. They were all commissioned officers, and Major Andrew E. McKeever of Number 11 Squadron leads them with a score of thirty aircraft. When Major McKeever returned to Canada after the war he was tragically killed on Christmas Day, 1919, when an automobile he was driving skidded on an icy road.

The list of Bristol Fighter pilots who became aces, and their scores follows:

|                              | Squadron | Victories |
|------------------------------|:--------:|:---------:|
| Major Andrew E. McKeever      | 11       | 30        |
| Captain Edward McKelvie       | 22       | 29        |
| Captain Henry G. Luchford     | 20       | 29        |
| Captain J. E. Gurdon          | 22       | 27        |
| Captain E. J. K. McLoughry    | 20       | 23        |
| Lieutenant W. McK. Thompson   | 20       | 22        |
| Captain D. Latimer            | 20       | 22        |
| Captain W. Beaver             | 20       | 19        |
| Lieutenant Thayer Iaccaci     | 22       | 18        |
| Captain T. P. Middleton       | 20       | 16        |
| Lieutenant Clive T. Warman    | 22       | 15        |
| Captain Fred Libby            | 20       | 14        |
| Lieutenant Paul Iaccaci       | 20       | 11        |

Libby, Warman, and the Iaccaci brothers were Americans serving with the Royal Flying Corps.

It should also be explained that Captain McKelvie has often been confused with Major McKeever of Number 11 Squadron. Their names were somewhat similiar, both flew Bristol Fighters, and both of them had at one time gunner-obervers named Powell. McKeever's back-seat man was Lieutenant L. F. Powell, whereas McKelvie's gunner was Sergeant Edward Powell, a hut-mate of mine. McKelvie was an Englishman, who, when last heard of, was living in Wiltshire.

McKelvie became an important member of our Number 22 Squadron and after a few weeks of flying in the Brisfit, as she was affectionately called, he engaged an Albatros D.3 on a fighter-to-fighter basis. He had no trouble outmaneuvering and shooting down the German, and from that time on persisted in using the Bristol two-seater in that manner. McKelvie did not claim the distinction of originating this mode of fighting, he just worked out variations of the two-seater attack, and by July 10 had racked up his fifth victory with a spectacular display.

McKelvie had decided early that NCO gunners were better trained fighting airmen than the officer observers, because most of these ex-infantrymen were putting in more hours than the commissioned gunners. He therefore selected Eddie Powell of A Flight, and these two became famous.

One morning McKelvie was leading an early patrol when Powell spotted a two-seater Roland just below them. He gave his pilot a signal and they nosed down. The Roland was hit hard and went up in flames. Then Powell's gun started chattering, and McKelvie turned and saw five gaudy Albatros fighters diving on them. In a running battle that lasted all the way back to the British lines, McKelvie downed two, and Powell shot the wings off another. The pilot was awarded the Military Cross, but his gunner was not even mentioned in the combat report sent to Wing headquarters.

In August, with Powell's assistance, McKelvie received a Bar to his Military Cross when he led a low-altitude bombing attack against a German airfield. Loaded to capacity with twenty-pound Cooper bombs, the Brisfits of A Flight wrecked three hangars and destroyed eleven planes. On their way back they were intercepted by a formation of enemy Pfalz fighters, but the Brisfit gunners easily took them apart, downing five in the ensuing melée.

There was no stopping the McKelvie-Powell combination for a time. Unofficially, Powell was credited with eight enemy aircraft and before the end of 1917 was sent back to England for a commission and pilot training.

On August 28 McKelvie and Powell scored another triple, downing an Albatros and a new Pfalz scout. Powell then torched an Albatros. As were the rest of us, they were also engaged in trench strafing, and on one occasion Mac downed a kite balloon while Powell wiped out the winch crew and knocked down a Pfalz that was guarding the gasbag.

This represents a typical day with a Bristol Fighter squadron. We might escort D.H. bombers to the airship sheds at Gontrode or we might hound road transport just behind the front lines. We bombed machine-gun posts, shot up trench-mortar redoubts, attacked any enemy aircraft, or made photographic reconnaissance well over the German lines. As can be imagined, there was no military aircraft to compare with the Bristol Fighter.

McKelvie and Powell fought their last battle together on November 30, a dud-weather period in the Battle of Cambrai. I recall this episode very well because I was involved later in the general activity, and remember that the weather was abominable.

Soon after breakfast on that day, GHQ called for a special look-see flight over an area of much activity, but the weather was so dreadful only volunteers were considered. McKelvie and Powell were the first pair selected, and before they were sixty feet off the ground, they were enveloped in fog. Cambrai was nearly eighty miles away and the pilot had only a simple compass to guide him. As they prowled about looking for a hole in the gloom, a tremendous roar punched a great gout of flame through the mist. An ammunition dump had erupted, and in the sharp illumination of the explosion McKelvie saw German infantrymen trying to subdue the flames—at least, that is what he thought he saw.

Powell, however, was suspicious. He thought it was not an accident, or a lucky long-range hit by British artillery, but rather that the dump had been exploded by intent, and he asked his pilot to go down to make sure. As they churned about at one thousand feet, attempting to make sense of the furor below, they were attacked by a flight of nine Albatros scouts. A burst of gun-fire shot the drum off Powell's gun, and more bullets tore into McKelvie's cockpit and smashed several instruments. Powell replaced the drum and opened fire on an Albatros that zoomed over their top wing. The enemy plane rolled over and exploded. Another D.3 crossed McKelvie's line of flight and the pilot blasted it out of the sky. Powell turned on a third Albatros and three German fighters were falling to the ground at the same time—all within thirty seconds.

The remaining Albatros pilots drew off, re-formed, and then accepted the challenge once more. McKelvie was still prowling about in his attempt to interpret the confusion below, and he and Powell stated later that they were positive the Germans were pulling out of Cambrai to a new line of defense. When McKelvie saw enemy planes roaring at them again, he nosed up, pressed his gun control, and another Albatros burst into flames, and still another was harried into a crazy spin from which it had no space to recover.

The Bristol was now perforated from rudder to prop boss. A piece of metal had slashed Powell's cheek, a bullet had cut one of McKelvie's boots, and suddenly both men were out of ammunition, so McKelvie zoomed into the murk, evaded their adversaries, and then went down, hedge-hopping all the way back to Estrée Blanche. For their performance McKelvie was awarded the Distinguished Service Order and Powell the Distinguished Conduct Medal.

McKelvie's suspicion of the German intent at Cambrai caused GHQ to ask for more volunteers, and another Bristol Fighter went out into the fog and hit the slag heaps around Lens. A third took off and was not heard from again. About noon of that day I accompanied a Lieutenant Davidson to Cambrai, and we had an experience similar to that of McKelvie's and Powell's. We came back with further evidence that the Germans *were* pulling out of Cambrai, but because neither Powell nor I were commissioned officers, our reports were not accepted immediately. By the time GHQ decided that there might be something in what we had seen, the Germans had consolidated their positions, counterattacked, and retaken most of the ground the British had won in the previous three weeks.

Cambrai might have been a major victory in 1917, had the observation reports of two NCO gunners been accepted, but no doubt greater campaigns have been won or lost on items of lesser importance.

### The Black Triplanes

One of the most colorful, but least known of the long list of Canadian aces, is Major Raymond Collishaw, who is credited officially with destroying sixty-eight enemy aircraft. Today, he lives in retirement in British Columbia where he was born in 1893.

The lure of adventure claimed Collishaw early, for while he was still in his teens he served as a second mate aboard a vessel plying between Victoria, B.C., and Alaska. Before he was twenty he sailed with the ill-fated Scott expedition to the South Pole. At the outbreak of the war he was twenty-one years of age and an officer on a Pacific coast steamer. He resigned, crossed a continent and an ocean to enlist. At first, he had considered the Royal Navy, but learned of the Royal Naval Air Service and, by January 1916, was a qualified pilot assigned to coastal patrol duty. In August of that year he was sent to the RNAS Third Wing, which consisted of bombers and their escorts. This organization went to France, and Collishaw flew a Sopwith Pup as escort to the heavier bombers. While engaged in this dreary work, Ray downed his first enemy plane, a Fokker fighter over Oberndorf on October 12, 1916. He downed two more of the same type over Lunéville on October 25 for which the French honored him with the Croix de Guerre.

Early in 1917 Collishaw was posted to Number 3 (Naval) Squadron on the Somme. This squadron was under command of R. H. Mulock, another Canadian who had already destroyed a submarine and a number of enemy aircraft. Collishaw had little luck here, but was transferred later to Number 10 (Naval) Squadron and sent back to the coast. He was promoted to flight commander and he personally hand-picked four other Canadian pilots to make up a special fighter flight. They were Flight Sub-Lieutenants Ellis V. Reid of Toronto, J. E. Sharman of Winnipeg, J. A. Nash of Hamilton, and W. M. Alexander of Montreal, all in their early twenties and keen on individual scrapping.

The Sopwith triplane had started to move off the production line at this time, and although not in particular favor with the RFC, two squadrons of the RNAS Numbers 8 and 10, were eager to have them, and were the first squadrons to fly the British three-decker on active service.

Collishaw's flight had a set of these most maneuverable aircraft, having chosen them over the earlier Spads that had been available.

After some secret deliberation, and in bold disregard for British rules, the pilots painted their new triplanes black, and when this personality touch was winked at, they gave them fitting names. Collishaw started it by naming his mount *Black Maria,* and the others were christened *Black Death, Black Prince, Black Roger,* and *Black Sheep.* This was a harmless, youthful spirit, but these five pilots ran up an extraordinary record.

Their first assignment was with the Home Fleet, but they saw few enemy aircraft. On April 28, however, Collishaw caught a venturesome Roland scout out beyond Ostend, and soon shot it to wreckage. He scored three times more in the first twelve days of May while patrolling the coastline. Then his unit was transferred to the Ypres front and attached to the Eleventh Wing of the RFC where the black Tripes made their presence felt. Four enemy scouts were downed by Collishaw's guns in five days, and the other members of the unit all tasted victory. On June 5 Collishaw shot down his first two-seater, and on June 6 nailed three in one day, making his score sixteen.

Disaster then touched the Black Flight when Lieutenant Nash crashed on June 26 from a mass attack by a section of the Richthofen Circus. Seeking revenge, Collishaw went looking for the gaily painted Fokkers and Albatros fighters, the next day, and caught up with a wide formation of red-daubed Jerries. The all-black Tripes flashed about seeking the particular Albatros that had followed Nash down to the ground. Collishaw swooped down on a green-striped plane, and cut it away from the rest of its formation. They were equally matched; the

German flew and fought well, but Ray was inspired with the spirit of vengeance, and they were circling high over the outskirts of Lille when the break came. The German had gained a momentary advantage from above and behind, but Ray tilted up on one wingtip, and the Albatros missed and swooped past. Ray pivoted on his horizontal axis and his gun spat flame.

The Albatros hung on for a second in a sharp turn, and then its nose snapped down and a white scarf trailed behind it; the white turned gradually to black, there was a brief flicker of flame, then a shattering crash on the old fortifications of Lille. When Collishaw looked around to take stock he saw that he had been carried well over the German lines, but his Black Flight was re-forming. The Germans had scattered, and three of the Circus, besides Ray's victim, had gone down. High up in the blue, two thousand feet above the combat, a blood-red Albatros that had not come down during the fight, wheeled, and flew back to Germany.

The pilot in that red Albatros may not have been Baron von Richthofen, but the man who died in the green-striped Albatros was Karl Allmenröder, second highest ranking ace in Jasta 11, and reputed to be the Baron's closest friend. It may be interesting to note that while Allmenröder was downing Nash the day before, and other members of the Circus were tying up the Black Flight, Richthofen had brought down a two-seater that Collishaw's group had been escorting.

But Collishaw had little respect for any German airman, ace or neophyte. In the first twelve days of July he added twelve more to his list; and on July 30, with his score at thirty-seven, he was sent to Canada for a leave of two months. He was back again by mid-November and given command of Number 13 (Naval) Squadron, and on December 1 added to his score when he downed two seaplanes and an L.V.G. two-seater.

When the Royal Air Force was formed in April 1918 Collishaw was commissioned a major—this was before the present rank of squadron leader was devised—and he was placed in command of Number 203 Squadron, flying Sopwith Camels. Over the next four months while flying against the new Fokker D.7s and Pfalz he accounted for twenty more victories, ten of which were the much vaunted Fokker. He scored "doubles" on seven occasions during that period. He had been awarded the British Distinguished Service Cross, the Distinguished Service Order, the Distinguished Flying Cross, and on August 3 was given a Bar to his DSO. He was returned to England about October 1, promoted to lieutenant colonel, and joined Billy Bishop, Andy McKeever, and other famous Canadian airmen who were laying the basic plans for a Royal Canadian Air Force, but the war ended early in November, and the proposed RCAF did not emerge until 1924.

Although Ray Collishaw had done more than his share, unlike most of the others, he stayed on when the war ended, and took command of an Allied air force that went to the aid of the Czarist cause under General Anton I. Denikin, who was attempting to oust the Bolsheviki. It is not known how many planes Ray destroyed in this almost forgotten campaign, but the British government has admitted that twenty would be a very modest figure, none of which, of course, was added to his World War I score.

When the Russian White Army collapsed in 1920, Collishaw was brought back to England, given a tropical uniform and sent out to command Number 84 Squadron in Persia where the Bolsheviki were menacing a British protectorate. He was still flying Camels, and by April 1922 was back in Mesopotamia for service against insurgent Arabs. There he was raised to the rank of wing commander.

Collishaw stayed with the RAF and was in action again in 1939 when World War II erupted. This time he was in command of a Fleet Air Arm Fighter Group that swarmed off Royal Navy aircraft carriers. He fought all through that war with distinction—but with little publicity—and when last heard of had accepted honorable retirement to a country home in Nanaimo, British Columbia.

*The Birth of Strategic Aviation*

Ignoring the headlines being written by the aerial fighters, the British made some effort in the spring of 1917 to develop tactical aviation to give necessary support to the ground forces. The primitive wireless had been improved by this time, artillery observation and target-spotting had become a well-developed science. Aerial photography and intelligent interpretation of its prints had been broadened to include the preparation of valuable mosaic maps. Skilled observers were as valuable as skilled pilots, and their training had been augmented to include many new subjects to meet the demands of GHQ.

British aviation was brought down to more workable levels, and aircraft and equipment modified for tactical activity. Machines, formerly considered fighters, were re-designed for low-level missions, and multi-gun aircraft for trench strafing were well beyond the blueprint stage. In fact, by late 1918 the Sopwith Salamanders with six machine guns mounted for this type of work, were ready for squadron delivery. Even the rocket was unearthed from the old Congreve days, and mounted in tubes that were fastened to the interplane struts and fired by electric contact. They were originally intended for anti-balloon work, but there were instances where they were used against enemy aircraft with notable success.

It may seem to be stretching credulity to add that the British were also planning for, and experimenting with, a guided missile, a radio-controlled aircraft that was designed to carry a load of high explosive to enemy targets, but an illustration of this device will be found in the photographic section of this book.

This naturally brings up the subject of strategic aviation, a program that was a long time in developing, but which actually reached a stage of fruition before the end of World War I. In other words, strategic aviation is not the sole property of the USAF, or General Curtis E. LeMay; it was conceived and carried to its initial effort by General Sir Hugh "Boom" Trenchard who had headed the First Wing of the RFC that went to France in 1914. In a service that had been so intent on keeping its activities within the bounds of military reconnaissance, or the limitations of fighting other aircraft, this idea of carrying the air war to the enemy's heartland and his industrial centers was wishful thinking, or visionary, to say the least.

One of the most provocative men in the British service, "Boom" Trenchard was born in 1873, and began his soldiering as a subaltern in the Royal Scots Fusiliers. He served in India, was seriously wounded in the Boer War, and did not return to England until 1912. The Royal Flying Corps was in its infancy, and although approaching forty, Trenchard saw a new future and applied for a transfer. He was shocked to learn that the limit for admission to the RFC was forty years of age, that a man had to have a Royal Aero Club certificate, then had to pass the Central Flying School examinations before his application could be acted on.

As soon as he heard of these conditions, Boom, who was now a major, rushed off to the Sopwith Flying School and explained his problem to the chief pilot, T. O. M. Sopwith, who was doubtful; men of that age were not as adaptable as younger ones, and he would have to learn to fly in a few weeks in order to negotiate the rest of the red tape and examinations before his fortieth birthday.

Trenchard soloed in four days, gained his certificate two days later, and passed his Central Flying School tests on August 13, 1912. Few majors of that era knew how, or even wanted, to fly, and Trenchard was eventually made CO of the Military Wing of the RFC. At the outbreak of war he was in charge of all British military flying in France.

He flew as many patrols, as time would allow, in the hated R.E.5, one of the worst products of the British Royal Aircraft Factory, and he continued to fly this notorious heap as long as his pilots overseas had to accept them. He was a strict disciplinarian which perhaps saved the RFC of those days, since the service had attracted many playboys who had joined mainly for the sporty uniform and the pleasure of wearing silken wings on their chests.

He also fought bureaucracy in London and demanded the best for his airmen, insisting on aircraft that fitted the situations, and guns and gun mountings that matched anything the enemy produced. He demanded regular leave every three months for his flying men, and fought for their comforts and conveniences.

One of Trenchard's pet theories was that Allied flying men and machines were being wasted on the routine patrols assigned to them. "Aces are worth about four-a-penny," he argued. "This business of knocking Hun planes down, one at a time, is senseless. Let's dig them out where they thrive, destroy their hangars wholesale, and then go even further and halt their aircraft before they can take off and be flown. I want long-range bombers that will go direct to the enemy heartland."

The War Office was too engrossed with the U-boat threat, and the frightful carnage on the Western Front to bear with Trenchard's fantastic theories, and after the formation of the Royal Air Force in April 1918, he was returned to Great Britain and given the post of Chief of the Air Staff. The Air Minister was Lord Rothermere, a suave politician who soon tangled with Boom, and within a month Trenchard resigned his post, a move that almost wrecked the British Air Service; airmen, mechanics, and administration personnel abroad deluged the War Office with letters of protest. Many of these entreaties spelled out mutiny, for the writers exhorted: "Lead us, rank or no rank, and we'll follow you!"

Alone, and to some extent dishonored, Trenchard continued his plea for pilots and aircraft that could carry the war deep into enemy territory. Only one other man of any importance at the time seemed to agree, or at least understand him. He was Colonel William Mitchell of the U. S. Air Service. Billy Mitchell had sought Trenchard early in 1917 and listened to his views and theories and agreed with them, so much so in fact, he had made a strong effort to get long-range bombers for his own squadrons. He echoed Trenchard's phrases: "The airplane is an offensive weapon, not a defensive weapon. Air power, properly organized, will make it possible to attack and to continue to attack, even though the enemy is on the offensive. We have been using the airplane improperly. No amount of flying machines can prevent an enemy aircraft from crossing the lines. The sky itself is too large to defend. We must plan military aviation to attack the rear areas of any enemy and destroy all means of supply."

Just before the war ended, Mitchell had gone to Pershing with the most advanced idea of air-infantry co-operation. He was determined to capture Metz, and proposed using sixty squadrons of British Handley Page bombers, and fill them with one of America's crack infantry divisions. He had no idea where these planes were to come from, but he believed Boom Trenchard would get them for him.

Inspired by Trenchard's views, Mitchell had actually gathered a force of 1500 Allied aircraft that he used in mass strikes during the battle for the Saint-Mihiel salient; and in the Meuse-Argonne offensive he sent more than six hundred American aircraft into the attack. Great bombers, escorted by fighters, flew deep into enemy territory, breaking supply lines, entangling transport, and cutting important communications. Some losses were suffered, but heavy critical damage was inflicted.

Meanwhile, in London, Trenchard had convinced the War Office that some form of independent aviation should be organized, a force designed to attack important industrial cities deep in Germany and so break up their manufacturing potential.

Oddly enough, the greatest opposition to this plan came from British "humanitarians," who had suffered for years from bombings by German Gothas and Zeppelins, but still refused to condone the bombing of German cities. Trenchard won out in the end, and was sent back to France in May 1918 to organize the Independent Air Force.

Probably no fighting organization is so little known as the old Independent Air Force; no one who served with it ever bothered to put the record down on paper. A handful of writers did weave tales of crusading heroism, and created myths about this so-called suicide outfit. The personnel consisted of dedicated airmen, not wild, undisciplined mavericks, as was so often reported. This, again, was the standard tale, and the characters were pictured as the no-goods, and dissolute, black-balled from more respectable squadrons. Such was not the case; they never would have been accepted by Boom Trenchard, and what few did seep in were soon turfed out and relegated to roles of lesser importance.

There were four squadrons in the original Independent Air Force; only one, Number 216, was equipped with the two-engined Handley Page. Number 55 had D.H.4s, Number 99 flew D.H.9s, and Number 100 was furnished with black-painted F.E.2b two-seater pushers that were resurrected from the discards of early 1917. The pilots and observers were Britishers, Canadians, and a few Americans who had been flying with Royal Flying Corps squadrons. All had volunteered for this new program, unrealistic as it was, and knowing that in most cases the aircraft had had to be modified for extra fuel tanks so as to get anywhere near the list of targets Trenchard had selected.

Boom wasted no time. On his first day back in action he started bombing Germany's supply lines with whatever he had, and did not give up until the Armistice was signed. When Billy Mitchell started his air offensive, he persuaded Trenchard to give him some assistance, particularly with a few bombers. Boom willingly agreed and sent every plane he had available, and even borrowed an S.E.5 squadron from the RAF to fly escort. This force raided Fére-en-Tardenois, a German center of supply, and although the armada was intercepted by flights of Fokkers and Pfalz and many British bombers were lost, the German supply base was wiped out.

Trenchard mourned his loss, but did not give up, and the pilots and observers who did return were convinced that his theory was right and were more than willing to go again. Boom literally worked his men to death, but he scored time and time again.

He continued to badger Parliament for bigger and better bombers. He spent money like water in improving fields, communications, and in planning night-flying operations. He was determined to strike by day and by night. By now many Americans, training in England, who had no United States squadrons to go to, transferred willingly to Trenchard's Independent Air Force.

In the next few months the Independent Air Force made 709 strategic bombing raids, 374 of them on German towns, 209 on enemy airfields, and 126 on particular military objectives. Its fighters downed 150 of the enemy in combat, and lost 111 machines of its own. None of this was of especial importance to Boom; he was far more concerned with the destruction of the enemy's manufactures, supplies, and potentials.

As the weeks went on, and the raids increased in fury and tempo, there was no restraining the enthusiasm of the aircrews. "Bomb Berlin!" they cried, but the one aircraft, the Handley Page V/1500, capable of such a flight, was not ready in squadron strength in time. When the Armistice was signed only three were available, although 255 had been ordered.

It is interesting to speculate what impact a full-scale bombing raid on Berlin might have had. The people of Germany had felt little of the thud of war, their main cities had not been bombed, and very little of their territory occupied. Would Hitler have been able to inspire his Nazi followers to begin World War II, had they known what a toll mass-bombing could take?

## Aircraft Carrier Operations

The aircraft carrier was conceived and designed during the latter part of World War I, a disclosure that may surprise many readers. The British Navy had designed several forms of flight-deck vessels, and as early as 1916, had flown aircraft from them and retrieved these machines. It will be recalled that *Campania*, a seaplane carrier, missed going to glory at Jutland through a communications failure. Had she and her aircraft taken part, Jutland might have been fought to a more satisfactory conclusion.

The development of the carrier was not simple or easy. The trick of "marrying" the aircraft of the time to the contemporary warship necessitated considerable thought, planning, courage, and imagination. Its development is a dramatic example of the old proverb, "Necessity is the mother of invention."

The military potential of the airplane, particularly in naval warfare, was appreciated by a few farsighted tacticians shortly after its birth. The Wright brothers, who invented the machine, also devised a primitive catapult, the forerunner of the launching mechanism used aboard today's carriers.

Fleet commanders saw the extension of visibility for their surface ships, but no one in naval circles considered the airplane as a weapon of offense; the flying boat and float plane were obviously suitable for naval-air operations because they could take off from, and land on water, and as their employment was extended, special vessels had to be designed to accommodate and service them.

There always were a number of handling problems connected with these early aircraft. They could only be launched or landed during favorable weather conditions. They occupied much valuable space aboard their tenders. They were difficult to handle aboard ship, or to retrieve after a patrol. Because of their size and lack of maneuverability they were limited to simple scouting missions, and were no match for land-based aircraft. Their hulls and floats that afforded their primary ability to work with the fleet were their major hindrances.

What Navy men wanted was a light, long-range aircraft that could defend itself, scout out the enemy, range the big guns, and take off from, and land back on the mother ship. These last two qualities would save an enormous amount of time, and, more important, would permit the vessel concerned to keep station with its own flotilla. This was of prime consideration with the increased speed of surface operations. If an aircraft could be launched from a vessel of war while she was under way and brought back again under the same conditions, the art of naval warfare would be vitally improved.

The Wright brothers had used a dropped-weight catapult to launch their first successful biplanes. The problem of a short-strip landing was partly solved by another American, Eugene Ely, who made the first known carrier-deck landing and take-off on January 19, 1911. He took off from the Presidio in San Francisco in a Curtiss June-Bug biplane, and flew out to the U.S.S. *Pennsylvania,* a cruiser of that day, and landed on a short platform mounted over the stern of the deck.

The Curtiss pilot put the biplane down at about forty miles per hour and used a variation of today's hook-and-cable arrester equipment—a series of ropes with sandbags at each end were laid across two wooden rails that ran lengthwise along the landing platform. Suspended a few inches high, the ropes caught and held a trailing hook, and furnished the means of snubbing the forward speed, slowing down the plane, and limiting it to the short platform.

Later that day Ely's biplane was turned around, the ropes removed, and he took off safely and flew back to the Presidio field. The landing-cable idea became the basis of today's deck-arrester system used on all naval carriers. The United States Navy did not pursue the venture at that time, however, and the aircraft carrier, as such was first developed by the British.

In 1908 a new post of Naval Air Assistant was created at the British Admiralty, but heavier-than-air machines were not seriously considered for naval operations until 1912, since it was widely believed that having planes alight on warships was not only dangerous, but of no practical value. But the young bloods of the Royal Navy had other views and pushed their "impractical" plans with determination.

Late in 1911 Commander Oliver Swann made Britain's first successful take-off from water while flying a thirty-five horsepower Avro biplane. Almost a year before Glenn H. Curtiss had made America's first floatplane take-off at San Diego, although the first airman to perform this feat was Henri Fabre, a Frenchman who in 1910 succeeded in getting off the water, but since his "floats" were simple curved sections of veneer, he had to land on a sandy beach. This brings up the question: was this the first amphibian plane?

Lieutenant Charles R. Samson of the Royal Navy flew a Short S.27 from an improvised deck built on the forecastle of H.M.S. *Africa* while she was at anchor in Chatham, and then made a safe descent alongside, using flotation bags lashed to the wheels. But it was not until 1912 that the first real seaplane and the first flying boat made their appearance. The first British flight from a vessel under way was made by a Lieutenant R. Gregory on May 9, 1912, when he flew another Short S.27 biplane from the deck of H.M.S. *Hibernia* as she steamed at ten knots in Weymouth Bay.

The United States Navy neglected its early success in deck take-offs, but gave some attention to catapult-assist launchings, but not until 1916 was a catapult, suitable for active-service conditions, fitted to the U.S.S. *North Carolina.*

During the 1913 annual maneuvers, aircraft took part for the first time, and two seaplanes were launched from a wheeled trolley off a platform that was mounted forward on H.M.S. *Hermes.* One of these aircraft, known as the Short Folder, was fitted with wings that could be folded back parallel with the fuselage. Aircraft manufactured by the brothers Horace and Eustace Short were having important roles in the development of the Royal Naval Air Service. A Short seaplane was the first to carry a torpedo, and one of these combinations sank a Turkish transport in the Sea of Marmara. All in all, it would appear that British naval aviation was outstripping the military arm.

When the war started it was evident that special ships were urgently needed to act as seaplane carriers, and in September of that year an ancient merchantman was hurriedly converted and named *Ark Royal.* This old lugger could carry ten seaplanes that were launched from wheeled trolleys, as they had been aboard *Hermes.* This early carrier arrangement was so successful that three cross-Channel steamers, *Empress, Engadine,* and *Riviera,* were converted to accommodate four seaplanes each.

Later, an Isle of Man packet, the *Ben-My-Chree,* was added to
this early carrier force. The *Hermes* was sunk by an enemy submarine off Calais on October 31, 1914.

The history of *Campania* has been reviewed. She continued
her career as a flight-training vessel until lost in a gale in the
Firth of Forth. However, so much had been learned aboard this
mother ship, that by early 1918 flight decks were part of the
planning, and H.M.S. *Argus,* that had been started before the
war as a merchantman for Italy, was turned out with a 550-foot
flight deck, an offset bridge and navigation area, and with her
funnels trunked horizontally aft. Thus, it was the first true flush-
deck carrier, and as close to the design of the modern carrier as
one would expect to find in those early days. The first actual
flight-deck landing was made aboard this vessel on August 3,
1917, when Squadron Commander E. H. Dunning safely landed
a Sopwith Pup, but in trying to repeat this performance two
days later, a tire burst, the Pup rolled over the side, and Dunning
was lost.

Following this misadventure, the British devoted a great deal
of time to perfecting an arrester gear, and devised a rope-net
buffer to protect the bridge. *Furious* was also the first aircraft
carrier that was equipped with elevators to lower her aircraft
to the hangars below. It should be stated here that none of these
flight-deck vessels engaged in any important naval action. A
German Zeppelin was destroyed, however, the first to be brought
down by an aircraft launched from a naval vessel.

On the evening of August 5, 1918, the British destroyer H.M.S.
*Redoubt* left her mooring at Harwich on the east coast of England, towing an ungainly craft known as a lighter. It actually was
a creaky old raft mounted on the gunwales of a barge-like hull.
A single-seater Sopwith Camel was perched on this precarious
platform, and a young Anglo-Canadian-American, Stuart D.
Culley, sat in the cockpit hoping this array of grotesque gadgets
would enable him to clamber off this thirty-knot deck to attack
a Zeppelin reported to be heading for a naval-air patrol.

Surprisingly, this fantastic experiment worked, and naval historians of the day recorded the first successful shipborne fighter interception. The German gasbag was destroyed, but, more important, the marriage of the airplane and the surface vessel was consummated. The fact that the airplane had to land on the sea near its mother ship was not important; unlimited range had been made for the airplane, and the firepower of the surface fleet greatly increased.

Flight Lieutenant Stuart D. Culley was born in Nebraska in 1895, the son of a Canadian mother and an English father. He enlisted in Canada in 1916, was accepted by the Royal Naval Air Service, and on completion of his flight training in England, was transferred from the light cruiser *Cassandra* to a shore base at Great Yarmouth. Up till then his deck flying had been limited to early variations of primitive carrier decks that were built over the hulls of converted cruisers or merchantmen, and in these operations Sopwith Pups—forerunners of the Camel—were successfully launched, but no deck landings were made. The aircraft either landed on the surface of the sea to be picked up, or returned to some nearby land base. In a few instances the landing gear was jettisoned to make the water landings less hazardous. Culley had had some experience in taking off from a seagoing platform, but flying a more powerful and very tricky aircraft off a deck that was only fifty-eight feet long and sixteen feet wide, was something else.

Apparently, Culley went into the adventure with an open mind. A destroyer was to tow the lighter at thirty knots, and at the appropriate moment one of the lighter's crew would start the engine of the Camel by swinging the propeller. To offset any chance of the mechanic's tumbling into the airscrew, he was anchored to the lighter deck by a safety belt and a line that permitted him just sufficient reach to perform the duty. As soon as the Bentley engine was started, the mechanic pulled himself clear by the safety line, unshackled the cordage, and darted to the shelter of the lighter's deck. The airplane itself was launched by a conventional bomb-release gear that was operated from the pilot's cockpit. Steel cables were attached to the ends of the wheels' axle and run over simple claw pieces that allowed the plane to move forward freely at any time, but until Culley pulled the release toggle there could be no upward or backward movement. Culley had made an initial trial of this arrangement off Great Yarmouth on August 1, 1918. In this trial the *Redoubt* and the lighter were worked up to thirty-six knots before Culley released the Camel and was airborne with scarcely any run over the deck. Once in the air, he turned away and landed safely at a shore base.

Five days later Commodore—later Admiral—Reginald Y. Tyrwhitt, aboard the light cruiser *Curacoa*, took his complete Harwich force of four light cruisers and thirteen destroyers out to sea to make an offensive sweep in the southeastern sector of the North Sea. *Redoubt* again hauled the lighter and its Camel fighter; other destroyers towed lighters on which reconnaissance flying boats had been embarked; and cruisers of the force were burdened with CMBs—coastal motorboats—that were to attack German minesweepers operating off the coast of Holland.

The CMBs were put overboard at dawn on August 11 twenty-five miles northwest of the island of Vlieland, and an attempt was made to launch the flying boats, but there was not sufficient wind to get them into the air. They had to be reloaded aboard the lighters and finally returned to the harbor waterborne. The six CMBs that were to be escorted by the flying boats had to make their attacks off Terschelling without this support, and were intercepted by German seaplanes. Three motorboats were sunk and the remainder limped back to safe areas along the Dutch coast.

While this air-surface action was taking place, Culley and the lighter crew left the destroyer's deck and prepared to launch the Camel. It was reasoned that the Germans would investigate the activity of Tyrwhitt's force, and at eight that morning the Admiralty monitored a signal that indicated that a Zeppelin was cruising over Heligoland Bight. Every man in the force searched the sky, but Culley was the first to spot a great silver cigar floating at 10,000 feet. It was *L.53*, commanded by Lieutenant (s.g.) Proell of the Imperial German Navy, and had been flown out of Nordholz in northwest Germany early that morning to investigate the intrusion of Tyrwhitt's flotilla.

Lieutenant Culley jumped into the cockpit of the Camel, and *Redoubt* worked up speed. When the lighter was hitting thirty knots, Culley checked his engine and gave the conventional "thumbs-up" signal, and the Camel roared into the air at 8:14. Culley climbed straight over the stacks of *Redoubt*, saw the whole flotilla spread out before him, and realized that he had suddenly become the leading actor in this drama. Probably no airman had ever played to such a breathless audience, but when he looked again, the Zeppelin was nowhere in sight.

"Oh, no! Please . . ." he pleaded.

As if in answer, the silver airship reappeared, and from that instant on Culley, flying like an automaton, never took his eyes off the glinting bag. At 5000 feet she appeared to have changed little—a disturbing thing—and the young flier finally saw that he was climbing fast instead of making great forward speed. He remembered that Zeppelins of this "50" category were noted for their ability to gain height rapidly, but he stuck to his task, keeping a discreet distance from the airship.

At 15,000 feet the controls of the Sopwith began to mush-out and become sluggish. The Bentley gave a disturbing cough, but picked up the rhythm again and Culley worked her up to 18,000 feet at which time he was positive that the Zeppelin had altered course and was heading out to sea.

Culley said afterward: "I hoped she would try to get back to Germany. I knew I would never head her off if she steered farther out to sea."

With his hopes gradually dying, he continued to watch the airship until suddenly the light changed and he saw that the silver raider was heading directly toward him. He figured, as close as he could, that she was a few hundred feet above his present level and approaching at a relative 150 knots.

His chief had ordered that he must dive on this target. "You must avoid any position behind or below the tail. Dive on her from above, and then race past just along her beam to avoid any flames. If you fail in this method, dive on her from behind the port quarter. You will perhaps come under heavy fire, so don't use up all your ammunition in the first attack. They are not likely to use the gun mounted on the top of the main frame, and you'll be able to get in closer by going in from above."

From Culley's position, and judging the speed at which the Zeppelin was approaching, it was obvious that an attack from above and behind was out of the question; he had no choice but to attack head-on and from below. In a matter of seconds the great bulk of the airship loomed ahead, and Culley could see the forward control car and the outboard engine gondolas, their propellers flailing like broadswords. For a short instance he was spellbound by the spectacle, then his eyes searched for some crew activity, his hand instinctively drew back on the stick, the nose of the chunky biplane came up and she almost stalled.

"I can hardly remember doing all that," Culley related later, "and I only came to when I discovered I was attacking that great thing. One gun operated beautifully and fired its first drum without slip-up, but the other jammed after pooping off a few rounds." (The Vickers guns had been replaced by two Lewis guns for this operation.) "By then I sensed I was about to stall out so I leveled off and raced along under the massive belly of the craft and saw something either fall or jump from a slit in the framework and disappear below." (This object was the only survivor from *L.53*, and his parachute descent from around 19,000 feet must have been a record for those days. The man was spotted and picked up by a German destroyer.)

The instant Culley's guns stopped firing, and as the Camel faltered in the stall, it nosed down some 2000 feet before the pilot could ease it out. He lost sight of his target during this time, but when he leveled off again and stared up he saw, to his consternation, that *L.53* was cruising along as though nothing had happened. He turned to make an adjustment to his throttle to regain the lost altitude when a glint above caught his eye.

Yellow flame was cascading from three widely separated points and within a minute all of the airship except the tail section was enveloped in fire. The huge conflagration burned out in a few seconds, leaving a blackened skeleton floundering in the sky, and a flag fluttered pathetically from a rudder post as *L.53* started her final dive. Culley saw the airship writhe and break her back before she hit the water. The clock on his instrument panel showed 9:14, exactly one hour after he had become airborne from the bobbing lighter.

Culley had scored, but now a new problem arose. Valor and training had been devoted to the destruction of an enemy raider, now it was time to consider a safe return. He knew there would be a number of German seaplanes in this area, and they would have great firepower, whereas one of his guns was empty, the other jammed. It was then that discretion replaced the spirit of valor; he opened the throttle wide, went into a steep dive and headed for the area parallel to the Netherlands coast.

In a hurried arrangement made just before he bounced off the lighter, it was agreed that one of Tyrwhitt's ships would rendezvous with him in the vicinity of the Texel Lightship, but whether this plan could be carried out was mostly a matter of luck. So, Culley studied a small-scale map and tried to locate some outstanding landmark. While thus engaged, his engine cut out and he knew that he had used all the fuel in the main tank while struggling to get to the level of the Zeppelin. He switched over to a small reserve container in an upper wing panel and throttled back, holding just enough power to remain airborne.

He probed his way through a light coverlet of offshore mist and thought he spotted a couple of Dutch fishing vessels, but when he had eased down into the clear he was overjoyed to see they were British destroyers, and another look told him the whole Harwich force was in the vicinity.

Now he could pick and choose, but he selected *Redoubt* because he saw that she had stopped, and was transferring the lighter's crew and lowering a whaleboat. While these rescue arrangements were being conducted, Culley circled the rest of the force, and during his triumphal circuit Commodore Tyrwhitt turned to his officer of the watch and said, "Do we have anyone aboard who knows the hymnbook well?"

The O.O.W. replied, "I used to be a choirboy, sir."

"Remember the hymn that begins, 'O happy band of pilgrims'?"

"Of course, sir."

When a hymnbook was found, the commodore sent a general signal to his fleet that read, *"Attention is called to the last verse of Hymn 224."*

The last verse is as follows:

*O happy band of pilgrims,*
*Look upward to the skies,*
*Where such a light affliction*
*Shall win so great a prize.*

And since the day was Sunday, the ships' companies of the Harwich force bellowed the hymn with unusual enthusiasm, and Lieutenant Culley was many months living down the "light affliction" tag.

In the meantime, he put the Camel down so skillfully on the water, it was soon hoisted out with little damage, and returned to the lighter. It was patched up some time later and put on exhibition in the Imperial War Museum where it remains to this day. Lieutenant Culley was awarded the Distinguished Service Order, although many men, who were closely involved, thought he should have been given Great Britain's highest award, the Victoria Cross.

And thus began the art of air interception by shipboard fighter aircraft.

## EPILOGUE

War kills men, and men deplore the loss; but war also crushes bad principles and tyrants, and so saves societies.

—Colton

# BIBLIOGRAPHY

*The War in Outline*, B. H. Liddell Hart; Random House, Inc.

*Deeds of Bravery and Heroism*, Elwyn A. Barron; Harper & Brothers.

*The Great War*, Louis E. Orcutt; The Christian Herald.

*Per Ardua*, Hilary St. George Saunders; Oxford University Press.

*History of the World War*, Francis A. March; United Publishers of U.S. & Canada.

*The Real War*, B. H. Liddell Hart; Faber & Faber, Ltd. (London).

*The World War*, H. S. Canfield; B. C. Forbes Publishing Company.

*The United States and World Sea Power*, D. B. Potter; Prentice-Hall, Inc.

*A Short History of the Great War*, A. F. Pollard; Harcourt, Brace & Howe.

*America in France*, Frederick Palmer; Dodd, Mead & Company.

*Landing Operations*, Alfred Vagts; Military Service Publishing Company.

*America*, Original Sources; Veterans of Foreign Wars.

*These Men*, Maurice J. Swetland; Military Service Publishing Company.

*Mr. Punch's History of the Great War;* Frederick A. Stokes Company.

*Revolt in the Desert*, T. E. Lawrence; George H. Doran Company.

*The Great Push*, Patrick MacGill; Grosset & Dunlap.

*The First Hundred Thousand*, Ian Hay; Houghton Mifflin Company.

*Over the Top*, Arthur Guy Empey; G. P. Putnam's Sons.

*War Is War*, Ex-Private X; E. P. Dutton & Company, Inc.

*Diplomatic Documents;* H.M. Stationery Office (London).

*Eye-Witness, Origin of the Tanks*, Ernest D. Swinton; Doubleday, Doran & Company, Inc.

*Carry On*, Coningsby Dawson; Grosset & Dunlap.

*The Paris Gun*, Henry W. Miller; Cape and Smith (London).

*Now It Can Be Told*, Philip Gibbs; Harper & Brothers.

*All's Fair*, Henry Landau; G. P. Putnam's Sons.

*New England Aviators*, Caroline Ticknor; Houghton Mifflin Company.

*American Fighters in the Foreign Legion,* Paul Ayres Rockwell; Houghton Mifflin Company.

*High Adventure,* James Norman Hall; Houghton Mifflin Company.

*The Tanks,* B. H. Liddell Hart; Frederick A. Praeger.

*My Experiences in the World War,* John J. Pershing; Frederick A. Stokes Company.

*The Years of the Sky Kings,* Arch Whitehouse; Doubleday & Company, Inc.

*The Lafayette Flying Corps,* James Norman Hall and Charles B. Nordhoff; Houghton Mifflin Company.

*America's First World War,* Henry Castor; Random House, Inc.

*John J. Pershing,* Frederick Palmer; Military Service Publishing Company.

*Black Jack Pershing,* Richard O'Connor; Doubleday & Company, Inc.

*Legion of the Lafayette,* Arch Whitehouse; Doubleday & Company, Inc.

*Great Events of the Great War,* Charles F. Horne; National Alumni Publications.

*The Australian Flying Corps,* F. M. Cutlack; Angus & Robertson, Ltd. (Sydney, Australia).

*The Aeroplane Speaks,* Horatio Barber; Robert M. McBride & Company.

*Great Exploits of the Air,* F. V. Monk & H. T. Winter; Blackie & Son, Ltd. (London).

*Subs and Submariners,* Arch Whitehouse; Doubleday & Company, Inc.

*There Shall Be Wings,* Leslie Roberts; Clarke, Irwin & Company, Ltd. (Toronto, Canada).

*Mitchell, Pioneer of Air Power,* Isaac Don Levine; Duell, Sloan and Pearce.

*The Great Adventure,* Edwin C. Parsons; Doubleday, Doran & Company, Inc.

*Raiders Approach!,* H. T. Sutton; Gale and Polden, Ltd. (Aldershot, England).

*U-Boats Westward!,* Ernst Hashagen; G. P. Putnam's Sons.

*Squadrons of the Sea,* Arch Whitehouse; Doubleday & Company, Inc.

*The Great Adventure,* America in the First World War, Pierce G. Fredericks; E. P. Dutton & Company.

*Tank,* Arch Whitehouse; Doubleday & Company, Inc.